# Living to Tell about It

# Living to Tell about It

*A Rhetoric and Ethics*
*of Character Narration*

## JAMES PHELAN

CORNELL UNIVERSITY PRESS

ITHACA AND LONDON

First published 2005 by Cornell University Press
First printing, Cornell Paperbacks, 2005

Printed in the United States of America

Library of Congress Cataloging-in-Publication Data

Phelan, James, 1951–
    Living to tell about it : a rhetoric and ethics of character narration / James Phelan.
        p. cm.
    Includes index.
    ISBN 0-8014-4297-4 (cloth : alk. paper) — ISBN 0-8014-8928-8 (pbk. : alk. paper)
    1. American prose literature—20th century—History and criticism.    2. Characters and characteristics in literature.    3. Ethics in literature.    4. Narration (Rhetoric).
I. Title.
    PS369.P48 2004
    810.9′23′0904—dc22

                                                                    2004007166

Cornell University Press strives to use environmentally responsible suppliers and materials to the fullest extent possible in the publishing of its books. Such materials include vegetable-based, low-VOC inks and acid-free papers that are recycled, totally chlorine-free, or partly composed of nonwood fibers. For further information, visit our website at www.cornellpress.cornell.edu.

Cloth printing            10 9 8 7 6 5 4 3 2 1
Paperback printing        10 9 8 7 6 5 4 3 2 1

For Betty, Katie, and Michael
Stories and funnies, oh my!

# Contents

# Preface

Some of us are born storytellers, some of us acquire the storytelling habit, and some of us have it thrust upon us. But for almost all of us living and telling are inextricably connected: we make sense of our experiences through the stories we tell about them, even as those stories influence our future experiences. What's more, most of us are almost as interested in other people's stories (or at least some other people's stories) as they are. My interest in other people's stories, in the ways their living gets converted into their telling, has led me to this investigation of how such stories—as distinct from those in which the storyteller is not a character—create their effects. This interest has also led me to choose both fictional and nonfictional narratives as part of my investigation: how, if at all, does the telling of a fictional character about his experience work differently from the telling of a real person about hers, even acknowledging that such telling is constructed through the same textual devices as the fictive teller's? Furthermore, my interest in the effects of these stories focuses on three main dimensions, which are themselves inextricably connected: the cognitive (what do we understand and how do we understand it?); the emotive (what do we feel and how do those feelings come about?); and the ethical (what are we asked to value in these stories, how do these judgments come about, and how do we respond to being invited to take on these values and make these judgments?). My hope is that, by answering these questions as they apply to a range of rich narratives, I can offer some insight into the workings of the pervasive and fascinating phenomenon of living and telling.

Narrative theory has long distinguished between narratives in which the narrator is also the protagonist and those in which the narrator and the protagonist are distinct figures. Even traditional taxonomies of point of view based on grammatical person distinguish not only between "first-person" and "third-person" narration but also between "first-person-protagonist" and "first-person-observer" narration. Gérard Genette's more precise taxonomy, which separates vision (who perceives) from voice (who speaks) and recognizes that any narrator can employ the first person, distinguishes between heterodiegetic narration, in which the narrator cannot directly interact with the characters, and homodiegetic narration, in which the narrator has (or, in retrospective narration, once had) the ability to interact with the characters. Genette's taxonomy goes on to mark off that subset of homodiegetic narration in which the narrator is the protagonist and to label it autodiegetic narration. I follow these taxonomies in making the major division between narration by a character and narration by a figure other than a character, but I am less concerned with refining taxonomies than with identifying and exploring a range of effects that follow from narration by a character.

As it turns out, almost all of my examples involve narratives in which the narrator is also the protagonist, but I believe that the rhetorical principles I deduce from these examples also apply to narratives in which the narrator is a secondary character. In the epilogue I take up the question of what might be distinctive about character narration by a character other than a protagonist. As it also turns out, my examples are all narratives written in English in the twentieth century, and all but one are narratives written in the United States. Again I believe that the rhetorical principles are applicable beyond these examples, though I do not have the hubris to claim that they apply across all time periods and all cultures.

More generally, this book is an exercise in what Peter J. Rabinowitz and I have called "theorypractice" (see the introduction to *Understanding Narrative*). The term describes a critical inquiry that has both a theoretical and a practical dimension and that develops a feedback loop between those two dimensions. Theory helps illuminate narrative texts even as elements of those texts challenge theory and lead to its extension or revision. My goal is to offer a set of theoretical principles that can account for the complex phenomenon of living and telling, even as I offer a set of extended engagements with striking examples of that phenomenon. The principles can of course be tested against other narratives, just as the engagements can be tested against those of other readers. And where the principles or the engagements are found wanting, they can be revised. Narrative theory and interpretation are both collective enterprises.

A few initial notes on terminology. First, given past taxonomies of narration, I want to explain why I use the term "character narration" rather than the more common "first-person narration" or narratology's more specialized "homodiegetic narration." "First-person narration" is, as Genette points out, insufficiently precise because any narrator, regardless of the grammatical person used to refer to the protagonist, can say "I." But Genette's more precise terms have not caught on beyond the field of narratology; they have simply proven to be infelicitous coinages for most other contemporary critics in the United States. Indeed, experience has taught me that these terms have the unfortunate effect of making the eyes of non-narratologists glaze over—or, if used in combination with other narratological neologisms ("there's a paralipsis in the proleptic homodiegesis"), making some think they should call 911. I have adopted "character narration" and "noncharacter narration" as a way to combine Genette's greater precision with a more user-friendly set of terms. At the same time, I realize that my term "character narration" can be seen as including a set of narratives that I have defined as outside the scope of this book: those in which the protagonist, the narrator, and the narratee are all the same figure and in which the narrator addresses himself with the second-person pronoun. Although I believe that some of the principles I articulate here are relevant to such narratives, I also believe that the effects of such narratives are different enough from the character narration I analyze here to deserve their own study.

Second, I have found it desirable, for the sake of precision and for ease of reference, to employ a cadre of other technical terms. Some of these are from narratology, some are from my previous efforts in the rhetorical analysis of narrative, and some are fresh coinages for this effort. When I have found it necessary to devise a new term, I have tried to make it both descriptive and user-friendly. But I remain aware of the paradox of a specialized vocabulary: even as it makes possible precise and efficient discussion among those who already share or easily adopt it, such a vocabulary runs the risk of shutting others, especially newcomers, out of the conversation. In order to counter this risk, I have included a glossary of key terms at the end of the book.

During the many years that I have been living with this book, I have done a lot of telling about it, and I have benefited greatly from responses to that telling. I am grateful to lecture audiences at Northern Illinois

University, the University of Louisville, the University of Maryland, Hamilton College, the University of Toronto, and the College English Associations of Indiana and of Ohio for good-spirited questions and comments that have made me think harder about my theoretical constructs and my engagements with the narratives. I am indebted to audiences at the annual Society for the Study of Narrative Literature conferences, and especially to the participants in the Contemporary Narratology seminars, for their numerous helpful questions and comments. I have learned greatly from conversations with students in graduate seminars at Ohio State University and the University of Toronto, and from working with Elizabeth Preston as she did her dissertation on "homodiegesis." My research assistants, Molly Youngkin and James Weaver, have been consistently conscientious and good-humored regardless of the task I assigned them, and James deserves most of the credit for the index. I have had helpful conversations about parts of the book with more individuals than I can mention here, but I want to single out Brian McHale, David Richter, David Herman, Wayne Booth, James Battersby, Brian Corman, Melba Cuddy-Keane, Linda Hutcheon, and especially Harry Shaw for their willingness to listen and support my various tellings about it. My creative writing colleagues, Michelle Herman and Lee Martin, offered helpful readings of chapters 2 and 4 respectively. Another creative writer, Kyoko Mori, has given perceptive feedback on many of my ideas about both the fictional and nonfictional narratives I discuss. Emma Kafalenos helped me formulate the distinction between disclosure functions and narrator functions. Leigh Gilmore productively engaged with my analysis of *The Kiss*. Mary Pat Martin, who taught *The Remains of the Day* at the same time as I did, engaged me in a weeks-long conversation in person and via e-mail about the novel that we eventually transformed into a major section of chapter 1 and that remains a highlight of my teaching career. Peter J. Rabinowitz has listened to more of my telling about this book than anyone else, and he has always responded with generosity, trenchant questions, helpful disagreements, and specific suggestions. Peter embodies the ideal of rhetorical reading.

Finally, as a small recognition of my great good fortune to live and tell—and observe and listen and love—in their company, I dedicate this book to my wife, Betty Menaghan, and to my children, Katie and Michael.

Earlier versions of certain chapters have previously appeared in print, and though I have often made substantial revisions in this material, I am grateful for permission from the publishers to draw on it here.

"Charlie Marlow, Character-Narrator, Discourses on 'Youth.'" *Col-*

# Living to Tell about It

# Introduction

*Disclosure Functions, Narrator Functions,
and the Distinctiveness of Character Narration;
Or, A Rhetoric and Ethics of "Barbie-Q"*

Character narration, it will surprise no one to hear, is an art of indirection: an author communicates to her audience by means of the character narrator's communication to a narratee. The art consists in the
author's ability to make the single text function effectively for its two
audiences (the narrator's and the author's, or to use the technical terms,
the narratee and the authorial audience) and its two purposes (author's
and character narrator's) while also combining in one figure (the "I") the
roles of both narrator and character. Even when the "I" who is the author appears to be identical with the "I" who is the narrator—in, for example, much autobiographical narrative—that "I" will sometimes speak
from the perspective of her former self, thereby making the communication shift from the direct to the indirect. I begin this book with the
conviction that narrative theory, despite all the attention it has given to
narrative discourse over the past forty years—attention sparked by such
major works as Wayne C. Booth's *Rhetoric of Fiction,* Gérard Genette's
*Narrative Discourse,* and Mikhail Bakhtin's "Discourse in the Novel"—
has not yet done justice to the complexities of the indirect art of character narration.[1] Let me begin to justify this claim by calling attention

---

1. I do not mean to claim that there has not been good work done on character narration,
but rather that there is still much to be done. In addition to Genette's groundbreaking work
on voice, see especially Romberg, Riggan, Yacobi, Preston ("Homodiegetic Narration"),
Lanser (*Fictions*), and Case. Romberg offers a helpful survey of types of character narratives,
notes the importance of distinguishing between the narrating-I and the experiencing-I, and

to what I regard as some curious phenomena across a range of texts employing character narrators, phenomena whose curiosity includes the fact that it is very easy to read the texts without registering that there is anything unusual going on.[2]

1. In lines 49–51 of Robert Browning's brilliant dramatic monologue "My Last Duchess," the Duke says to the envoy from the father of his next duchess,

> The Count *your master's* known munificence
> Is ample warrant that no just pretence
> Of mine for dowry will be disallowed. (Emphasis mine)

What is curious here is that the Duke knows that the envoy knows that the Count is his master, and so this reminder seems uncharacteristically gratuitous in the context of the Duke's carefully calculated speech.[3]

---

does extended analyses of a good range of examples. But his approach is more strictly formal than the one I develop here, and he does not draw upon the French narratological tradition. Riggan's title, *Picaros, Madmen, Naifs, and Clowns*, indicates his way of classifying unreliable narrators, and his book offers insightful analysis of a wide range of individual narratives. His attention to the naïve narrator, with Huckleberry Finn and Holden Caufield as his main examples, is an especially worthwhile contribution. In my view, however, Riggan's classification system is limited because it mixes kinds of unreliability with traits of character in unequal parts and because some unreliable narrators do not fit very snugly into their assigned categories. Yacobi, in effect, develops a productive approach to the indirection of character narration by focusing on readerly strategies for coming to terms with gaps and anomalies in texts. Preston offers worthwhile contributions to our understanding of the concepts of the implied author and of the self-conscious character narrator, among other things, as well as skillful analyses of a range of individual character narrators.

Lanser and Case have each done work in feminist narratology that offers excellent insights into some connections between the technique and ideology. Lanser is especially interested in how women fiction writers establish authority, and she offers compelling analyses of how some writers use character narrators to create what she calls a "personal" voice and, in some instances, a "communal voice." Case focuses on the difference between character narrators who actively shape the designs of their narratives and those who record experience without shaping it toward particular ends. Case persuasively argues that throughout the eighteenth and nineteenth centuries this second kind of character narration, whether the character narrator is male or female, is marked as "feminine."

2. Similar phenomena can be found in drama, where playwrights must use their own version of character narrators—think of asides to the audience, characters who tell others what they already know so that the audience can also be in the know, and so on. I believe that my discussion here is relevant to an investigation of these phenomena in drama, but my focus remains on fictional and nonfictional narrative.

3. It is, I realize, possible to argue that the Duke's reminder is not gratuitous, that he deliberately wants to call the envoy's attention to the power differential between them. As I will explain below, however, this reading seems to me less motivated by the rhetoric of the poem than by the impulse of readers to preserve the mimetic.

2. In Sandra Cisneros's "Barbie-Q," a short story of six paragraphs, the young girl who is the character narrator spends the first five telling the narratee, her sister, about events that they both have been present for. What is curious here is that there is no clear evidence of the character narrator's motivation for the address to the narratee, certainly nothing comparable to the evidence of the Duke's motivation in Browning's monologue, and so these five paragraphs seem to be an instance of a narrator needlessly telling a narratee something that she already knows.

3. In the "Weymouth" section of *The Remains of the Day*, Kazuo Ishiguro's character narrator, Stevens the butler, offers the following present-tense justification to his narratee for inquiring into Mrs. Benn's marital happiness.

> I am aware, of course, that such matters were hardly any of my business, and I should make clear I would not have dreamt of prying into these areas were it not that I did have, you might recall, important professional reasons for doing so; that is to say, in respect to the present staffing problems at Darlington Hall. In any case, Miss Kenton did not seem to mind at all confiding in me over these matters and I took this as a pleasing testimony to the strength of the close working relationship we had once had. (233–34)

What is curious here is that this present-tense justification does not jibe with Stevens's later admission that he had very personal motives for his inquiry, yet the discrepancy does not mark Stevens as a deliberately deceptive narrator or Ishiguro as a sloppy craftsman.

4. In *Angela's Ashes*, Frank McCourt employs the historical present tense and narrates the events of his childhood largely from his perspective as a child at the time of the action; in effect, he creates a three-year-old narrator, then a four-year-old narrator and so on until the end of the narrative when the nineteen-year-old Frankie arrives in the United States from Ireland. Yet McCourt has the six-year-old Frankie narrate this scene of his Limerick neighbor Nora Molloy exposing Mrs. McGrath's manipulation of her grocery scale:

> I think there was a little accident there the way your hip was pressed against that paper and you didn't even know the paper was pulled down a bit. Oh, God, no. A woman like you that's forever on her knees before the Virgin Mary is an inspiration to us all and is that your money I see on the floor there?
> Mrs. McGrath steps back quickly and the needle on the scale jumps

and quivers. What money? she says, *till she looks at Nora, and knows. Nora smiles.* Must be a trick of the shadows, she says, and smiles at the scale. There was a mistake right enough for that shows barely half a pound of flour. (67, emphasis mine)

What is curious here is that in order for young Frankie to report that Mrs. McGrath "knows" and that Mrs. McGrath and Nora share their knowledge of each other's intentions, Frankie must know at least as much as the two women. But since Mrs. McGrath's knowledge is registered only in her look, he can't report that "Mrs. McGrath knows" unless he also knows both Nora's intention and the significance of Mrs. McGrath's look. But six-year-old Frankie can't know all that, so, in the interest of narrative economy and effectiveness, McCourt drops the restrictions of Frankie's perspective and gives him an adult's understanding of the scene.

5. In chapter 8 of *The Great Gatsby*, Nick Carraway reports the scene at Wilson's garage involving Michaelis and Wilson as if he were a noncharacter narrator with the privilege of moving between his own focalization and that of Michaelis. What is curious here is not just that Nick narrates a scene at which he was not present but also that Fitzgerald does not try to justify how Nick came to know what Michaelis must have been thinking.

The list could go on to include (a) stories such as Ernest Hemingway's "My Old Man" in which a naïve character narrator, Joe Butler, loses some of his naïveté at the end of the tale but whose past-tense narration is not informed by that new knowledge; and (b) the increasingly frequent use of character narration in the simultaneous present tense, that is, narratives in which living and telling occur at the same time.[4]

Part of my effort in this book will be to account for the rhetorical dynamics of these curious phenomena, dynamics that involve the complex relationships between the functions of the narrator in relation to the narratee and the functions of the implied author in relation to the authorial audience as well as the complex relationships between the functions

4. I conduct fuller discussions of line 49 of "My Last Duchess" and of "Barbie-Q" as a whole later in this introduction, and I more fully examine the passages from *The Remains of the Day* and *Angela's Ashes* in subsequent chapters. I have written about *The Great Gatsby* and "My Old Man" in *Narrative as Rhetoric* and about the simultaneous present-tense narration of J. M. Coetzee's *Waiting for the Barbarians* in my contribution to *Understanding Narrative,* and won't rehearse my arguments about those phenomena here. For more on the phenomenon of simultaneous present-tense narration, see Dorrit Cohn's illuminating discussion in *The Distinction of Fiction.*

of the I as narrator and the functions of the I as character.[5] (I will discuss the concept of the implied author at some length in the next chapter; for now I will just define it as the streamlined version of the real author responsible for the construction of the text.) In other words, part of my effort here will be to offer a more adequate account of the formal principles underlying character narration. But I will be equally concerned with the ethical consequences of those formal principles because my approach to character narration is not formalist but rhetorical. That is, rather than focusing only on textual features and their relationships, I am concerned with the multilayered communications that authors of narrative offer their audiences, communications that invite or even require their audiences to engage with them cognitively, psychically, emotionally, and ethically. I will have more to say about this view of narrative as rhetoric later in this introduction (and, indeed, throughout the book), but here I want to emphasize that my conception of rhetoric not only includes both form and ethics but also sees them as interconnected: the formal logic of character narration has consequences for our emotional responses to character narrators, and these emotional responses, in turn, have consequences for the ethical dimension of our engagement with them and with the narratives in which they appear.

These points, and, indeed, the rhetorical approach as a whole, will become clearer as I demonstrate how it can address the curious phenomenon of the character narration in Cisneros's "Barbie-Q," a story from her 1991 collection *Woman Hollering Creek and Other Stories*, and one that is short enough to reproduce in full:

Barbie-Q
for Licha

Yours is the one with mean eyes and a ponytail. Striped swimsuit, stilettos, sunglasses, and gold hoop earrings. Mine is the one with bubble hair. Red swimsuit, stilettos, pearl earrings, and a wire stand. But that's all we can afford, besides one extra outfit apiece. Yours, "Red Flair," sophisticated A-line coatdress with a Jackie Kennedy pillbox hat, white gloves, handbag, and heels included. Mine, "Solo in the Spotlight," evening elegance in black glitter strapless gown with a puffy skirt at the bottom like a mermaid tail, formal-length gloves, pink chiffon scarf, and mike included. From so much dressing and undressing, the

---

5. Although all fictional and some nonfictional narration also involves one text with distinct audiences and purposes, noncharacter narration often elides those differences while character narration rarely does.

black glitter wears off where her titties stick out. This and a dress invented from an old sock when we cut holes here and here and here, the cuff rolled over for the glamorous, fancy-free, off-the-shoulder look.

Every time the same story. Your Barbie is roommates with my Barbie, and my Barbie's boyfriend comes over and your Barbie steals him, okay? Kiss kiss kiss. Then the two Barbies fight. You dumbbell! He's mine. Oh no he's not, you stinky! Only Ken's invisible, right? Because we don't have money for a stupid-looking boy doll when we'd both rather ask for a new Barbie outfit next Christmas. We have to make do with your mean-eyed Barbie and my bubblehead Barbie and our one outfit apiece not including sock dress.

Until next Sunday when we are walking through the flea market on Maxwell Street and *there!* Lying on the street next to some tool bits, and platform shoes with the heels all squashed, and a fluorescent green wicker wastebasket, and aluminum foil, and hubcaps, and a pink shag rug, and windshield wiper blades, and dusty mason jars, and a coffee can full of rusty nails. *There!* Where? Two Mattel boxes. One with the "Career Gal" ensemble, snappy black-and-white business suit, three-quarter-length sleeve jacket with kick-pleat skirt, red sleeveless shell, gloves, pumps, and matching hat included. The other, "Sweet Dreams," dreamy pink-and-white plaid nightgown and matching robe, lace-trimmed slippers, hairbrush and hand mirror included. How much? Please, please, please, please, please, please, please, until they say okay.

On the outside you and me skipping and humming but inside we are doing loopity-loops and pirouetting. Until at the next vendor's stand, next to boxed pies, and bright orange toilet brushes, and rubber gloves, and wrench sets, and bouquets of feather flowers, and glass towel racks, and steel wool, and Alvin and the Chipmunks records, *there!* And *there!* And *there!* And *there!* and *there!* and *there!* and *there!* Bendable Legs Barbie with her new page-boy hairdo. Midge, Barbie's best friend. Ken, Barbie's boyfriend. Skipper, Barbie's little sister. Tutti and Todd, Barbie and Skipper's tiny twin sister and brother. Skipper's friends, Scooter and Ricky. Alan, Ken's buddy. And Francie, Barbie's MOD'ern cousin.

Everybody today selling toys, all of them damaged with water and smelling of smoke. Because a big toy warehouse on Halsted Street burned down yesterday—see there?—the smoke still rising and drifting across the Dan Ryan expressway. And now there is a big fire sale at Maxwell Street, today only.

So what if we didn't get our new Bendable Legs Barbie and Midge and Ken and Skipper and Tutti and Todd and Scooter and Ricky and Alan and Francie in nice clean boxes and had to buy them on Maxwell Street, all water-soaked and sooty. So what if our Barbies smell like smoke when you hold them up to your nose even after you wash and wash and wash them. And if the prettiest doll, Barbie's MOD'ern cousin Francie with real eyelashes, eyelash brush included, has a left foot that's melted a little—so? If you dress her in her new "Prom Pinks" outfit, satin splendor with matching coat, gold belt, clutch, and hair bow included, so long as you don't lift her dress, right?—who's to know.

Applying the principle that character narration is an art of indirection, one in which the same text simultaneously communicates two different purposes to two different audiences, we can say that the success of "Barbie-Q" depends on the implied Cisneros's ability to communicate her perspective to her audience while restricting herself to the vision and voice of the unnamed character narrator as she addresses her narratee. Indeed, this difference between Cisneros's perspective and the character narrator's, a difference that by definition creates some unreliability in the narration (for more on this definition and on types of unreliability see the next chapter), is far more important for the effectiveness of the narrative than its main events—the acquisition of the damaged Barbie dolls and outfits by the character narrator and her playmate and (probably) sister. Consider, for example, the relative flatness of this alternative version that employs a reliable noncharacter narrator and focuses primarily on the events:

> Two sisters who lived in Chicago loved to play with their Barbie dolls. Because their family was poor, each girl had only one doll and one extra outfit. One Sunday, however, the girls went with their family to the flea-market on Maxwell Street and discovered that, as a result of a fire in a local toy warehouse, the vendors had plenty of damaged Barbie merchandise. After pleading with their parents, the sisters took home ten new dolls and several new outfits and happily played with them for many months.[6]

Cisneros develops the interplay between her perspective and the character narrator's in multiple ways, but it makes sense to start by noticing what she chooses to make present and what to leave absent, though im-

---

6. Let me be clear that I do not regard this text as an adequate paraphrase of Cisneros's, a simple transformation of the original into noncharacter narration, or even the only way to render the tale with a reliable narrator and a focus on the events (it would of course be possible to do a version that is less flat). But this version serves my purpose of highlighting the difference between Cisneros's focus on the relation between author's and narrator's perspectives and a telling that focuses on the events.

plied, about the character narrator's identity. Cisneros does not have the character narrator explicitly reveal her age, but the dialogue between the two Barbies in the game the girls play ("You dumbbell! He's mine. Oh no he's not, you stinky!") indicates that this "I" is a pre-adolescent. Cisneros also shows how impressionable the character narrator is by having her voice echo the language of the marketing division of Mattel toys: for example, "sophisticated A-line coatdress with a Jackie Kennedy pillbox hat, white gloves, handbag, and heels included." Notice that as Cisneros reveals the character narrator's approximate age through these features of voice, she also reveals the character narrator's naïveté—and thus establishes substantial distance between herself and her speaker.

Unlike the character narrator's age, her race or ethnicity has no implicit or explicit markers within the text itself.[7] The first effect of this absence is to highlight the narrative's focus on socioeconomic class. Above all, this is a story about the desire of a lower-class girl. Nevertheless, the absence of an explicit textual marker of the character narrator's race or ethnicity does not mean that Cisneros wants us to hear the voice of an unracialized Everypoorgirl. Much in the context of the story collection invites us to read the character narrator as Chicana: every other story in *Woman Hollering Creek* explicitly explores some aspect of Chicano/a experience, and every other one of the seven stories in Part One of the collection, "My Lucy Friend Who Smells Like Corn," is explicitly about Chicano/a children. This part of the character narrator's identity is especially important, given the cultural narratives Cisneros is using as intertexts.

By a cultural narrative, I mean one that has a sufficiently wide circulation so that we can legitimately say that its author, rather than being a clearly identified individual, is a larger collective entity, perhaps a whole society or at least some significant subgroup of society. Cultural narratives typically become formulas that underlie specific narratives whose authors we can identify, and these narratives can vary across a spectrum from totally conforming to the formula to totally inverting it. Thus, for example, a list of current cultural narratives in the United States would include, among numerous others, the story of the triumph of the individual over hardship due to hard work and intelligence, and the story of the individual's corruption, the abandonment of worthy

7. There are also no explicit markers that identify the narrator's sex, but there are so many implicit ones in the attitudes expressed (toward Ken, toward Barbie fashions) that we can confidently infer that the narrator is female. To put it another way, if Cisneros wanted to destabilize our inferences about the sex of the narrator, she would need to include another set of markers pointing more strongly toward the narrator as male.

ideals in exchange for money, sex, or power—or some combination of the three. Cultural narratives fulfill the important function of identifying key issues and values within the culture or subculture that tells them, even as they provide grooves for our understanding of new experiences. My two examples clearly point to American culture's concern with the individual, with success, with definitions of success, and with obstacles to it.

Cisneros's choice of title, the other stories in her collection, and her note "About the Author," as well as the general cultural significance of Barbie dolls, provide a useful guide to our recognition of the cultural narratives relevant to "Barbie-Q." The title is both good-humored and aggressive as it puts the image of burnt Barbie dolls before the audience. The other stories and the author's note are consistent with this attitude as they highlight Cisneros's Chicana feminism. The title story, for example, is an account of a Mexican woman who learns from a Chicana something of the power of women's voices, including her own.[8] The author's note plays off the genre's standard descriptions of the author's family: "The daughter of a Mexican father and a Mexican American mother, and a sister to six brothers, she is nobody's mother and nobody's wife" (n.p.). In light of this feminism and the cultural significance of Barbie dolls, two cultural narratives are especially relevant. The first we might call "Dangerous Role Model Barbie."[9] In this narrative, Barbie's plastic body—white, curvaceous, blond, tall, and thin—becomes an impossible ideal created by corporate America against which American girls can't help but compare themselves negatively. Consequently, Barbie and her corporate producers are partially responsible for eating disorders and self-hatred among women, especially teenagers and young adults. The second relevant cultural narrative is one we might call "Endlessly Acquisitive Barbie." In this one, Barbie's outfits and other accessories, which proliferate incessantly to keep up with changing fashions in clothes and other personal items as well as with changes in society, become a sign of Barbie's upper-middle-class identity and the conspicuous consumption that goes along with it. In this narrative too, Barbie is a dangerous role model because she seems to carry the message that happiness depends on acquiring the right clothes and other possessions—on becoming Madison Avenue's ideal female consumer. This narrative is all the more compelling because it applies so well to the phenomenon of

8. For a fuller analysis, see Phelan, "Sandra Cisneros."

9. This cultural narrative underlies Marge Piercy's poem "Barbie Doll," in which the speaker tells the story of a girl who is so aware of the gap between her own body and the ideal image projected by Barbie that she commits suicide.

Barbie herself. The Barbie industry is a microcosm of a capitalist economy based on creating needs in consumers that the consumers can only partially satisfy. As happens in Cisneros's story, one Barbie and one outfit only engender the desire for more Barbies and more outfits. And no matter how many of each one acquires, new products are always coming on the market.

In the basic materials of "Barbie-Q," then, Cisneros has the potential for a story that would score high on anybody's scale of Political Correctness: the character narrator's monologue about her desire for All Things Barbie, a monologue inflected with the language of Barbie's advertisers, could demonstrate the speaker's interpellation into the value system of mainstream culture, particularly its norms about beauty, fashion, and consumerism, even though those norms implicitly exclude or denigrate someone of her race and class. In such a story, the relationship between Cisneros's politically informed perspective and the character narrator's naïveté would be a highly ironic one even as that irony would also generate sympathy for the girl and antipathy for dominant culture. Cisneros incorporates elements of this story into "Barbie-Q," but she adds a few crucial twists that make it a more subtle—and more ethically challenging—narrative.

Although "Barbie-Q" includes a story of change—the story of how the girls acquired their new Barbies—its overall progression is lyric. That is, the story of change is used in the service of Cisneros's revelation of a more static condition: what it is like to be this poor Chicana girl living with—and responding to—the strong desire for more than she has. More specifically, the first two paragraphs of the monologue begin to reveal the girl's condition and her desire, the next three paragraphs describe the change brought about by acquiring the new dolls, and the last paragraph both finishes the revelation begun in the first paragraph and indicates the girl's attitude toward her situation.

Lyric progressions, as I will show in the final chapter, ask for a fundamentally different response from their audiences than progressions built around a character's change. Our judgments and emotions focus not on characters' choices and what they mean for what does and does not happen to them but rather on the progressive revelation of characters and their static situations. In some lyric progressions, judgment drops out of our response to be replaced by sympathetic identification: rather than viewing the speaker from an observer position, we take on his or her perspective. In others such as "Barbie-Q," judgment is tied not to characters' choices but to the relation among their vision of their condition, that of their implied author, and ours; at the same time, these judgments will be mediated by our emotional responses to the characters.

We can best understand the way judgment and emotion work in Cisneros's story by focusing on the final paragraph, since the most crucial communications of their different perspectives are located there, but in order clearly to see the dynamics of the two perspectives at that point, we should look more closely at the overall construction of the narrative. First, it is not until we reach the last paragraph that we can infer the occasion for the narration. The present tense of the first five paragraphs as well as the shift from the iterative narration of the second paragraph to the singulative narration of the next three makes it difficult to locate the speaker in time. Once, however, we reach the last paragraph, with its shift to the past tense ("didn't get") and its indications that some time has passed since the acquisition ("smell like smoke . . . even after you wash and wash and wash them"), we can reinterpret the tense of the first five paragraphs as historical present and plausibly surmise that the occasion is within a few weeks of the Sunday on which the girls got their new dolls and outfits—perhaps even as early as that afternoon or evening.

But even this plausible inference does not resolve all the puzzling signals about the relation between time of the action and time of the telling: the reference to "next Sunday" in paragraph three is difficult to naturalize since the apparent reference point for "next" is a specific time prior to what happened next. The iterative, however, does not specify a single temporal point from which we can orient ourselves to "next Sunday," and so we have a "next" but not a clear "then." We can, however, naturalize this temporal problem by understanding it as another signal that the character narrator is a young girl, one who has not fully mastered the handling of temporality in storytelling.

This small recalcitrance about temporality pales beside the larger puzzling feature of the technique in the first five paragraphs, what I referred to above as the narrator needlessly telling the narratee what she already knows. I will call this technique *redundant telling,* and will define it as a narrator's apparently unmotivated report of information to a narratee that the narratee already possesses.[10] Since the girl's sister has been present for all of the events narrated, this telling is redundant from her perspective, and Cisneros does not supply—or guide us to infer—any clear

10. Redundant telling is different from what Genette calls repeating narration, the telling of one event *n* times.

motivation for the narrator's address to the narratee. The motivation for redundant telling resides in the *author's need* to communicate information to the audience, and so we might use the longer phrase *redundant telling, necessary disclosure* to describe it.

Most authors who are interested in involving readers in the mimetic component of their creations avoid redundant telling or use it sparingly. For example, what I have called curious about line 49 of Browning's "My Last Duchess" is the tiniest piece of redundant telling Browning can manage in order to achieve his purpose of letting his audience know that the Duke's auditor is a representative from the father of his next Duchess and to maintain the remarkable illusion that we are not just reading a poem but overhearing a conversation. "Barbie-Q" is a very different example of the technique not only because Cisneros does not gesture toward a motivation for the telling such as having the monologue begin with a statement like "Let's tell the story of how we got our new Barbies" but also because the redundancy is so extended. Before I turn to the specific effects of Cisneros's redundant telling, I want to consider how the technique highlights the distinctiveness of character narration.

As my discussions so far have indicated, the standard rhetorical approach to character narration is to assume that the narrator directly addresses a narratee and, through that direct address, the implied author indirectly addresses the authorial audience. Redundant telling indicates that we should refine this description, because the technique reveals that the implied author's indirect address to the authorial audience can interfere with the narrator's direct address to the narratee. This potential for interference, in turn, suggests that communication in character narration occurs along at least two tracks—the narrator-narratee track, and the narrator-authorial audience track. Along the narrator-narratee track, the narrator acts as reporter, interpreter, and evaluator of the narrated for the narratee, and those actions are constrained by the narrative situation (a character narrator, for example, cannot enter the consciousness of another character); let us call these actions "narrator functions." Along the narrator-authorial audience track, the narrator unwittingly reports information of all kinds to the authorial audience (the narrator does not know that an authorial audience exists); let us call this reporting "disclosure functions." Let us call both sets of functions "telling functions," and understand them as distinct from the "character functions" of a character narrator, the ways in which characters work as representations of possible people (what I have called their mimetic function), as representative of larger groups or ideas (their thematic functions), and as artificial constructs within the larger construct of the work (their synthetic functions).[11]

Consider, for example, the first three sentences of *Adventures of Huckleberry Finn*: "You don't know me without you have read a book by the name of *The Adventures of Tom Sawyer*, but that ain't no matter. That book was made by Mr. Mark Twain, and he told the truth, mainly. There was things which he stretched, but mainly he told the truth" (32). Huck begins to establish his relationship with the narratee by reporting a little about himself (he's an unknown quantity unless the narratee happens to have read *Tom Sawyer*) and by evaluating Twain's truthfulness. At the same time, Huck's narration discloses to the authorial audience not only Twain's initial view of Huck as an unassuming boy who knows something about the difference between stretched and unstretched truth but also Twain's comic self-awareness and delight in playing with his audience. Furthermore, the sentences begin to characterize Huck mimetically as that unassuming boy, thematically as someone concerned with issues of truth and falsehood, and synthetically as a device for Twain's indirect communication to his audience. Understanding these sentences involves tacitly understanding the simultaneous—and compatible—operation of the two telling functions and of the character functions.

As in the first three sentences of *Huckleberry Finn*, often the two sets of telling functions converge, or, we might say, the two tracks of communication exist one on top of the other with no space between. This situation is likely to obtain whenever the narrator is the narratee's only source of information about the narrated: in such cases, the narratee and the authorial audience are in the same position with respect to the narrated; both are fully dependent on the narrator for their information. In fact, this situation is the standard case for noncharacter narration, and that's one of the reasons for the differences between the two modes of telling.

In "My Last Duchess," the convergence between the two tracks of communication can be found in every line except 49 where the Duke utters the phrase, "the Count your master's." In that phrase, and in redundant telling more generally, the disclosure functions become dominant over the narrator functions: indeed, if Browning were concerned only about the Duke's narrator functions, he would never have used this

---

11. Noncharacter narration also has this same rhetorical structure; however, it is far less likely that the two tracks of communication will interfere with each other because the noncharacter narrator has more freedom in the range of his/her reporting to the narratee and so the conflicts can be more easily avoided.

phrase.[12] But of course it makes sense that disclosure functions would *ultimately* trump narrator functions since the communication between implied author and authorial audience ultimately subsumes that between narrator and narratee. I say "ultimately" trump because at times an author may temporarily let the narrator functions dominate as a way to create a tension between a narrator's knowledge and the authorial audience's knowledge. In the foreword to *Lolita*, for example, Vladimir Nabokov lets John Ray Jr.'s narrator functions dominate his disclosure functions by having Ray report on the fates of characters Nabokov's audience has not yet met. Indeed, by having Ray refer to Dolores Haze as "Mrs. Richard F. Schiller," Nabokov disguises the fact of her death until Humbert reveals her married name toward the end of his narrative, when he quotes Dolores's letter to him. Interestingly, with Humbert's revelation, Nabokov completes the disclosure of Dolores's death without Humbert's having any knowledge of that disclosure; in other words, the disclosure function of his narration, because it depends on something he cannot know (John Ray Jr.'s preface), occurs entirely without Humbert's awareness.

The distinction between disclosure functions and narrator functions helps us recognize at least part of what is involved in the other curious phenomena I cited at the beginning of the chapter. Ishiguro does not allow Stevens's narration to be informed by his knowledge because to do so would be to have Stevens disclose too much too soon. McCourt violates the restrictions he has placed upon Frankie's narration in order to disclose the silent, mutual understanding between Nora Molloy and Mrs. McGrath. Fitzgerald has Nick narrate the scene in Michaelis's garage for similar reasons: he needs to disclose the events that occurred there to his audience as efficiently as possible.

With her use of redundant telling, Cisneros not only gives us an example of the divergence between the two tracks of communication but also exposes the fault line between the character functions and some of the narrator functions of her character narrator. On the one hand, the narration works hand in glove with the events to create a vivid sense of the character as a possible person—or, in the terms I developed in *Read-*

---

12. This model of dual track communication can also help explain the omissions in the early stages of *The Gambler* discussed by Peter J. Rabinowitz in his essay "'A Lot Has Built Up': Omission and Rhetorical Realism in Dostoevsky's *The Gambler*": the narrator functions become dominant over the disclosure functions. The narrator's information is intelligible to the narratee—himself—but not to the authorial audience because our contextual knowledge is so much less than the narratee's.

*ing People, Reading Plots,* to foreground the mimetic component of the character.[13] On the other hand, the extended use of redundant telling—as well as the story's resistance to a fully satisfactory account of its temporal occasion—calls attention to the artificiality of the narration and, thus, to the synthetic component of both the character narrator and the narrative as a whole. It's striking that the narration in "Barbie-Q," unlike that in "My Last Duchess," where the Duke has clear designs on his audience, is rooted not in the character's need to say certain things on this occasion to this audience but rather in Cisneros's need to communicate certain things about the character to us. It's also striking that Cisneros, unlike Browning, flaunts rather than tries to disguise the predominance of disclosure functions over narrator functions. As usually happens when both the mimetic and the synthetic components of the protagonist are emphasized, the thematic component of both character and narrative gets foregrounded.

That thematic component emerges most strongly through the relation between the specifics of the character narrator's story and the cultural narratives about Barbie identified above. Cisneros plays off rather than conforms to the narrative about Barbie as a Dangerous Role Model and, thus, emphasizes that the character narrator is not simply a victim of mainstream culture's ideas about female beauty. She has little to say about Barbie's body, and that little is either matter of fact or negative: her notice of Barbie's breasts is subordinated to her interest in the "Solo in the Spotlight" outfit ("the black glitter wears off where her titties stick out"), and she describes her sister's doll as "mean-eyed Barbie" and her own as "bubblehead Barbie." Furthermore, she makes it clear that she and her sister would prefer another outfit for Barbie to a Ken doll: "Only Ken's invisible, right? Because we don't have money for a stupid-looking boy doll when we'd both rather ask for a new Barbie outfit next Christmas."

The narration about the fire sale further emphasizes the girls' primary interest in fashion: what the girls notice first are the boxes with the "Career Girl" and "Sweet Dreams" ensembles. (Note how neatly these outfits divide the world of work and the world of home—and how they are both complemented by the social world represented in "Solo in the Spotlight" Barbie.) And it is the very prospect of acquiring *the outfits* that leads the narrator to say "On the outside you and me skipping and

13. For a brief sketch of what I mean by the mimetic, thematic, and synthetic components of narrative, see the discussion of my rhetorical approach in the next section of this introduction.

humming but inside we are doing loopity-loops and pirouetting." The
character narrator's focus, in other words, is not on Barbie's figure or her
whiteness but on her wardrobe and the affluence and social status and
other elements of appearance it represents. This focus makes the relation between the cultural narrative about "Endlessly Acquisitive Barbie"
and "Barbie-Q" more important even as it gives a twist to the relevance
of "Dangerous Role Model Barbie."

The girls clearly share the desire for acquisition identified in "Endlessly Acquisitive Barbie," but their very poverty gives that desire an
edge that the activity of steady acquisition lacks, and that edge is crucial to the story's emotional effect. The middle paragraphs not only emphasize the girls' excitement at the prospect of acquisition, but they also
show how their desire lifts the Barbies out of their mundane surround-
ings, transforming them from the rest of the odd lots on Maxwell Street
into sublime objects: "next to boxed pies, and bright orange toilet
brushes, and rubber gloves, and wrench sets, and bouquets of feather
flowers, and glass towel racks, and steel wool, and Alvin and the Chipmunks records, *there*! And *there!* And *there!* And *there!* and *there!* and
*there!* and *there!*" Cisneros uses this combination of desire and excitement to heighten her audience's sympathy with the girls and even to
induce us to wish, despite our awareness of the relevant cultural narratives, that their desires will be fulfilled.

As noted above, in the final paragraph Cisneros drops the technique of
redundant narration as the character narrator tells her sister—and, indeed, herself—about her attitude toward their new acquisitions. Cisneros asks us, first, to recognize that the character narrator's defensive
rhetorical questions—"So what if . . . ? . . . So what if . . . ? . . . so? . . .
who's to know?"—indicate that she is protesting too much, trying to
convince not just her sister but also herself that the soot, the melted plastic, and the smell of smoke on the dolls do not make any difference. Even
at her young age, she intuitively recognizes, though she cannot consciously admit that she does, the difference between her fire sale Francie and a flawless one. And given the thematic emphasis of the story, the
Barbies function as a synecdoche for the other desirable objects of mainstream culture. Most generally, the character narrator notices the difference not only between her Maxwell Street doll and the ones sold in
Marshall Fields but also the difference between herself and the girls represented by Francie. But her intuitive awareness of the difference does
not at all lessen her desire. This aspect of the paragraph in combination
with the cultural narrative of "Endlessly Acquisitive Barbie" underlines

Cisneros's first thematic point, one that the character narrator does not herself see: the girls will continually be encouraged by mainstream culture to desire what they cannot have. The character narrator's intuitive recognition of her difference is of course accompanied by her explicit denial that it matters, and this double response makes her situation particularly poignant even as it introduces the subtleties that move the story away from one that would score high on the scale of Political Correctness.

Just as the character narrator is not deeply affected by the message in "Dangerous Role Model Barbie" about bodily appearance, she is not fully socialized into the values implied in "Endlessly Acquisitive Barbie" and thus is not just a victim. If she were fully socialized, she would reject the dolls and their outfits as too sooty, smoky, and water damaged to be any good. Instead, the same spirit and desire that transformed the damaged toys into sublime objects when she first saw them gives her response a tone of proud defiance. Her insistence that there is no difference between their dolls and ones bought in "nice clean boxes" and its accompanying implicit insistence that there's no insuperable gap between her and her sister and the girls of mainstream culture are her way of claiming that their poverty and ethnicity do not make all the difference, that she and her sister can pass as the equals of more socioeconomically advantaged white girls. Just as Francie's barbequed leg can be hidden under her outfit, so too can the character narrator's poverty and even her ethnicity become beside the point: "who's to know." Neither the burnt bodies of the dolls nor the child's poverty will disappear, but each can be rendered unimportant through the skillful deployment of the right "outfit." In this respect, the character narrator escapes a full socialization into the value system of "Endlessly Acquisitive Barbie," because she refuses to define her worth solely in terms of her socioeconomic status.

Thus, Cisneros uses the difference between her implied perspective and the character narrator's in some very productive ways. On the one hand, the character narrator's defiance underlines her naïveté, her inadequate understanding of the way the world works. On the other, that defiance is a sign of her strong spirit, something that Cisneros asks us to admire. If the first thematic emphasis of the final paragraph points to the character narrator as victim, this second one points to her as an agent who is not totally defined by her socioeconomic and racial position and who is determined to cope with her situation. This emphasis neither cancels nor supersedes the first one, and the power of the story arises from their coexistence. The story's last paragraph, then, with its revela-

tion of the character narrator as being inculcated with dangerous messages from the dominant culture, and as someone capable of retaining
some independence from those messages, not only completes the lyric
progression but invites us to respond to that completion with sympathy
and respect. I will build on this analysis when I turn to the ethical dimensions of the story but first I need to discuss the general approach I
have taken, one that conceives of narrative as rhetoric.

## Character Narration and Narrative as Rhetoric

The approach includes the following key ideas. First, narrative itself
can be fruitfully understood as a rhetorical act: somebody telling somebody else on some occasion and for some purpose(s) that something happened. In fictional narrative, as I have emphasized throughout the
analysis of "Barbie-Q," the rhetorical situation is doubled: the narrator
tells her story to her narratee for her purposes, while the author communicates to her audience for her own purposes both that story and the
narrator's telling of it. In nonfictional narrative, the extent to which the
narrative act is doubled in this way will depend on the extent to which
the author signals her difference from or similarity to the "I" who tells
the story.

Second, my conception of narrative as rhetoric assumes the possibility that different readers can share similar experiences, and it locates
meaning in a feedback loop among authorial agency, textual phenomena
(including intertextual relations), and reader response. In other words,
for the purposes of interpreting narratives, the conception assumes that
texts are designed by authors in order to affect readers in particular ways,
that those designs are conveyed through the language, techniques, structures, forms, and dialogic relations of texts as well as the genres and conventions readers use to understand them, and that reader responses are
a function, guide, and test of how designs are created through textual and
intertextual phenomena. Methodologically, this view of the relationship
among author, text (including the narrator), and reader means that the
interpreter may begin the interpretive inquiry from any one of these
points on the rhetorical triangle, but the inquiry will at some point consider how each point both influences and can be influenced by the other
two. My own typical method, which I have followed in the discussion of
"Barbie-Q," is to start with the textual phenomena.

Third, this conception of the recursive relationship among authorial agency, textual phenomena, and reader response entails the possibility of shared readings among different flesh-and-blood readers. The author designs the textual phenomena for a hypothetical audience (what I call the authorial audience), and the individual rhetorical reader seeks to become part of that audience. When I start the task of interpretation with my readerly response, I seek not simply to find support for that response in the text as constructed in this way rather than that but also to test that response by considering other ways of construing the text and comparing the adequacy of the different understandings. Rhetorical reading acknowledges that individual readers will find some authorial audiences easier to enter than others, and it stops short of ever declaring any one reading as definitive and fixed for all time. But it assumes that one significant value of reading narrative is the opportunity it offers to encounter other minds—that of the author who has constructed the narrative and those of other readers also interested in shared readings. For these reasons, throughout this book, I will often use the first-person-plural pronoun to refer to the activities of the authorial audience.[14]

Fourth, as I noted earlier, the rhetorical act of narrating entails a multileveled communication from author to audience, one that involves the audience's intellect, emotions, psyche, and values. Furthermore, these levels interact. Our values and those set forth by the narrator and the implied author affect our judgments of characters (and sometimes narrators) and our judgments affect our emotions. The trajectory of our feelings is itself linked to the psychological, thematic, and, as we shall see, ethical dimensions of the narrative. These considerations underlie my attention to the poignancy of the lyric revelation in "Barbie-Q."

Fifth, the principle about the feedback loop among authorial agency, textual phenomena, and reader response comes together with the principle about the multileveled nature of narrative communication to give an important place to the concept of narrative progression, my term for the synthesis of the narrative's internal logic, as it unfolds from beginning through middle to end, with the developing interests and responses of the audience to that unfolding. Narratives typically proceed by the introduction and complication of instabilities, unsettled matters involving elements of story, typically characters and their situations, and/or tensions, unsettled matters involving elements of discourse such as unequal knowledge among authors, narrators, and audiences (as in mys-

14. For more on the model of audience in the rhetorical approach, see Rabinowitz, "Truth in Fiction" and *Before Reading*, as well as chapter 7 of my *Narrative as Rhetoric*.

teries) or matters of different values and perceptions (as in narratives with unreliable narrators). Narratives conclude by resolving at least some of the instabilities and tensions (narratives that resist closure will leave more instabilities and tensions unresolved than those that seek strong closure).

As audiences follow the movement of instabilities and tensions, they engage in many kinds of responses: judging characters, developing hopes, desires, and expectations for them, and constructing tentative hypotheses about the overall shape and direction of the narrative. Furthermore, audiences develop interests and responses of three broad kinds, each related to a particular component of the narrative: mimetic, thematic, and synthetic. Responses to the mimetic component involve an audience's interest in the characters as possible people and in the narrative world as like our own. Responses to the thematic component involve an interest in the ideational function of the characters and in the cultural, ideological, philosophical, or ethical issues being addressed by the narrative. Responses to the synthetic component involve an audience's interest in and attention to the characters and to the larger narrative as artificial constructs. The synthetic component is always present because any character is constructed and has a specific role to play within the larger construction of the narrative, but the synthetic may be more or less foregrounded. Realistic fiction seeks to create the illusion that everything is mimetic and nothing synthetic, or, in other words, that the characters act as they do by their own choice rather than at the behest of the author; metafiction, on the other hand, foregrounds the synthetic component, making us aware of its own construction. More generally, different narratives establish different relationships among these three components. Some narratives are dominated by mimetic interests, some by thematic, and others by synthetic, but developments in the progression can generate new relations among those interests.

Sixth, the doubled communicative situation of fictional narration and even much nonfictional narration—somebody telling us that somebody is telling somebody else that something happened—is itself a *layered* ethical situation. Any character's action will typically have an ethical dimension, and any narrator's treatment of the events will inevitably convey certain attitudes toward the subject matter and the audience, attitudes that, among other things, indicate his or her sense of responsibility to and regard for the told and the audience. Similarly, the author's treatment of the narrator and of the authorial audience will indicate something of his or her ethical commitments toward the telling, the told, and the audience. Further, the audience's response to the narrative will indicate their commitments to and attitudes toward the author, the narrator, the narrative situation, and to the values expressed in the narrative.

These considerations provide a way of discussing the ethical dimension of the rhetorical communication. Work on ethical criticism has exploded in the last decade or so, and there have been many valuable contributions. My approach, like that of such figures as Martha Nussbaum, Wayne C. Booth, Adam Zachary Newton, and Charles Altieri, starts from the general principle that literature in general and narrative in particular, through their attention to the concrete particularities of human situations and their capacity to engage our emotions, provide an especially rich arena for the exploration of ethical issues. More specifically, my approach has most in common with the work of Wayne C. Booth and of Adam Zachary Newton.[15] Each of them, like me, sees ethics as inextricably connected to narrative. Indeed, Booth emphasizes the pervasiveness of ethics in critical responses to literature, and Newton says that he wants to conceive of "narrative *as* ethics." Each of them moves, in his own way, from narrative to theoretical treatments of narrative and then back to narrative. In Booth's case, those theoretical treatments can be found in his own earlier work on the rhetoric of literature. His title, *The Company We Keep*, and his main metaphor, books as friends, grow out of his earlier exploration of the way that writing and reading make possible a meeting of minds between author and reader. *The Company We Keep* moves beyond Booth's earlier major emphases

15. Booth and Newton are themselves part of a broader ethical turn in literary studies over the past fifteen years or so, a phenomenon that should be seen in relation to other, larger developments in the institution. The ethical turn is part of the general reaction against the formalism of Yale-school deconstruction in the wake of the revelations of Paul de Man's wartime writings; it is also compatible with, though distinguishable from, the continuing power of feminist criticism and theory and the influence of African American, postcolonial, multicultural, and queer criticism and theory, all of which ground themselves in sets of ethico-political commitments. The ethical turn in narrative studies is also part of a growing attention to the uses of narrative across the disciplines and in "everyday life."

From this perspective, we can see J. Hillis Miller's work on ethics as an effort to address the connection between the formal concerns of Yale deconstruction and the turn toward ethics. That ethics becomes, for Miller, another way of doing deconstruction is testimony to both the power and limits of deconstruction's conception of language as undecidable. We can also see interdisciplinary interest in the ethics of narrative in Martha Nussbaum's philosophical investigation into narrative's capacity to take advantage of the cognitive power of the emotions as it offers thick descriptions of moral problems and of moral reasoning. For other important work, see Harpham, Davis and Womack, and the special issue of *PMLA* devoted to ethical criticism.

on the cognitive, the aesthetic, and the emotive aspects of that meeting to the contemplation of how our values are engaged as we read, especially the ethical dimension of desiring as the text invites us to desire, and what the ethical consequences of those engagements are likely to be. *The Company We Keep* also gives greater emphasis to the communal nature of ethical response, suggesting that the activity of discussing the ethics of texts, what Booth calls coducing, is more important (ethically) than getting the text "right."

Newton investigates the "ethical consequences of narrating story and fictionalizing person, and the reciprocal claims binding teller, listener, witness, and reader in that process" (11), an investigation that leads him to describe three kinds of ethical structure in narrative: the narrational, the representational, and the hermeneutic. Narrational ethics are those associated with the telling; they occur along the line of narrative transmission from author to narrator to narratee to reader. Representational ethics are those associated with "fictionalizing person" or creating character. Hermeneutic ethics are those associated with reading and interpreting, the obligations readers and critics have to the text. Newton synthesizes work of Mikhail Bakhtin, Stanley Cavell, and Emmanuel Levinas as he does his analyses, borrowing especially Bakhtin's concept of *vhzivanie* or live-entering (empathy with the Other without loss of self), Cavell's concept of acknowledging (being in a position of having to respond), and Levinas's concepts of Saying (performing a telling) and Facing (looking at or looking away).

While I have learned much from Booth and from Newton, I do not want to adopt Booth's overarching metaphor of books as friends, because it seems too limiting, or Newton's idea that narrative is equivalent to ethics because that seems not to recognize all the other things narrative is as well. In one respect, I am trying to go further in the direction that Booth and Newton take, one that ties ethical response to the techniques of narrative itself, as I focus on the links among technique (the signals offered by the text) and the reader's cognitive understanding, emotional response, and ethical positioning. To achieve this end, I have deliberately not followed Newton's example of looking to thinkers such as Levinas, Bakhtin, and Cavell for the ethical categories of my analysis. Instead, I seek to let those categories arise out of the examination of narrative technique and to place as much emphasis on the audience's ethical engagement as on the ethical situations represented in the narrative.[16] To

16. In this connection, the difference between Newton's analysis of *The Remains of the Day* and the one I offer in the next chapter is instructive. He focuses on a number of ethical issues either enacted in the narration or dramatized in the action—"looking away,"

put this point another way, my effort will be to trace how the technical choices of the narrative entail ethical consequences and to stage my own engagements with those consequences. I do not offer my engagements as definitive or comprehensive, but I do hope that they provide the grounds for what Booth would call a productive coduction.

The central construct in my approach is *position, a concept that combines being placed in and acting from an ethical location.* At any given point in a narrative, our ethical position results from the dynamic interaction of four ethical situations:

1. that of the characters within the story world; how they behave— and judge others—is inescapably tied up with ethics;

2. that of the narrator in relation to the telling, to the told, and to the audience; unreliable narration, for example, constitutes a different ethical position from reliable narration; different kinds of focalization also position the narrator differently;

3. that of the implied author in relation to the telling, the told, and the authorial audience; the implied author's choices to adopt one narrative strategy rather than another will affect the audience's ethical response to the characters; each choice will also convey the author's attitudes toward the audience;

4. that of the flesh-and-blood reader in relation to the set of values, beliefs, and locations operating in situations 1–3.

Let me illustrate the method by returning to Cisneros's story.

## The Ethical Dimension of "Barbie-Q"

In a story that depends so heavily on the relation between the implied author's and the narrator's perspectives, it is not surprising that the most important ethical position is the third one, that of the implied author in relation to the narrator and the audience. But the first two positions also matter. With regard to the first, there are two main situations, that of the girls in relation to each other, and that of the girls in relation to the

---

"leaving home," "throwing voice," and others—but his analysis is very much text-centered rather than reader-centered. My concern is much more with the reader's response to specific choices Ishiguro makes in constructing Stevens's narration. Booth's attention to the way in which narratives ask readers to follow a pattern of desires is more in line with what I do in this book, but, again, my effort is to offer more systematic attention to the reader's ethical positioning by the text and by his or her own values.

messages of corporate capitalism and mainstream culture. The relationship between the girls is not greatly developed but what we see is admirable: they play together with pleasure, and they successfully collaborate in the acquisition of the new dolls. Indeed, this aspect of the relationship is another reason we sympathize with the character narrator. We have already touched on the ways that the messages of mainstream culture are ethically deficient, though I want to note here that this deficiency is not dramatized but assumed in the story as Cisneros focuses on the girl's response to her situation.

The most unusual position in the story is the narrator's relation to her audience throughout the redundant telling. In telling her sister what she already knows, the character narrator is violating what H. P. Grice has called the Cooperative Principle of Conversation, which says that one should make one's contribution relevant and appropriate to the situation. More particularly, the character narrator is violating the Maxim of Quantity, which stipulates that one should not tell someone something that he or she already knows. Such violations have the potential to mark the speaker as not just inattentive or socially inept but also self-centered. In this case, however, because the effects of the redundant telling are to foreground the synthetic component of the narrative and to signal Cisneros's greater concern with the thematic purposes of the narrative, those ethical consequences don't occur. Instead, the effect of the redundant telling is to transfer even greater ethical weight to the third ethical situation, the relations among Cisneros, the character narrator, and the authorial audience.

One key to these relations is the lyric progression, the kinds of emotional responses it elicits, and the kinds of judgments Cisneros asks us to make within it. I have noted the importance of our response to the girls' excitement at seeing the Barbie dolls and the way it increases our desire for them to attain their desires. With respect to judgments, it's striking that Cisneros does not ask us to judge specific actions—for example, we do not come away convinced that the character narrator's relentless repetition of "please" means that she is a whiny child—but Cisneros does ask us to see the narration as unreliable in the sense that the character narrator partially misreads and partially misjudges her situation. In this sense, Cisneros positions herself and her audience above the character narrator, looking down on her with superior knowledge and understanding. The ethical risk of such a position is condescension toward the character narrator and even toward our emotional response toward her and her situation: we may end up comfortably reinforced in our superiority, pitying the poor girl who really does not understand what is happening to her and shaking our heads about our own willingness to be taken in by her hopeless desires. If Cisneros had written the Politically Correct version of the story, then she would have invited this kind of condescension from her audience. But the actual story is more ethically challenging, because our superior understanding of the character narrator's situation is accompanied by three other elements of our response: (1) our sustained emotional investment in her desire; (2) our recognition of Cisneros's departure from stereotyped treatments; and (3) our positive judgments of some aspects of the character narrator's response to her situation. Throughout the story Cisneros invokes stereotypes that initially seem to apply to the situation only to show that they are inadequate: the girls are interested in Barbie dolls but not in Ken, who is initially "invisible"; they are interested in Barbie's fashions but not her body; the character narrator is susceptible to the messages of dominant culture but she is not defined by them. By working this way, the story exposes the limits of stereotype-based—or cultural narrative-based—thinking about the character narrator. As she does this exposing, Cisneros does not condescend to the character narrator and does not ask the audience to turn on its own emotional investment but instead guides us to share her respect for the girl. Consequently, flesh-and-blood readers—or at least this flesh-and-blood reader—respond to Cisneros with similar respect. In this way, the story provides an ethically satisfying reading experience.

## Redundant Telling and the Impulse to Preserve the Mimetic

In discussing both "My Last Duchess" and "Barbie-Q" with other readers, I have found that many want to propose alternative explanations of what I have called their redundant telling, explanations that seek to preserve the mimetic component of the story by finding a plausible, naturalistic rationale for the narration. I believe that these alternatives are very revealing because they point to readers' default assumptions about the relation between character functions and narrator functions and about the power of those assumptions to affect our interpretations.

With "My Last Duchess," the alternative explanation is that the Duke's reference to "The Count your master" is motivated by the Duke's interest in reminding the envoy of the significant power differential between them, thereby putting the envoy back in his place after the more deferential treatment of him during the display of the portrait. While this account is sensible, it is also very general: the Duke's interest in exercising his power can be invoked to explain every line of the poem, but such an invocation does not give us a very precise account of Browning's craft in each line. Furthermore, upon closer inspection, the account gives us a different kind of redundancy in the Duke, since the story he has just told the envoy about the fate of his last duchess is all about his audacious exercise of his power. The envoy would have to be extremely dense not to be keenly aware of the place in which he has already been put. For these reasons, I believe that the more persuasive account of the line is that it is an instance of redundant telling. At the same time, our default interest in preserving the mimetic means that we are very likely not only not to notice the redundancy on a first reading but also to try to explain it away when it is pointed out.

With "Barbie-Q," there are three main ways to counter the explanation that Cisneros is employing redundant narration, and there are variations on each of the last two ways: (1) to read the narrator and the narratee as the same character—that is, to understand the narrator's monologue as addressed not to a playmate or a sister but to herself, perhaps in the guise of an imaginary friend; (2) to define a specific occasion for the narration that makes it mimetically plausible; and (3) to find a specific rhetorical purpose for the narrator's telling the story to the narratee. Each of these hypotheses, however, either encounters some significant recalcitrance from the text itself or is grounded less in the details of the text than in the conviction that there must be a mimetic explanation for the telling.

In relation to this last point, it will be helpful to consider briefly the difference between Browning's communication about the occasion and motive for the Duke's telling and Cisneros's communication about these matters in "Barbie-Q." Understanding that the Duke is speaking to the emissary from the father of his next bride shortly before the marriage in order to deliver a warning without seeming to stoop—such an understanding is what I call a necessary inference, since the force of the poem depends crucially upon it. Furthermore, Browning supplies all the relevant clues to the occasion, most of them in lines 49–51,

> The Count your master's known munificence
> Is ample warrant that no just pretence
> Of mine for dowry will be disallowed.

but some in other lines such as "We'll meet / The company below then" (ll. 47–48). Cisneros includes no similar clues to the occasion and motive of her character narrator's monologue, and, consequently there is no necessary inference about them analogous to the one in "My Last Duchess." Consequently, we are left either to supply these matters or to see the first five paragraphs as redundant telling. Experienced readers are of course very good at supplying mimetic justifications, but my argument is that (a) without any clear guidance from Cisneros, any one justification is as good—or bad—as any other, and, thus, (b) the hypothesis about redundant telling is more compelling; furthermore, (c) the mimetic justifications are unnecessary because the conventions of character narration, particularly the principle that disclosure functions will trump narrator functions, allow for the redundant telling to foreground the synthetic and thematic components of the story without eliminating its mimetic interest. But let's look more closely at the mimetic justifications.

With respect to the hypothesis that the narrator and the narratee are the same person, the recalcitrance includes the opening sharp split between "yours" and "mine" and their respective possessions, a split that is reinforced by the subsequent references to what "we'd *both*" rather have and to "our one outfit apiece." The recalcitrance also includes the narrator's remark that directs the gaze of the narratee to the toy warehouse on Halsted Street: "see there?" These recalcitrant details can be accounted for with the variation of this hypothesis that the character narrator is addressing an imaginary friend. But there is nothing in the story that decisively marks the friend as imaginary, and so the move to the variation seems motivated less by textual details than by the need to preserve the mimetic. Furthermore, seeing the character narrator as addressing herself weakens the thematic force of the story because it locates the desire for Barbie and what she represents in a single character, whereas seeing the narratee as a distinct real person expands the horizon of desire.

One can also attempt to preserve the mimetic by specifying the occasion of narration as a time much later than the events reported when the narrator wants to reminisce with the narratee. A related move is to see the shared remembrance as itself something that repeats: this is not the first time that narrator and narratee have gotten together and shared this story. Once again, however, this hypothesis encounters significant recalcitrance: as noted above, the diction of the story marks the narrator as a pre-adolescent, and the shift from the historical present of the first five paragraphs to the simultaneous present of the last ("who's to know") indicates that the narration occurs shortly after the events reported. A variation on this hypothesis admits the redundancy but sees it as part and parcel of the girls' pleasurable sharing of their common experience, a conversion of that experience into narrative. This variation is initially appealing until we realize that it leaps over the story's silence about the narratee's response, and that it deals much more satisfactorily with the story's first five paragraphs than with its concluding sixth.

The hypothesis that the narrator is trying to persuade the narratee to view the dolls in the same way that she does has the advantage of giving a motivated progression to the narrator's discourse: all strokes lead to the argument that they can do just fine with the barbequed Barbies. The problem with this hypothesis, however, is the disjunction between the apparent naïveté of the character and the sophisticated rhetorical purpose attributed to the narrator. In other words, the impulse to preserve the mimetic is not successful on mimetic grounds.

Apart from the specifics of these approaches, I am struck by the power of the interpretive habit to preserve the mimetic. That power is not at all surprising: the mimetic component of narrative is responsible for our emotional responses to it, and those responses are a crucial part of the distinctive quality and power of narrative. Furthermore, the impulse to preserve the mimetic also contributes to the effectiveness of a poem such as "My Last Duchess" by contributing to our willingness to gloss over the redundant telling. The impulse also suggests two other, related conclusions. (1) In reading character narration, we regard the character functions as more prominent than the narrator functions. We are inclined to explain away redundant telling and other examples of disclosure functions trumping narrator functions because we think that such narrative situations will detract from the mimetic function of the character. But my point is that (2) violations of strict mimesis in the narrator functions—or, to put it another way, narrator functions and techniques that depend on the narrator's synthetic rather than mimetic status—can be introduced without entirely breaking the mimetic illusion, provided that they enhance a story's overall purpose and effect. In "Barbie-Q," Cisneros's use of redundant telling exposes the fault line between the "I"'s character functions and narrator functions, but it does not overpower the story's mimetic component. Instead, the redundant telling makes possible the authorial audience's simultaneous understanding of events and the character narrator's perspective on those events, and in so doing provides the basis of our emotional response to her, the response upon which Cisneros builds the thematic component of the story. In sum, it is not possible to account adequately for the redundant telling as a mimetic strategy, but that impossibility is a sign not of Cisneros's flawed construction but of her ingenuity.

## Looking Ahead

In the following chapters, I will examine narratives that raise a broad range of other questions about the rhetoric and ethics of character narration. More specifically, I will start with the question of unreliability and its consequences for ethical engagement in both fiction and autobiography through the analysis of Kazuo Ishiguro's *Remains of the Day* and Frank McCourt's *Angela's Ashes* and *'Tis*. From a formal perspective, the key issues in developing an adequate account of unreliability are (a) determining the scope of the concept and (b) specifying the relations among author, narrator, and audience, a specification that necessarily includes a consideration of the concept of the implied author. From an ethical perspective, the key issue is how the author's treatment of the narrator affects our ethical responses to both. The discussion of unreliability will also lead to my consideration, during the analysis of *Angela's Ashes*, of what I call "restricted narration," by which I mean narration that records events but does not interpret or evaluate them. Restricted narration is typically reliable but, like unreliable narration, it requires the authorial audience to infer communication from the author beyond what the narrator tells the narratee.

I then move to consider Vladimir Nabokov's *Lolita* and Kathryn Harrison's *Kiss*, two narratives that are linked by a kind of inverse relationship: the fictional Humbert Humbert tells the story of his pedophilia and its consequences for his stepdaughter Dolores Haze; Harrison by contrast tells the nonfictional story of her four-year incestuous affair with her father that began when she was twenty. These narratives have generated considerable debate as critics argue for and against their value, and these debates once again demonstrate the interconnections between form and ethics. The discussion in these chapters will pay even more attention to the ethical dimensions of the character narration than in the previous chapters. But with these narratives too there are important formal considerations: in *Lolita*, Nabokov employs what I call "dual focalization," narration in which Humbert the narrator perceives Humbert

the character perceiving Dolores; furthermore, the effect of the dual focalization is to influence Humbert to shift the motives for his telling, a
shift that has major consequences for the ethical dimension of the narrative. In *The Kiss* Harrison employs what I call "suppressed narration,"
a technique in which she withholds relevant information about certain
key scenes, information that we know is relevant not from our beliefs
about what must be relevant to such a situation but from other passages
in the memoir. As this description suggests, suppressed narration complicates the relation between author and authorial audience and so has
significant ethical consequences.

In the last extended chapter, I will return to some matters I have
touched on in the discussion of "Barbie-Q," as I look at two lyric narratives, Ernest Hemingway's "Now I Lay Me" and John Edgar Wideman's
"Doc's Story." The formal and ethical considerations here involve questions about narrative progression and audience engagement: when the
narrative is not telling a story of change, how does it provide a sense of
movement from beginning through middle to end? And how does our
ethical engagement differ when our responses are rooted not in our judgments of characters but in our sympathetic participation in their attitudes, feelings, and situations? More specifically, "Now I Lay Me"
provides a paradigm case of a lyric narrative in which the monologue of
the character narrator, Nick Adams, about past events sheds light on his
current condition. "Doc's Story" presents a more unusual case because
it is a frame tale in which the outer lyric narrative employs a noncharacter narrator and the embedded tale is a standard narrative which the
protagonist of the outer tale tells to himself. Examining "Doc's Story"
will help clarify the nature of both lyric narration and character narration. I will conclude the book with an effort to synthesize and extend the
work of the detailed discussions of these diverse narratives, and then, in
the appendix, I will yield the floor to Charlie Marlow and some of his fellow character narrators as they discuss Joseph Conrad's "Youth."

By the end of this investigation, then, I hope to have offered some gen-
eralizable conclusions about character narration as well as some theoretical principles for approaching variations and deployments of the
technique that I have not explicitly addressed. In other words, while I do
not claim that *Living to Tell about It* addresses every formal use and ethical consequence of character narration, I do hope that it will provide
worthwhile tools for analyzing the diversity of character narration to be
found across the history of storytelling.

# 1 The Implied Author, Unreliability, and Ethical Positioning

*The Remains of the Day*

In "Weymouth," the concluding section of Kazuo Ishiguro's *Remains of the Day*, the character narrator, an elderly butler named Stevens, recounts the climactic moments of his life, a narrative situation in which the distinction between character functions and telling functions is especially relevant. As character, Stevens is so overcome by commingled feelings of love and loss, recognition and regret that his heart breaks. As narrator, Stevens is so complexly reliable and unreliable that Ishiguro places the authorial audience in a very challenging ethical position. Furthermore, Stevens's narration is so richly layered that existing accounts of unreliability cannot do either him or Ishiguro justice. Indeed, during "Weymouth," Ishiguro deftly and unobtrusively offers several lessons in sophisticated character narration and its relation to the ethics of reading, lessons that his audience needs at some level to register in order to feel the depth and power of Stevens's experience. In this chapter, I want to unpack the details of those lessons, paying close attention to how Ishiguro's technique guides our inferencing, where it leaves us to our own devices, and how both the guidance and the freedom affect our ethical engagement with Stevens. In the discussion of this ethical engagement, the chapter will become a collaboration with another reader, Mary Patricia Martin, whose ideas about the novel have deeply influenced mine and whose disagreements with me have enriched my ethical encounter with Ishiguro's narrative. Ishiguro's lessons will lead me to propose a new account of unreliability[1] and, in connection with that ac-

1. In a very fine essay on Ishiguro's technique, Kathleen Wall also recognizes that Stevens's narration provides challenges to existing theories of unreliable narration, but my

count, to redefine the concept of the implied author. But let us look first
at some of the problems of reliability in Ishiguro's narrative.

## Reliably Reading the Unreliable Stevens

Stevens tells the story of his trip in the summer of 1956 from Darlington Hall in eastern England to the West Country, where he meets
with his former coworker, Miss Kenton, who has recently written to him
in some distress about her marriage. Stevens has been having some problems with his new staff plan for Darlington Hall, and he reads in Miss
Kenton's letter a desire to return to her old post and, thus, a solution to
his staffing problems. Ishiguro arranges Stevens's narration into eight
distinct installments, recounting the successive events of his journey;
all the installments are addressed to the same minimally characterized
narratee, a fellow butler. Each act of narration, except "The Prologue"
and "Weymouth," also leads Stevens into memories of his more distant
past. This arrangement means that Stevens narrates each installment
from a different place, both literally and emotionally, because in those
memories Stevens almost unwittingly conducts an examination of his
life. More specifically, the act of narrating leads Stevens to reflect on key
moments in his life, on his three significant relationships with others—
his father, Lord Darlington, and Miss Kenton—and on the two main
ideals that have consistently guided his behavior: (1) a great butler always acts with dignity; and (2) a butler's greatness depends on his loyal
service to a distinguished household. Acting with dignity means always
remaining in control of a situation and one's emotions, never giving way
to sorrow, love, sympathy, never literally or metaphorically "removing
one's clothing in public" (210). Loyal service to a distinguished household means striving to be part of the great affairs of the world through
service to one's distinguished employer. As Stevens moves, mile by mile,
day by day, and narrative installment by narrative installment toward his
meeting with Miss Kenton, he shows intermittent signs of recognizing
the deficiencies of his ideals. It is the meeting itself that leads him si-

---

rhetorical model places greater emphasis on the reader's activity than her more strictly formal model. Consequently, my discussion moves toward the ethics of reading, while hers
moves toward the relation between contemporary ideas of subjectivity and unreliability. For
other helpful commentary on the novel, see Raphael and Shaffer. Raphael is especially insightful about how Stevens's pride affects his interactions with other characters.

multaneously to recognize and regret just how seriously mistaken his ideals have been and how much he has foolishly sacrificed for them. Ishiguro's difficult task is to communicate the psychological complexity, emotional richness, and ethical difficulty of Stevens's climactic realization by means of Stevens's generally reticent and often unreliable narration. Part of my purpose will be to show how well Ishiguro's choice of means serves his narrative ends.[2]

Early in Stevens's meeting with Miss Kenton (now Mrs. Benn), he learns not only that she does not want to return to Darlington Hall but also that she had recently "returned home and [that] Mr Benn had been very pleased to have her back" (233). Stevens comments:

> I am aware, of course, that such matters were hardly any of my business, and I should make clear I would not have dreamt of prying into these areas were it not that I did have, you might recall, important professional reasons for doing so; that is to say, in respect to the present staffing problems at Darlington Hall. In any case, Miss Kenton did not seem to mind at all confiding in me over these matters and I took this as a pleasing testimony to the strength of the close working relationship we had once had. (233–34)

The locus classicus for discussions of unreliability is Wayne C. Booth's 1961 study *The Rhetoric of Fiction*, and although Booth's account has recently come under serious challenge in ways that I will discuss, it remains the dominant approach. A narrator is *"reliable,"* Booth writes, "when he speaks for or acts in accord with the norms of the work (which is to say the implied author's norms), *unreliable* when he does not" (158–59). Booth goes on to explain that a narrator may be unreliable about either facts (what I will call the axis of events) or values (what I will call the axis of ethics) and to describe the special communication— the "communion and even . . . deep collusion" (307)—between implied author and audience that goes on behind an unreliable narrator's back.

Adopting Booth's approach, we can recognize that this passage is a case of unreliable narration: Ishiguro's audience infers a great deal more from Stevens's narration than he is aware that he is communicating. But

---

2. Terrence Rafferty's review of the novel in the *New Yorker* provides an instructive contrast to this chapter's analysis. For Rafferty, Stevens and his unreliability are too easily seen through, rendering the novel too neat and bloodless. In my view, Rafferty underreads not just the subtlety of the technique but the depth of psychological insight and emotional sensitivity it contains.

Booth's approach does not adequately explain our inferencing. That approach would have us take four steps: (1) determine through evidence either in the passage or in the larger context of the narrative that unreliability exists; (2) specify the kind of unreliability it is—about facts, values, or both; (3) link the unreliability to inferences about the narrator as character; (4) reflect on the kind of communion established among implied author, narrator, and authorial audience. The main problems arise in steps 2 and 3.

The seven previous installments of Stevens's narration have cumulatively indicated that although he does have legitimate professional reasons for inquiring about the state of Miss Kenton's marriage, he has even more pressing personal ones. Indeed, the authorial audience recognizes that Stevens's professional purpose is actually a pretext for his personal interest in finding out how Miss Kenton now feels about him. For similar reasons, we can also infer that Stevens's pleasure in Miss Kenton's "confiding in [him] over these matters" is a reminder not just of their former close professional relationship but also of the intimacy that they once shared and that he has been hoping, without ever quite admitting it to himself, they could share again. Yet, the passage is reliable *as far as it goes*; the problem is that it doesn't go far enough. Recognizing that Stevens here is both reliable and unreliable in this way also means recognizing that trying to locate the unreliability only on the axis of facts or values may be inadequate to the complexity of the passage.

Given what we know about Stevens and what he tells us, we can infer that he is seriously either underreporting or underreading his motives here. By "underreporting," I mean that Stevens does not admit to his narratee what both he and the authorial audience know about his personal interest. If he is underreporting, the unreliability does exist along the axis of ethics: Stevens is being intentionally deceptive. By "underreading," I mean that he does not consciously know—or at least is not able to admit to himself—what we infer about his personal interest. If he is underreading, then the unreliability exists along neither the axis of ethics nor the axis of events but along a different axis, one that Booth's work and its various supplements have not sufficiently noticed: the axis of knowledge and perception.[3]

One way to determine whether Stevens is underreading or underre-

---

3. For an important exception, see Riggan. Naïve narration such as we find in *Adventures of Huckleberry Finn* is typically unreliable along this axis. For a discussion of Twain's novel that calls attention to the unreliability resulting from Huck's lack of "cultural literacy," see Preston, "Homodiegetic Narration."

porting is to follow step 3 of the standard approach and examine the link between narrator and character. This method initially produces a clear result: Stevens is underreading. His strict adherence to a code of dignity, which for him has meant denying his feelings, has prevented him from obtaining conscious awareness of those feelings. Thus, it is very much in character for him to locate the motive for his questions to Miss Kenton in professional rather than personal reasons. But if we continue to examine the relation between the roles of narrator and character, the situation becomes less clear. Shortly after this passage, Stevens admits that Miss Kenton's report of being content with her life breaks his heart. I will have much more to say about this moment, but for now I just want to note how it complicates the authorial audience's decisions about Stevens's unreliability. Because Stevens the narrator speaks in the present tense—that is, at the time of the narration, after the anagnorisis of Stevens the character—the standard approach would now lead us to conclude that he is not underreading but underreporting. Although he says, "I am aware," he clearly leaves out much that has entered his awareness by the time of the narration.[4]

Faced with these conflicting conclusions, our analysis may go in one of several directions. If we choose to follow the standard approach, we have two choices: either (1) account for the conflict as a positive contribution to Ishiguro's narrative project, a step that would require explaining how the project benefits from our reading the passage as both underreading and underreporting; or (2) conclude that Ishiguro has mismanaged the narration here, at best producing an incoherent view of Stevens and at worst cheating by making Stevens appear to be underreading when in fact he is underreporting. Alternatively, we could bracket the standard assumption and seek to explain—even perhaps resolve—the conflict by turning back to the detailed workings of Ishiguro's technique. Armed with the distinction between two kinds of telling functions, narrator functions and disclosure functions, I will take this alternate route.

---

4. This information, regardless of how we decide the question of unreliability, establishes the passage as an instance of what Genette calls paralipsis: the narrator not telling as much as he or she knows. My question is about how to read the paralipsis, what kind of effect it has on our understanding of the narrative. In previous work, I have analyzed what I called "paradoxical paralipsis," situations where the narrator's withholding of information seems to violate conventional mimesis but is nevertheless effective within the larger narrative (see my discussions of Hemingway's "My Old Man" and *A Farewell to Arms* in *Narrative as Rhetoric*). In what follows, I offer what I regard as a new and fuller account of the way paradoxical paralipsis works. For more on these passages in Ishiguro's novel, see Wall.

Let us consider the choices Ishiguro faces in his handling of Stevens's narration in "Weymouth" as he builds to the climactic moment. As with the other installments, in this one Stevens narrates the events shortly after they occur; in this case, he is narrating "two days since my meeting with Miss Kenton" (231). Thus, Ishiguro either can have Stevens's narration be informed on every page by the awareness Stevens achieves as character late in the scene, or he can have Stevens the narrator retain his general lack of awareness until Stevens the character experiences his painful éclaircissement. This choice is also one about the timing of the disclosure to both the narratee and the authorial audience of the outcome of Stevens's meeting with Miss Kenton: should there be full disclosure at the beginning of "Weymouth" or some other point prior to that moment in Stevens's recounting of the meeting, partial disclosure through hints or cryptic comments, or no disclosure until Stevens reaches that moment? The distinction between narrator functions (how Stevens's telling establishes and is governed by his narrative situation and his relation to the narratee) and disclosure functions (how Ishiguro's management of that telling establishes and is governed by his relation to the authorial audience) and especially the recognition that these functions do not always operate in concert help uncover the logic of the passage.

If we read the passage as a standard case in which the mimetic logic is preserved and the direct address to the narratee works simultaneously as an indirect address to the authorial audience primarily governed by narrator functions, then it initially appears more plausible to conclude that Stevens is underreporting: as he addresses the narratee, he withholds relevant information about his current state of awareness. This conclusion, however, raises the question of Stevens's motivation for that withholding, a question for which there are no good answers. If we see the withholding as deliberate, then we have to conclude either that (1) Stevens is trying to deceive the narratee—a conclusion for which we have no other evidence and which has no real consequence since Stevens does soon reveal the outcome of the meeting with Miss Kenton—or that (2) Stevens is a consummate storyteller whose ability to build to a climax is comparable to Ishiguro's. Stevens's previous unreliability, which shows him not to be a narrator who, in Alison Case's terms, "plots" his narration, casts grave doubt on this hypothesis.

If we consider Stevens's narration here as a nonstandard case in which the disclosure functions do not neatly converge with but override the narrator functions, then it is more plausible to conclude that Stevens is underreading. This conclusion raises the question of motivation on *Ishiguro's* part even as it invites another look at the narrator functions. Ishiguro's motivation is not far to seek. Withholding the information allows him to build the scene to its climactic revelation: Stevens's confession that Miss Kenton's statement of being satisfied with her life breaks his heart. To put it another way, Ishiguro's motivation is to make the narrative more effective. Furthermore, concluding that Stevens is underreading fits with the narrative progression to this point. As we read the passage in the course of the progression, we do not know that Stevens will achieve his breakthrough, and so we assume that Stevens the narrator, like Stevens the character, is operating with the level of knowledge he has achieved by the end of the previous installment. That assumption renders the passage perfectly intelligible as underreading. Then later, when we get to the climax, this passage of underreading adds to the power of that moment by implicitly underlining the magnitude of his self-recognition.

Returning to the relation between the disclosure functions and the narrator functions, I would suggest that the disclosure functions override the narrator functions in such a way that Stevens's agency as narrator is largely restricted to the axis of reading. While we can see, in retrospect, that it would have made mimetic sense for Stevens's narration to have been informed by what happened later in his meeting with Mrs. Benn, the requirements of Ishiguro's disclosure to the authorial audience effectively block that option. Interestingly, this restriction does not reduce the mimetic illusion, as a comparison with "Barbie-Q" will help illuminate.

Like Cisneros's story, *The Remains of the Day* demonstrates that character narration allows for some divergence between the roles of a character narrator's disclosure functions and narrator functions when that divergence serves the larger purposes of the narrative. Unlike Cisneros in "Barbie-Q," who flaunts the redundant telling, Ishiguro does not want the authorial audience to register the divergence in Stevens's functions until after it affects our reading experience. This difference between on-the-spot and after-the-fact recognition of divergence in the functions does not add up to a difference between an effective and an ineffective technique. Instead, the difference is that between generating one set of effects and another; and each set may or may not serve the larger purposes of the narrative. If we register divergence as it occurs, as we are likely to do in "Barbie-Q," the mimetic component of the narrative will be reduced and the synthetic and thematic enhanced. If we register divergence after it occurs, as in *The Remains of the Day*, the mimetic component of the narrative will not be affected. In each case, the set of effects serves the larger purposes of the narrative.

## The Implied Author and the Location of Unreliability

To this point, I have proposed revising Booth's model of unreliability by highlighting the importance of the axis of perception and understanding and by employing the distinction between the two kinds of telling functions, disclosure functions and narrator functions. I have retained the concept of the implied author, and I have analyzed Ishiguro's narration according to my principle that rhetorical reading involves a feedback loop among the implied author's agency, textual phenomena, and reader response. Since narrative theorists have debated the utility of the concept of the implied author almost from the day that Booth introduced it in *The Rhetoric of Fiction*, and since many of those who want to eliminate the category seek to relocate unreliability only in the interaction of reader and text, I want to reexamine the concept and reconsider the location of unreliability in light of the debate. This effort should clarify both the underlying theoretical issues of the debate and the rhetorical approach I am developing and demonstrating throughout this book. My discussion of the debate does not survey every contribution but rather seeks to highlight the main issues it raises for a rhetorical theorist.[5]

When Booth defines the implied author as a second self that a writer creates in the construction of a text, he is in part responding to two contemporary theoretical positions: (1) the aesthetic ideal of impersonality, the driving force behind the dictum that authors should show not tell and, in that showing, should remain neutral toward their representations; (2) the New Critical stance against authorial intention as a guide to interpretation, famously expressed in W. K. Wimsatt and Monroe Beardsley's "Intentional Fallacy" and its dictum that what the author in-

5. Among other contributors to the debate, see especially Diengott, Toolan, and Nelles. Diengott points to the problem created by conceptions of the implied author that make the figure both the source (what she calls the personalized approach) and the product (the depersonalized approach) of the text and argues in favor of the latter. Toolan offers the intriguing position that the implied author, like the implied reader, is a potentially useful concept but not essential in the way that the concepts of author, narrator, and reader are. Nelles is very good on distinguishing the implied author from the historical author.

tended to achieve is not relevant to the critic's judgment of that achievement. In practice the New Critical position ruled out reference to biography or to any other extratextual evidence of authorial intentions. Booth's definition of the implied author fits nicely with his overall refutation of the ideal of impersonality. In Booth's view, an author will necessarily construct a version of himself or herself (Booth calls this version a "second self") as someone with certain attitudes, beliefs, and values, and these matters necessarily inform the narrative text. Implied authors cannot choose whether to be neutral or partisan; they can choose only the ways in which they will express their partisanship.

Booth's definition responds in a more nuanced way to the anti-intentionalist position of the New Critics. His definition posits a clear continuity between the flesh-and-blood author and the author in the text, while also insisting that flesh-and-blood and textual authors are not identical. (Indeed, Booth tends to regard implied authors as ethical beings who are superior to their real creators.) In this way, Booth suggests that the real author's intention is relevant to the construction of the implied author—the real author chooses a second self appropriate for a particular narrative project—but also allows for a clear distinction between the two by positing the implied author as an entity that can be known from the text itself. Booth's notion of continuity without identity is the logic behind his insistence that the same real author can create different implied authors (a stance that later leads him in *Critical Understanding* [1979] to develop the concept of the career author, defined as a synthesis of the various implied authors of a given author's oeuvre).

As Booth fleshes out his general conception of the implied author by specifying its relation to the text and to the reader, he makes three main points: (1) The implied author is the source for the assumptions, beliefs, norms, meanings, and purposes of the text. (2) Every feature of that text can be understood as a stroke in the service of the implied author's portrait. (3) The reader's task is to reconstruct both the implied author and his or her assumptions, beliefs, norms, meanings, and purposes. In developing these points in a way that will allow him to repudiate impersonality without being guilty of the Intentional Fallacy, Booth sometimes represents the implied author as an external agent who constructs the text and at others as a functional equivalent of the text. "Our sense of the implied author," he writes, "includes not only the extractable meanings but also the moral and emotional content of each bit of action and suffering of all the characters. It includes, in short, the intuitive apprehension of a completed artistic whole" (*Rhetoric*, 73). By positing this equivalence between the implied author and the form of the work, Booth weakens, if he does not entirely lose, his view of the implied author as constructive agent of the text. Interestingly, most narratologists who follow Booth seek to make the implied author a textual function rather than an independent agent.

Two of the most influential later commentators are Seymour Chatman and Shlomith Rimmon-Kenan. Chatman, in his 1978 synthesis of French narratology and Anglo-American narrative theory, *Story and Discourse*, defines the implied author as the structure of the text's norms, and he goes on to develop the still widely cited "communication model" of narrative ("R" stands for "real" and "I" for "implied"):

Narrative text

RA→ | I author→(Narrator)→(Narratee)→I reader | →R reader

Clearly, one of the appeals of this model is its symmetry: there are three entities on the left side and three on the right, and each entity can be seen as the mirror image of the other. As Chatman himself points out, this symmetric model presupposes that both the implied author and implied reader are located within the text. Because Chatman's model has been so widely adopted, Booth's initial point that the implied author is a version of the real author has become much less significant in the general understanding of the concept.

Shlomith Rimmon-Kenan, in her 1983 overview of narratology, *Narrative Fiction: Contemporary Poetics*, continues the move of the implied author into the narrative text. Rimmon-Kenan praises what she calls Chatman's "semiotic account" of the implied author as a voiceless "it" whose communication with the audience is always mediated by other voices: because the implied author is voiceless, Rimmon-Kenan asserts, it "must be seen as a construct inferred and assembled by the reader from all the components of the text. Indeed, speaking of the implied author as a construct based on the text seems to me far safer than imagining it as a 'personified consciousness' or 'second self'" (87). Developing these points further, Rimmon-Kenan concludes that if the implied author "is to be consistently distinguished from the real author and the narrator, the notion . . . must be de-personified, and is best considered as a set of norms rather than as a speaker or a voice (i.e. a subject)" (88). In her effort at analytical rigor, Rimmon-Kenan posits an implied author not as "a participant in the narrative communication situation" but as an aggregation of what is communicated (a set of norms). Indeed, as these quotations suggest, in Rimmon-Kenan's account, the implied author ceases to be either implied or an author.

As those narratologists who found utility in the concept of the implied author moved it further into the text, those who wanted to eliminate it made two main and related arguments. Mieke Bal, writing in 1981, is representative of the first: the concept is vague and ill defined, a kind of catch-all or "critical passepartout" for whatever aspects of narrative transmission were not covered by vision and voice; in other words, since the concept designates neither an author, a narrator, nor a specific kind of textual feature, it seems elusive and unnecessary. Gérard Genette, writing in *Narrative Discourse Revisited* in 1983, offers the second kind of argument: the concept is unnecessary because the categories of author and narrator are sufficient to account for the complexities of narrative communication; introducing an entity between the two violates Occam's Razor. The source of the whole narrative is the real author; the voices speaking in the text are those of the narrator and the characters; there is no pressing need for another entity in the model. Although Genette allows that the implied author is a useful category for apocryphal texts, ghost-written texts, and collaboratively written texts (in all these cases the real author and the implied author do not coincide), he does not see it as necessary for a general model of narrative communication.

Aware of these objections and others, Chatman attempts a redefinition and defense of the concept in his 1990 book *Coming to Terms*. The underlying logic of Chatman's case is as follows: (1) since we recognize that there is often a gap between what a narrator says and what we infer, we can also recognize that there is textual communication other than the narrator's or the characters'. (2) We ought not to identify the source of this communication as the real author because doing so would lead us to interpretations rooted in appeals to biography and authorial intention, appeals that have been largely rejected by current criticism and that have never had much support among narratologists. (3) If, however, we locate the source in the implied author, an entity that is logically prior to and thus can be understood as the "inventor" of the narrator and the rest of the text, we can both explain the gap and remain consistent with an anti-intentionalist approach to interpretation. We can maintain this consistency by conceiving the entity not as a human agent but rather as the "patterns of the text," or the "codes and conventions of the text," or, even, "the text intent." (4) The concept has the practical value of providing a way to make decisions about reliable and unreliable narration. The implied author provides a standard against which to test the reliability of the narrator's statements; if they are consistent with the patterns of the text, the narrator is reliable; if inconsistent, unreliable. In sum, while Chatman gives greater scope to the concept than Rimmon-Kenan, his redefinition reaffirms the conflation of implied author with the text. His concept may be implied, but it's not really an author.

In 1997 Ansgar Nünning launched the severest critique of the concept in his essay "Deconstructing and Reconceptualizing the Implied Author," and then in 1999 he proposed a new approach to unreliability in a companion essay, "Unreliable, Compared to What?" Strikingly, Nünning uses Chatman's 1990 defense as exhibit A in his deconstruction of the concept, an operation based on three main objections: (1) The concept, as introduced by Booth and elaborated and defended by Chatman, is incoherent. On the one hand, the term refers to a subject, an inventor or creator, but, on the other, it refers to a set of objects, a whole text, or the codes and conventions of the text. (2) The concept does not aid but only confuses the communication model of narrative. Echoing Rimmon-Kenan, Nünning asks, if the implied author is a silent agent in the narrative transmission, how does it communicate? Nünning's version of the question takes on even greater force in light of the basic incoherence he finds in Chatman: how can an entity be both a distinct agent in the sequence of narrative transmission and the text itself? Nünning points out that if the implied author is equivalent to the whole text, and if the implied reader is also a textual function, then the implied author is either equivalent to or a subsumption of the implied reader. (3) The main functions of the concept can be better attributed to the real author, but these functions do not have much power in our interpretations. The first part of this move is similar to Genette's: the agent responsible for inventing the text, for creating the narrator, and otherwise organizing the text is not the implied but the real author. The second part echoes the general anti-intentionalist strand of criticism that has persisted since the New Criticism and that characterizes the age of poststructuralism with its embrace of Barthes's proclamation of the death of the author and celebration of the multiple significations of texts. To locate the meaning of the text in the real author is a discredited approach to interpretation.

Nünning reconstructs the concept by proposing to replace it. Rather than invoking the "implied author," Nünning recommends that we refer to "the structural whole," a term that means something very close to what Booth means by "a completed artistic whole" and to what Chatman means by the "text intent." Nünning defines it this way: "an absent cause which is only identifiable on the basis of its consequences," or as Louis Althusser says, "not empirically present as an element, . . . not part of the whole or one of the levels, but rather the entire system of relationships among those levels" (quoted by Nünning, "Deconstructing," 111). More specifically, Nünning identifies the textual features that can be located at the level of the structural whole: book and chapter divisions; the order or sequence of narrative happenings (when not explicitly attributed to a narrator) and other aspects of the handling of time; the perspective structure; the constellation of characters and the contrasts and correspondences among them. Most generally, the whole structure is the "system of all superordinate formal relationships" (114) and their governing of the rest of the narrative's elements. Given the similarity between Booth's idea of "completed artistic whole," Chatman's "text intent," and Nünning's "structural whole," his proposal to this point is largely for clarifying terminology: since even Chatman is not really talking about an author, let's eliminate, once and for all, the notion of the implied author as an agent who constructs the text by eliminating the very term. We can then more clearly and consistently designate the textual properties narratologists want the term to designate by using the phrase "the structural whole."

With his final move, however, Nünning suggests another shift in the narratological communication model, because he contends that the structural whole does not inhere in the text but is constructed by the reader, and, thus, can vary from reader to reader. He opts, in other words, for what he labels a constructivist epistemology, because he finds it compatible both with the work of reception theory and with the empirical phenomenon of the polyvalent nature of literary meaning.

Having deconstructed the concept of the implied author and embraced constructivism, Nünning recognizes that he needs a new model to account for unreliability. This new model supplements constructivism with a cognitive approach to understanding narrative. While texts can contain signals of unreliability such as a narrator's inconsistent or contradictory comments, Freudian slips or linguistic markers of a high degree of emotional involvement, these alone, Nünning argues, will not be sufficient to account for all cases of unreliability. We need also to recognize that the "world model or conceptual information previously existing in the mind of the individual reader or critic" ("Unreliable," 66) interacts with textual signals to produce narrative interpretations. Nünning identifies two main kinds of conceptual frameworks relevant to reader's judgments of unreliability: (1) extraliterary, having to do with knowledge of the real world and cultural codes, assumptions about human behavior, awareness of the social, moral, and linguistic norms existing at the time of represented action in the narrative, and the reader's individual perspectives on these and other matters; and (2) literary, having to do with knowledge of conventions, stereotypes, genres, styles, intertexts, and with the specific structure of the text under consideration. Furthermore, Nünning argues that because these two frameworks change over time, readers at different times will respond to the same narrator differently. In determining unreliability at any one temporal point, the reader will first recognize some inconsistency between the text and one or more of these conceptual frameworks and then make a move to "naturalize" the text by attributing a specific kind of unreliability to it. Through this process of naturalization, the inconsistency, instead of being an unresolved problem in the text, becomes a part of the text's larger design.[6]

The debates about the implied author, then, entail several underlying and interrelated theoretical issues:

1. the elegance and effectiveness of the communication model: Booth, Chatman, and Rimmon-Kenan all find the implied author to be a necessary part of such a model; Genette finds it to be (largely) unnecessary; and Bal and Nünning find it to be an impediment to narratological analysis;

2. the role of human agents in the communication model: Booth's idea of the implied author as a second self entails the view that the implied author is a human agent; Chatman and Rimmon-Kenan, however, explicitly reject what they refer to as an anthropomorphic conception of the implied author; Nünning agrees with that rejection but wants to take the additional step of eliminating the category completely;

3. authorial intention: Booth's concept of the implied author does not explicitly embrace authorial intention as the key to interpretation, but it does not deny a role to intentionality either; Chatman, Rimmon-Kenan, and Nünning, on the other hand, carefully distance themselves from any allegiance to interpretations based on authorial intention;

4. the role of the reader: in Booth's model, the reader infers what the author implies; in Nünning's model, the reader constructs the text's structure and, indeed, various features of the author;

6. For an excellent related argument, see Yacobi.

5. the relation between narratology and other developments in criticism such as constructivism and cognitive models of understanding.

A successful response to the debate about the implied author should do
at least three things: (1) provide a coherent and widely applicable redefinition of the concept; (2) provide a coherent and cogent position on the
various underlying theoretical issues; and (3) provide a viable model for
reading unreliable narration. I'll start with the first task: *the implied author is a streamlined version of the real author, an actual or purported
subset of the real author's capacities, traits, attitudes, beliefs, values,
and other properties that play an active role in the construction of the
particular text.* As the phrase "actual or purported subset" indicates, the
initial adjective and the initial noun of the definition deserve emphasis:
"streamlined" indicates that the implied author is a partial representation of the real author and "version" indicates that the implied author
is a construction by the real author. Thus, this definition can account
both for the common situation in which the implied author is an accurate reflection of the real author's capacities, attitudes, beliefs, values,
and other properties and for the less common but significant situation
in which the real author constructs an implied author with one or more
significant differences from herself—for example, when a woman author
constructs an implied author who is male (Marianne Evans/George
Eliot), or a white author an implied author who is nonwhite, as Forrest
Carter did in his controversial *Education of Little Tree.*[7] This definition
also moves away from Booth's occasional conflation of the implied author and the text and sharply contrasts with Chatman's, Rimmon-Kenan's, and, in a different way, Nünning's efforts to make the implied
author solely a textual function. In my account, the implied author is
not a product of the text but rather the agent responsible for bringing the
text into existence.

This understanding moves my position closer to Genette's, while still
clearly distinguishing the author and the implied author; it will, however, be useful to address Genette's point that the communication model
would be both more elegant and more effective with just two agents of
communication, the author and the narrator. I, too, like Occam's theoretical shaving, and for that reason can agree with Genette that, for many
practical purposes, insisting on a distinction between the author and the

---

7. *The Education of Little Tree* purports to be the autobiography of a Cherokee growing
up within American Indian culture, whereas the real Forrest Carter is probably not a Cherokee and definitely someone who has espoused white supremacist doctrines.

implied author is multiplying entities beyond necessity. However, I believe that including the implied author in our general theoretical model of narrative communication allows for greater clarity, precision, and comprehensibility. First, the concept captures something important about the acts of writing and reading narrative. Writers create versions of themselves as they write, and readers understand both that a narrative is a communication from a real person and that they can come to know a version of that person through the narrative. Second, as suggested above, the concept allows for an effective way of talking about works in which a real author takes on values, beliefs, attitudes or even features of identity that he or she does not actually espouse or possess. Indeed, this way of talking about such works opens up a useful way of exploring their ethical dimensions: on what grounds do we say that one discrepancy between a real and an implied author constitutes an act of deplorable dishonesty, while a different discrepancy represents an ethically admirable act? Third, and closely related, as Genette notes, the concept helps explain such phenomena as hoaxes, ghost-written works, and collaborative works. In ghost-written narratives and one kind of hoax (e.g., the *Hitler Diaries*), the real author attempts to construct an implied version of himself or herself that can pass for someone else. In another kind of hoax, such as the one Alan Sokal famously perpetrated on the editors of *Social Text*, the relation between real and implied author is more complicated. The real author constructs an implied author who actually closely shares her beliefs, attitudes, and values but who seems sincerely to espouse quite different ones. Consequently, although it is possible to recognize the masquerade without being told one is being enacted, unsuspecting readers, especially those who share the values the implied author is pretending to espouse, are likely to be taken in. The implied Sokal, for example, writes a jargon-ridden prose into which he slips such questionable claims as "the pi of Euclid and the G of Newton, formerly thought to be constant and universal, are now perceived in their ineluctable historicity" (222). If one's antennae for irony are up, these claims point to the implied author as parodist; but, if one regards the jargon as a sign of the implied author's learning and one is a strong social constructionist, one will take the implied author as ploddingly earnest. To take Genette's third example, collaborative texts, we can recognize that different parts of multiple authors get synthesized into a coherent implied author (or, in some cases, the different parts remain unsynthesized and the implied author is an incoherent figure).

Fourth, the rhetorical definition of the concept clarifies the possible role of biography in rhetorical analysis. Reference to biography may or may not be helpful; such reference may give us insight into the real author beyond what we may infer from the narrative text, but this additional insight may or may not be relevant to that text's implied author, depending on the degree of overlap between the implied author and the real author.

In this connection, it is worth noting that reestablishing a closer link between the flesh-and-blood author and the implied author and regarding the implied author as the agent who is the source of the narrative enable us to acknowledge that there is no a priori reason to assume that a given implied author will be consistent in his or her attitudes, norms, and beliefs. Just as flesh-and-blood authors are full of inconsistencies so may implied authors be, and such inconsistency may very well accompany a real author's attempt to take on values and properties he or she does not really hold or possess. At the same time, this conception of the implied author also allows us to recognize that where flesh-and-blood authors may be inconsistent in their attitudes or values they may create implied authors who are far more consistent (for useful arguments about inconsistent implied authors, see Preston ["Implying"] and Lanser ["(Im)plying"]). Similarly, the conception allows us to recognize that real authors may, as Booth often notes, create implied authors who are more admirable than themselves—or, alternatively, less admirable than themselves. Furthermore, because the implied author is a version of a real author, an implied author has a version of the real author's unconscious.

My definition of the implied author not only suggests that we have, in effect, two human agents on the left side of the communication model (the real author and the implied author) but it also disrupts the neat symmetry of Chatman's model. The implied author moves outside the text, while the implied reader, which, in my rhetorical model is equivalent to the authorial audience, remains inside the text. The implied author as the constructive agent of the text builds into that text explicit and tacit assumptions and signals for the hypothetical ideal audience, the audience that flesh-and-blood readers seek to become.

My conception of the implied author also leaves room for authorial intention (as realized in textual phenomena) as an important component of interpretation, but it does not make authorial intention either the sole or the dominant determiner of a text's meaning. As I have previously noted, this model views meaning as arising from the feedback loop among authorial agency, textual phenomena, and reader response. Here I can add that the authorial agency is exercised through the implied author. Because the approach attends to the flesh-and-blood reader's effort to enter the authorial audience, it remains aware that there may be gaps between author's intentions and readers' conclusions about those intentions. At the same time, I do not want, as Nünning and so many other contemporary theorists do, to reject the notion that writers can fashion their texts to communicate sharable meanings and that readers can, and frequently do, apprehend those meanings. A more detailed response to Nünning's critique will clarify my position about the role of the reader and about the relations between (1) narratology and constructivism and (2) narratology and cognitive approaches to interpretation.

At one level, Nünning and I want to recommend different kinds of interpretive projects with different purposes. Nünning's constructivism suggests that he wants to focus on differences among readers, on the ways in which the same textual phenomena can and often will be construed in different ways by different readers, especially as readers and reading conventions change over time. As I noted above, I am interested in developing an approach that accounts for the ways in which readers might share understandings with authors and with each other. I acknowledge that readers often differ and that accounting for that difference can be a valuable critical enterprise. My main contention, however, is that Nünning's case for constructivism does not invalidate my case for rhetorical reading.

Indeed, to push that contention further, I find Nünning's specific proposal to replace the implied author with "the structural whole" and to locate the agency for determining the structural whole in the reader less satisfactory than the rhetorical model because it fails to identify the multiple constraints on readerly agency, constraints imposed not just by texts and conventions of reading but by the designers of those texts, implied authors. Nünning himself implicitly recognizes these constraints when he identifies the range of textual phenomena that point to unreliability: the interpretive move to read an inconsistency as a sign of unreliability rests on the assumption that someone designed the inconsistency as a signal of unreliability. More generally, the move to naturalize the text rests upon a similar assumption: the surface problem in the text has been planted by an agent who expects the audience to recognize that the problem signifies something beyond itself. Moving to the larger issue of the structural whole, we can also recognize that such a whole is originally designed, whether consciously, intuitively, or in some combination of the two, by the implied author and that the text contains legible evidence of that design, evidence that can be appealed to in order to adjudicate between different hypotheses about that design. While not all such appeals will be decisive—and, indeed, I will soon be examining a case where I believe they are not—many will. The analyses of "Barbie-Q" and the passage from *The Remains of the Day* offer examples of how one can use evidence of the structural whole to choose between different interpretive hypotheses.

Nünning's proposal to supplement narratological analysis with cognitive approaches to understanding is subject to a similar kind of analysis. The proposal makes good sense because textual phenomena always need to be construed within some kind of larger framework. But if readers need conceptual schema to construct interpretations, authors also need conceptual schema to construct structural wholes. In other words, writers work not just with words, sentences, characters, events, settings, and narrative discourse; they also work with conceptual schema as they find principles for structuring the elements of narrative. In rhetorical reading, part of the reader's task is to reconstruct the conceptual schema that give the text its particular shape.

For all these reasons, then, I want to include this revised concept of the implied author within my theoretical account of narrative communication and to regard the implied author as the source of unreliable narration. But I have also discovered that it is cumbersome to refer repeatedly and consistently to a given implied author with the phrase "the implied X." Consequently, from this point on, I will sometimes use the author's last name as a shorthand for "the implied X," but, when I want to refer to the real author, I will use the phrase "the flesh-and-blood X."

## Six Types of Unreliability

I turn now to consider kinds of unreliability. Consistent with my theoretical model, my taxonomy is focused on the relations among implied author, narrator, and authorial audience; more specifically, it is focused on the activities of the narrator as teller and as discloser and on those of the authorial audience as reinterpreter of what is told. Given these emphases, I want, first, to broaden Booth's original definition beyond just the axes of events and of values: a character narrator is "unreliable" when he or she offers an account of some event, person, thought, thing, or other object in the narrative world that deviates from the account the implied author would offer. I want to broaden the definition for two reasons: (1) regardless of the axis, all deviations require the authorial audience to infer an understanding of the narration different from that offered by the narrator; (2) there is a strong family resemblance among deviations, and, indeed, one kind of deviation will often be accompanied by its kin. Consequently, I prefer to label all deviations with the single term "unreliable" and then differentiate among kinds of unreliability rather than creating separate terms for different deviations.[8] The first reason for broadening the definition also points to my interest in offering a "thicker" rhetorical description of unreliability, one that attends to both narrator functions and disclosure functions. This attention will allow us to account more precisely for the double communication involved in unreliable narration: the narrator's communication to the narratee and the implied author's quite different communication to the authorial audience. In most unreliable narration, unlike the situation of redundant telling in "Barbie-Q," there is no incompatibility between the two functions; indeed, part of the challenge for the implied author in the standard case is to use the same text to send two different messages without the interference we saw in redundant telling.

Narrators perform three main roles—reporting, interpreting, and evaluating; sometimes they perform the roles simultaneously and sometimes sequentially.[9] They may, therefore, deviate from the implied author's views in one or more of these roles simultaneously, sequentially, or intermittently. With such deviations the disclosure functions and the narrator functions may very well work harmoniously, but in all cases, the authorial audience will recognize a communication from the implied author beyond the awareness of the narrator.

As we have seen, the metaphor of axes of unreliability helps to differentiate among different kinds of deviation: unreliable reporting occurs along the axis of characters, facts, and events; unreliable reading (or interpreting) occurs along the axis of knowledge and perception; and unreliable regarding (or evaluating) occurs along the axis of ethics and evaluation. The activity of the authorial audience allows us further to distinguish kinds of unreliability. Audiences perform two qualitatively different actions once they determine that a narrator's words can't be taken at face value: (1) they reject those words and, if possible, reconstruct a more satisfactory account; or (2) they do what I have done with

8. Commenting on Stevens, Daniel Schwarz, for example, writes, "Stevens is more an imperceptive than unreliable narrator; he is historically deaf to his implications rather than untruthful" (197).

9. See Ryan for a suggestive account of how we might differentiate among narrators in another way.

the passage from "Weymouth"—accept what the narrator says but then supplement the account. (Although it is possible to distinguish a third option here, namely "subtracting from" the narrator's account as, for example, when we have a narrator given to overstatement, I find "subtraction" or "discounting" similar enough to "rejecting and reconstructing" that I do not create a separate category of unreliability to describe it. When we add to a narrator's account, we have a stable base on which to do the addition; when we subtract, we don't have the same stability: in trimming the narrator's inflated account, we have to decide what should go and what should remain.)

Combining the activities of narrators and audiences, then, I identify six kinds of unreliability: misreporting, misreading, misevaluating—or what I will call misregarding—and underreporting, underreading, and underregarding. Misreporting involves unreliability at least on the axis of characters, facts, and events. I say "at least" here because misreporting is typically a consequence of the narrator's lack of knowledge or mistaken values, and, consequently, it almost always occurs with misreading or misevaluating. When Stevens says that he stood outside Miss Kenton's door and heard her crying after she learned of her aunt's death, he is misreporting. When he later corrects the report to say that he was in that position on the night she became engaged, we understand that his misreporting was a consequence of his mistaken value system, which denies the importance of his own emotions and so initially leads to a memory which locates all the dolorous emotions of the scene in Miss Kenton.

Misreading and misregarding may occur either by themselves or in combination with other kinds of unreliability. Misreading involves unreliability at least on the axis of knowledge/perception. When Stevens says that "any objective observer" will find the English landscape "the most deeply satisfying in the world" (28), he demonstrates a misperception analogous to his saying that "any objective observer" would find English cuisine the most satisfying in the world. Since his descriptions of the landscapes, however, are both accurate and sincere, one might argue either that the misreading exists by itself or, as I would, that the misreading is also sign of a mistaken value system that finds "unobtrusiveness" to be one of the greatest virtues. Misregarding involves unreliability at least on the axis of ethics and evaluation. When Stevens rationalizes his lying about having worked for Lord Darlington, he is misregarding: not only is his claim that "Lord Darlington was a gentleman of great moral stature" (126) untrue, but his denials suggest that at some level of consciousness he knows it is untrue.

Similarly, underreporting, underreading, and underregarding occur respectively on the axes of characters, facts, and events; understanding and
perception; and ethics and evaluation. Underreporting, which Genette
calls paralipsis, occurs when the narrator tells us less than he or she
knows. When Stevens reports that he has denied working for Lord Darlington but defers telling the narratee (and us) about Lord Darlington's
disgrace, he is underreporting. Not all underreporting, however, constitutes unreliability, and it is worth distinguishing unreliable underreporting from reliable *elliptical narration*, that is, telling that leaves a gap
that the narrator and the implied author expect their respective audiences to be able to fill.[10] At several places in the narrative, including later
in "Weymouth," we learn from the dialogue of other characters but
never from Stevens's direct report that he is crying in public. On those
occasions, Stevens is underreporting his emotions, and this underreporting is a clear sign of the reticence of his character. But Stevens's
telling at these points is reliable elliptical narration rather than unreliable underreporting: his report of the other characters' dialogue indicates
that he expects his narratee to infer that that he has been crying. Elliptical narration can of course also be unreliable, as, for example, when the
narrator deliberately guides the narratee to fill in the gap inaccurately;
in this case, the elliptical narration would fall under the rubric of misreporting. I will return to the category of elliptical narration in chapter
4 when I compare it with what I call suppressed narration.

Underreading, as we have seen in the passage from "Weymouth," occurs when the narrator's lack of knowledge, perceptiveness, or sophisti-
cation yields an insufficient interpretation of an event, character, or
situation. Underregarding occurs when a narrator's ethical judgment is
moving along the right track but simply does not go far enough. A possible instance of underregarding, one that I shall return to, occurs when
Stevens entertains the idea, at the very end of "Weymouth" that "in bantering lies the key to human warmth" (245).

Having sketched this taxonomy, I want to emphasize some important
points about its possible uses and abuses. As the illustrations from *The
Remains of the Day* indicate, a given narrator can be unreliable in different ways at different points in his or her narration. As we have also

10. It is also arguable that all narrators report less than they know, since narration necessarily involves selecting from among the welter of events, thoughts, feelings, and experiences that make up the raw material of "what happened" those that are most salient for the
narrator's account. But I distinguish this general condition of narrative from the underreporting of what is clearly salient.

seen, a narrator can also be unreliable in more than one way at any one point in his narration, and, indeed, misreporting will usually be accompanied by another kind of unreliability. Furthermore, even where the unreliability initially seems to be of one kind (located along only one axis), once the authorial audience makes inferences about the relation between the narrator's unreliability and his or her character, the unreliability is likely to reveal itself as multifaceted. Finally, in many cases the border between types, especially the one between two types identified by the same root (e.g., misreporting and underreporting) will be soft and blurry rather than hard and firm. For these reasons, debates about whether a particular instance of unreliable narration is of one type rather than another are likely to be far less productive than debates about whether a particular instance of narration is reliable or unreliable. And for the latter debate, the important question is what we can infer about the implied author's relation to the narration. For example, one could imagine an implied author who wished to present Stevens's views about the beauty of the British landscape as reliable narration that served primarily to characterize him, but such an implied author would be very unwise to have Stevens find fault with the "unseemly demonstrativeness" of the beauty to be found in Africa and America, for it is through such signals that Ishiguro makes it clear that he is both characterizing Stevens and indicating his unreliability.

In sum, I propose my taxonomy not as a new set of tools for an aging Procrustes but rather as a heuristic device designed to sharpen our perceptions of individual acts of unreliable narration. At the same time, recognizing these different kinds of unreliability allows us to move away from the common assumption that reliability and unreliability are a binary pair, that once any unreliability is detected all the narration is suspect, and, instead, to recognize that narrators exist along a wide spectrum from reliability to unreliability with some totally reliable on all axes, some totally unreliable on all, some intermittently unreliable on all, and some unreliable on one or two axes and not on others.

## Telling, Acting, and the Ethics of Reading

n.b. *From this point forward, the chapter has been coauthored with Mary Patricia Martin.*

As Ishiguro builds to Stevens's climactic realization in "Weymouth," the inferences he asks his audience to make become more complicated and the lessons of the narrative expand to the domain of ethics. Ishiguro guides our inferences not only through Stevens's underreporting but also through the extensive dialogue. Because the inferencing is so complex, we will review the major steps leading to Stevens's moment of recognition. As they wait for the bus that will take Miss Kenton back to her husband, Stevens explicitly requests her permission to ask "something of a rather personal order" (237), namely, whether she is "ill-treated in some way" (238). Stevens begs her forgiveness for asking but says it is something he's been concerned about for a long time and that he "would feel foolish had [he] come all this way and seen you and not at least asked you" (238). After Miss Kenton assures him that "my husband does not mistreat me at all in any way," Stevens remarks that, then, "one is rather mystified as to the cause of your unhappiness" (238). Miss Kenton revises his question, saying that she understands him to be asking something of an even more personal order, "whether or not I love my husband." She explains that, although she initially got married only to conduct "another ruse . . . to annoy you," she has grown to love her husband. However, she adds this reflection:

> "But that doesn't mean to say, of course, there aren't occasions now and then—extremely desolate occasions—when you think to yourself: 'What a terrible mistake I've made with my life.' And you get to thinking about a different life, a *better* life you might have had. For instance, I get to thinking about a life I may have had with you, Mr Stevens. And I suppose that's when I get angry over some trivial little thing and leave. But each time I do so, I realize before long—my rightful place is with my husband. After all, there's no turning back the clock now. One can't be forever dwelling on what might have been. One should realize one has as good as most, perhaps better, and be grateful." (239)

Stevens's response contains the climax:

> I do not think I responded immediately, for it took me a moment or two to fully digest these words of Miss Kenton. Moreover, as you might appreciate, their implications were such as to provoke a certain degree of sorrow within me. Indeed—why should I not admit it?—at that moment, my heart was breaking. Before long, however, I turned to her and said with a smile:
> "You're very correct, Mrs Benn. As you say, it is too late to turn back the clock. Indeed, I would not be able to rest if I thought such ideas were the cause of unhappiness for you and your husband. We must each of us, as you point out, be grateful for what we *do* have." (239)

Moments later, Stevens and Miss Kenton part, and as she goes, Stevens notes that "her eyes had filled with tears" (240).

Drawing on our previous inferences about both Stevens and Miss Kenton, we can recognize that much is going on beneath the surface of the scene. Miss Kenton's move to speak more directly and frankly reveals only the thinnest layer of the deep subtexts operating here. Just as Stevens's narration is marked by underreporting and underreading, his dialogue and Miss Kenton's are marked by some combination of what we might call understating (the character-to-character equivalent of under-reporting—they say less than they mean and so convey less to each other) and indirection (they say less than they mean but convey their meaning anyway). Reading the dialogue requires the same kind of inferential activity that reading Stevens's narration does.

Ishiguro wants us to recognize that Stevens's question to Miss Kenton about being ill treated is the first personal question he has ever asked her. But we also infer that it is a pale reflection of the question that he really wants to ask, though he himself does not yet fully realize what that question is. Miss Kenton's revision of his question shows that she recognizes both these facts, even as that revision, despite its move toward greater disclosure, also stops short of the real question. Miss Kenton's additional remarks about the life she might have had with Stevens then constitute her answer. That question, of course, is "Do you still love me?" and Miss Kenton's answer is "I used to love you, and, indeed, I loved you more than I love my husband now, but my feelings have altered and it's now too late for us to think about a future together." Stevens's heart breaks precisely because, in the "moment or two [it took] to fully digest these words of Miss Kenton," he is registering their subtext. He not only still loves Miss Kenton but his trip and his reminiscences have made his feelings more acute even as they've led him to value those feelings more. Reading the scene, we feel our hearts about to break in sympathy.

Part of the power of the scene derives from how Ishiguro orchestrates the movement of Stevens's narration from underreporting back to reliable reporting. Ishiguro uses the extreme formality and self-distancing rhetoric of the statement, the "implications [of Miss Kenton's words] were such as to provoke a certain degree of sorrow within me," to mark it as underreporting. Consequently, Stevens's shift to the frank, plain-spoken acknowledgment, "Indeed—why should I not admit it?—at that moment, my heart was breaking," stands out as his most directly honest statement in the narrative. Yet even here Ishiguro requires us to infer a lot beyond what the statement directly asserts: Stevens's admission is simultaneously (1) a realization that he loves Miss Kenton—and, indeed, has loved her for years; (2) an acknowledgment that she has told him what he had hoped was true and what he had undertaken the journey to find out, namely, that she too had loved him; and (3) an expression of his belief that he has lost his chance to have her return his love. Thus, the moment when he fully acknowledges to himself that he loves her is also the moment that he realizes he is too late.

In the authorial audience, our knowledge of Stevens's character and situation has been greater than his own throughout the whole course of the narrative. As the trip has progressed, however, Stevens has gradually, albeit inconsistently, moved toward what we know. In this sentence, Ishiguro not only shows that Stevens now knows his heart as well as we do but also that Stevens comprehends more about his situation than we are likely to do in the "moment or two" he takes "to fully digest" Miss Kenton's speech.

In his speech to Miss Kenton, however, Stevens does not disclose any of what he comprehends but rather replies in a kind, if conventional, turn toward closing off the topic: "You are very correct . . . , it is too late to turn back the clock. . . . You really mustn't let any more foolish ideas come between yourself and the happiness you deserve." This discrepancy between Stevens's narration and his speech (his telling as narrator and his acting as character) deepens the emotional poignancy of the scene: his heart breaks but he doesn't let her know. At the same time, the discrepancy increases the complexity of the ethical demands the scene places upon its readers.

Applying the approach to ethics outlined in the introduction, we can see that coming to terms with the ethical dimensions of the discrepancy between Stevens's telling and his acting in response to Miss Kenton involves addressing the following interrelated questions: (1) At the level of character-to-character relations: should Stevens have spoken differently to Miss Kenton, should he have told her that his heart has broken as she spoke? (2) At the level of narrator-audience relations: how is Stevens's treatment of the narratee related to his treatment of Miss Kenton? (3) At the level of implied author—authorial audience relations: how does Ishiguro guide us to answer the question about character-character relations, both through signals in the scene and through the patterns of ethical reasoning he has previously established in the narrative, including those connected with Stevens's relation to the authorial audience and to the narratee? What are the consequences of our once again being in the position of knowing more about the characters and their situations than they do about themselves? (4) At the level of the relation between the flesh-and-blood reader's beliefs and the other three positions: how do individual hierarchies of value affect the answers to the above questions? Articulating these questions shows how deeply intertwined the ethical positions of character, narrator, implied author, authorial audience, and flesh-and-blood audience are: the answer to any one has consequences for the answers to the others.

None of the questions, except perhaps the last, has a definitive answer. On the one hand, Stevens's speech to Miss Kenton appears to be one more failure, one more instinctive choice for dignity over honest emotion. Earlier in the narrative, Ishiguro has shown Miss Kenton asking Stevens with both exasperation and justice, "Why, Mr Stevens, why, why, why do you always have to *pretend*?" (154). Consequently, his pretending yet once more, on this occasion when his feelings are so strong and when he seems to have recognized something of the cost of his habitual pretending, seems to be a clear signal from Ishiguro that Stevens's self-understanding is still limited.

On the other hand, given the specific nature of Miss Kenton's revelation—"I loved you once but I now am content with my husband"—Stevens's decision not to speak about his own feelings can be understood as an act of unselfishness. This position becomes clearer if we imagine the likely consequences of his telling Miss Kenton how he feels. To say to her that his heart is breaking is not just to tell her that he loves her but also implicitly to appeal for help. And that appeal for help would, in effect, be an abuse of his new self-knowledge, an act in which he took his new awareness of the consequences of his own failures and used it to ask for relief from the very person those failures have most hurt in the past. The lesson of "Weymouth" for him is that he has lost any right to make such an appeal. Both Miss Kenton and Stevens are right: it is too late to turn back the clock.

Perhaps we can resolve the conflict between these views of Stevens's action and Ishiguro's signals about it by expanding our view of the scene to include Miss Kenton and the motives of her speech. Again we need to pay attention to the way the speech involves both disclosure and indirection. If, as we have argued, she is aware that her speech is indirectly answering Stevens's question about whether she still loves him, then she may be using the speech to appeal to him indirectly as well: "I'm willing openly to acknowledge that I did love you and still think about what-might-have-been; are you willing to reciprocate and, for once, talk about your feelings?—not because I want to leave my husband but because I want to hear you talk about the past." This view of Miss Kenton, then, would support the reading that the discrepancy between Stevens's telling and his acting is another wrong choice for dignity over honest expression of feeling.

But other elements of the scene point to another reading of the speech. Ishiguro sends us many signals that Miss Kenton takes control of their meeting: she comes to find Stevens at his hotel, rather than waiting, as they had planned, for him to come to her house; she asks most of the questions during their meeting and otherwise does more to direct the flow of their conversation; as we have seen, she takes the step of translating Stevens's question about being mistreated to one about whether she loves her husband, and she answers firmly and clearly that she does. The speech about what-might-have-been, then, is not an indirect appeal for an acknowledgment of Stevens's feelings but a further step in Miss Kenton's taking control. Its message is "let me be perfectly clear about the difference between the past and the present: I did love you, as even you must have figured out; further, as you may have seen in my letters over the years, I've occasionally wished we'd had a life together; but don't get any wrong ideas; I'm past all that and want to go on with the life I have." On this account, the last thing Miss Kenton wants to hear from Stevens is that his heart is breaking.

In short, we find that we cannot resolve the ambiguity of Stevens's ethical position at this point in the narrative because we cannot clearly determine the implied Ishiguro's relation to Stevens. And our inability to make that determination is a direct consequence of the character narration. While Ishiguro's rendering of Stevens's character and his narration has guided us to the complicated series of layered inferences that we have traced here, that rendering simultaneously prevents us from reading through the drama of the scene and its narration to Ishiguro's own position on the discrepancy between Stevens's acting and his telling. The most logical way for Ishiguro to resolve the ambiguity of the scene—to have Stevens disclose his motives for his response to Miss Kenton—is not really an option. First, it's not plausible that Stevens, given the way Ishiguro has characterized him, would disclose those motives, even if he knew them. Second, such a disclosure, even an unreliable one, would undesirably reduce the emotional intensity of the scene, which depends so much on what is not said.

To find such ambiguity in character narration is of course not a surprising phenomenon; even finding it at the climax of a narrative is not unheard of. (Can you say *The Turn of the Screw*?) Finding it, however, in the climax of an artfully constructed narrative that has depended on the reader's inferring clear, albeit complex, conclusions about the character narrator is a rare occurrence, certainly one that deserves further comment. Precisely because the narrative has, for most of its trajectory, rewarded rather than blocked our efforts to discern Ishiguro's positions behind Stevens's narration, this ambiguity has further consequences for our interpretive efforts: it transfers the responsibility for disambiguating the scene, and especially for coming to terms with the ethics of Stevens's action, from Ishiguro and the signals in the narrative to the flesh-and-blood reader.

In other words, to say that the authorial audience cannot disambiguate the scene is not to say that flesh-and-blood readers won't feel compelled to resolve the ambiguity, and it is also not to say that they will have difficulty finding one account more persuasive than the other. On the contrary, the pressure of the prior experience with the narrative is more likely to make it difficult for the flesh-and-blood reader who resolves the ambiguity one way to see the force of the argument for resolving it the other. Our own experience follows this pattern: Mary Pat is convinced that the right thing for Stevens to do is to let Miss Kenton see what he is feeling, while Jim remains persuaded that, in keeping silent, Stevens has done the right thing. Our extended conversations about the book and the scene, what Booth would call our coductions, have led us to recognize the persuasiveness of each other's case, but each of us in our heart of hearts believes that he or she has the better reading. In fact, we each initially saw our own readings as self-evident and were surprised to discover that what was so self-evident was not shared.

It is possible of course that the most compelling explanation of this phenomenon is that each of us has a wide stubborn streak, but we would like to propose an alternative account, one that would apply not just to us in this reading situation but also to other readers in other situations. Our account emphasizes not only the links among character narration, the cognitive, the emotive, and the ethical dimensions of response but also those between the patterns of the narrative and the flesh-and-blood reader's agency. As Jim has been arguing, within the model of rhetorical reading the flesh-and-blood reader will *attempt* to enter the authorial audience, but that entrance can be affected by the reader's own set of beliefs and values. Recognizing this phenomenon is one reason that the rhetorical model does not privilege authorial intention over textual phenomena or reader response but instead proposes a feedback loop among these three components of the rhetorical exchange. What we have encountered at the climax of *The Remains of the Day*, however, is a situation in which the efforts to allow the feedback to operate do not lead to a clear choice for one understanding and one ethical response over the other.

Because Ishiguro's particular use of character narration here blocks our access to conclusive signals about how to respond, the effect of his technique is to transfer the responsibility for disambiguating the scene to the flesh-and-blood reader, and the deciding factor in how we each carry out that responsibility is *our individual ethical beliefs as they interact with our understanding of Stevens as a particular character in a particular situation.* In other words, the consequence of Ishiguro's technique at this crucial point is that he invites our own ethics to play a crucial role in shaping our response to the scene. However, those ethics do not supply abstract rules of behavior for us to slap onto Stevens and his situation. Instead, our own individual ethical standards influence our view of which subset of Ishiguro's ethical norms is most relevant to this scene (in other words, Ishiguro renders the scene ambiguous but not indeterminate). In a sense, we each ask "what does Ishiguro think is the right thing for Stevens to do here?," and we find persuasive answers in a particular subset of the norms he has previously established. That the answers and the norms underlying them are different indicates the influence of our different ethical beliefs—or at least of our different hierarchy of such beliefs. For Mary Pat, Ishiguro's emphasis on the costs to both Stevens and Miss Kenton of Stevens's pretending is what is most salient. For Jim, Ishiguro's emphasis on Stevens's past selfishness is what matters most. While we might each think that we are getting out of ourselves and entering into Stevens's situation, we nevertheless continue, as our differences show, to carry our own ethical standards with us.

We are aware that our particular difference fits what some might predict on the basis of gender: of course the woman wants Stevens to express his feelings, and of course the man wants him to keep those feelings to himself. While we would not want to deny that gender has some effect on our beliefs, we would resist any single-cause explanation of our difference, since our ethical beliefs, like those of most people, have developed from a multitude of sources and causes, including experience, religious training, education—and reading narrative. We make this point not to swerve into confessional criticism but rather to underline the multifarious relations among the narrative texts and our responses to them.

## Knowledge, Desire, and the Narratee

Regardless of how we individually resolve the ambiguity of the climax, there is another dimension of our ethical positioning that deserves attention. In this scene, as in the one depicting the events on the night Miss Kenton gets engaged, Ishiguro gives us knowledge about Stevens that Miss Kenton does not have. In that earlier scene, Stevens remembers that he stood outside her room, convinced that she is inside crying:

> As I recall, there was no real evidence to account for this conviction—I had certainly not heard any sounds of crying—and yet I remember being quite certain that were I to knock and enter, I would discover her in tears. I do not know how long I remained standing there; at the time it seemed a significant period, but in reality, I suspect, it was only a matter of a few seconds. For, of course, I was required to hurry upstairs to serve some of the most distinguished gentlemen of the land. (226–27)

Stevens here corrects his earlier report that he stood outside Miss Kenton's room convinced she was crying after she had learned about her aunt's death. The psychological dynamics of Stevens's memory are telling: Stevens's misremembering is another sign of his repression of feeling. Where the earlier report locates Miss Kenton's sorrow in something external to Stevens, this scene locates it in Stevens himself: he is both its cause and its secret sharer. Indeed, he may even be projecting his tears onto Miss Kenton; shortly after he has been standing outside her room, we learn through the dialogue with young Mr. Cardinal that Stevens is himself crying. (Strikingly, however, while Stevens may be misreporting the facts about Miss Kenton here, we can be confident that she has not really wanted to leave Darlington Hall and marry Mr. Benn: earlier that evening, she indirectly appealed to Stevens to tell her that she should not go out.) That Stevens is able to recall this scene now is a sign of how his journey—both geographically across England toward Miss Kenton and temporally across decades of memory—is leading him to admit where he went wrong. Now that he reports the more accurate memory, we make new inferences about a future they once might have had together: if Stevens had knocked and entered or if Miss Kenton had opened her door and found him standing outside it, the entire course of their lives would have been changed. The scene is excruciating to read because their "whole dreams" (179) hang by a thread and Miss Kenton is not even aware of that fact. What, then, about our ethical position as readers who know what Miss Kenton does not?

Our knowledge has two main effects, one connected with ethical responsibility, the other with desire. With the privilege of this knowledge come a certain temptation and a certain responsibility. The temptation is to feel omniscient, or at least so superior that we begin look down at both Stevens and Miss Kenton, these foolish Brits who simply can't talk directly to each other; or we may decide that if they can't see the value of the relationship they treat so cavalierly, they don't deserve to be together. But these temptations are balanced against the demands our superior knowledge places on our sense of justice. In Stevens's case, justice means recognizing his desire to knock as well as his fear of the consequences of knocking. Indeed, recognizing his near breakthrough at this moment also means recognizing how close he came to having a very different life, a recognition that leads to empathy rather than superiority. In Miss Kenton's case, justice means recognizing how conflicted she must have felt: in love with Stevens but despairing of ever having him acknowledge his own feelings or even the possibility that anything matters to him beyond his service to Lord Darlington. She loves but knows that her beloved is someone whose emotions, while deep, are expressed only through indirection. The effect of exercising this responsibility is to deepen our sympathy for each of the characters and to intensify our desire for Stevens to act. But this desire itself exists alongside the knowledge, implicit in the retrospective nature of the narration, that Stevens does not knock. So even as our desire is activated, we know it cannot be fulfilled.

Nevertheless, this understanding of the scene allows us to regard the final meeting in "Weymouth" as Stevens's finally deciding to knock on Miss Kenton's door, a recognition that in turn increases our desire for the two of them to make a satisfactory emotional connection (though, given our own awareness of the passage of time, not necessarily an acknowledgment of their mutual love). In Mary Pat's reading, Stevens's failure to share his feelings, after traveling so far to knock and after having Miss Kenton open the door in her speech, again frustrates our desire. Miss Kenton has again opened herself to Stevens, and he ought to reply in kind; his feelings would not be a burden for her; she would welcome— and he owes her—the acknowledgment of their mutual regret for the life they now realize might have been. Consequently, the pain of Stevens's broken heart is doubled. And Miss Kenton's tears as she boards her bus are the objective correlative of the reader's unfulfilled desire. In Jim's reading, Stevens's knocking and Miss Kenton's answer give a twist to the reader's desire: although the emotional connection is not complete, something new has happened between them. Although Miss Kenton does not know all that Stevens is feeling, she does understand what it means for him to knock, however tentatively, and she can feel the tenderness with which he treats her throughout the scene. Her tears, then, signify her own recognition that if he'd acted this way twenty years before, her life would be different. In that important respect, her knowledge catches up with ours.

Despite their differences, both readings agree that our desire for Stevens remains unfulfilled, at least to some extent, and both lead to the conclusion that Stevens's anagnorisis leaves him with little to build on: he is broken-hearted about Miss Kenton and ashamed of his association with Lord Darlington. The final segment of the narrative, however, offers some consolation both to Stevens and to us. Again it will be helpful to recall the details of the scene.

Narrating the event right after its occurrence, Stevens tells of meeting an elderly gentleman on the pier at Weymouth, who turns out to be a retired butler. Significantly, in light of his earlier denials to others, Stevens tells this butler that he worked for Lord Darlington and then suddenly breaks into tears and confesses his feelings of professional failure: comparing himself to Lord Darlington, Stevens says, "I can't even say I made my own mistakes. Really—one has to ask oneself—what dignity is there in that?" (243). Stevens's companion, without being asked, advises Stevens that he needs to stop looking back and start looking ahead because "the evening's the best part of the day" (244). Stevens takes this advice to heart, and, inspired by the happy laughter of the crowd enjoying the evening on the pier at Weymouth, decides that he shall take up the art of bantering because it just may be "that in bantering lies the key to human warmth" (245).

If Ishiguro was not cheating in his handling of Stevens's narration leading up to the climax, surely he is cheating here. By what rule of literary probability can Ishiguro justify having Stevens meet a retired butler who just turns out to give him wise and consoling advice? We think that Ishiguro uses this last segment, including the seeming contrivance of Stevens's meeting with his "curious companion" to call attention to our experience as readers of this narrative and to readerly desires that have not yet been fulfilled.

In a number of ways, this section is set apart from the others in the novel. It is told in the present tense. Stevens's conversation with his new acquaintance is curiously intimate, its tone more like that of Stevens's narration than any other dialogue. As the two butlers share a cheerful conspiracy of "secrets" and "know-how," we are reminded of the professional camaraderie Stevens has consistently assumed with the narratee, as this reflection reveals: "The hard reality is, surely, that *for the likes of you and I,* there is little choice other than to leave our fate, ultimately, in the hands of those great gentlemen at the hub of this world who employ our services" (244, our emphasis). The retired butler, in other words, is a figure of the narratee—and he speaks as if he knows Stevens's whole story. Indeed, the conversation he has with Stevens roughly reiterates the trajectory of Stevens's prior narrative. Stevens's early reflections on the nature of greatness in a butler are recalled in the memories they share of professional life, and his gradual reexamination of his dedication to Lord Darlington results in the disillusionment he openly confesses to the sympathetic stranger. The greatest cost of Stevens's dedication is, of course, the life that he has missed with Miss Kenton, and we hear echoes of their final parting in the advice from Stevens's companion: "Don't keep looking back . . . make the best of what remains" (243–44).

In providing this figure of the narratee and this rough recapitulation of Stevens's story, Ishiguro also provides us some consolation after the deeply painful experience of the climactic scene. Since the narratee is only minimally characterized, he functions as a stand-in, first, for the authorial audience, and, second, for flesh-and-blood readers. Thus, the butler is ultimately a stand-in for us. When Stevens not only listens but heeds the advice we would like to give him, some of our desire is finally satisfied. The emotional satisfaction of having Stevens's reality partially conform to our desire and the ethical satisfaction of seeing Stevens resolve to make something of the remains of his days combine to relieve the bleakness of his final situation. His anagnorisis has led not just to his pain but also to a new direction even at this late period in his life.

In other ways, however, Ishiguro keeps the final scene within the boundaries of realism he has observed in the rest of the narrative. Stevens's remark that "in bantering lies the key to human warmth" is an example of underregarding, a sign that he still has much to learn about the sharing of human emotion. Bantering can convey warmth, but it does not equal the warmth generated by the intimate and frank disclosure of thoughts and feelings among people who trust each other. (If bantering were *the key* to human warmth, then male locker rooms would be the warmest places in the world.) Nevertheless, it is progress for Stevens to be underregarding rather than misregarding or misreading, and his resolution to seek greater human warmth in his life is more significant than his overestimation of bantering. In the final move of the narrative, then, Ishiguro shows Stevens trying to build on his new self-knowledge without showing him as an unrealistically transformed character. We can have some hope for the remains of his day, even as we ought not have any illusions about how much he has lost.

Ishiguro's communications to us, by contrast with Stevens's, are themselves a generous offer to share human warmth. Although the veil of fiction and the filter of Stevens mean that Ishiguro is not engaging in direct disclosure about himself, he is, nevertheless, sharing his concerns about lives not lived, sacrifices made for the wrong reasons, whole dreams irredeemably lost. And that sharing is one that implies a deep trust in our ability to read the disclosures behind his many strategies of indirection—and, in the key moment of the narrative, to fend for ourselves. *The Remains of the Day*, in that respect, is itself an ethical act of the highest order.

Having taken these lessons from "Weymouth," I will try to build on them in the next chapter by considering how Frank McCourt's unreliable narration works in his autobiographical narrative *Angela's Ashes*. There are, as we will see, both narrative theorists and writers of guidebooks for aspiring memoirists who say that unreliability should not—or indeed, cannot—appear in nonfictional narrative. My questions, then, are how the lessons of Weymouth can help illuminate—and eventually close—this gap between theory and practice, and how they might help explain the ethical dimension of McCourt's technique. McCourt's narrative also provides an opportunity to do more with the lesson about the three axes of communication because of his frequent use of what I call restricted narration, the limitation of the narrator to just one axis even as the implied author communicates along all three.

## 2 Unreliable Narration, Restricted Narration, and the Implied Author in Memoir

Angela's Ashes *and (a Glance at)* 'Tis

"Only in fictional narrative do we have true cases of unreliability," (100) writes Monika Fludernik in "Fiction vs. Non-Fiction," and Dorrit Cohn notes, "Though we often apply the term "unreliable" to voices we regard as wrong-headed in nonfictional works (historical, journalistic, biographical, or autobiographical), the narrator of such works *is* the author, the author *is* the narrator so that we can not attribute to them a significance that differs from the one they explicitly proclaim" (307). For memoirist Vivian Gornick, "Memoir writing shares with fiction the obligation to lift from the raw material of life a tale that will shape experience, transform an event, deliver wisdom. It differs from fiction writing in the way it approaches the task, the chief difference being that a fictional 'I' can be, and often is, an unreliable narrator; the nonfictional 'I' never can be. In memoir, the reader must be persuaded that the narrator is speaking truth" (vii–ix). And Jane Taylor McDonnell, author of a guidebook for aspiring memoirists, emphasizes the importance of reflection: "The reflective voice is so important to memoir writing because self-revelation without reflection or understanding is merely self-exposure. We want the author of a memoir to have grown up, to have learned from earlier mistakes or experiences, and to be the wiser for it. A writer who merely tells us (or even shows us) how awful life was will quickly lose our interest" (136). But Frank McCourt violates all these dicta in *Angela's Ashes* when his narrator reports incidents such as this one:

Billy Campbell says, We'll go back to St. Joseph's and pray that from now on everyone in Mickey Spellacy's family will die in the middle of the summer and he'll never get a day off from school for the rest of his life.

One of our prayers is surely powerful because next summer Mickey himself is carried off by the galloping consumption and he doesn't get a day off from school and that will surely teach him a lesson. (172)

McCourt's *Angela's Ashes* is the autobiographical exception that will either prove or falsify the theoretical rules because McCourt has built his narrative on the foundation of unreliability and the virtual absence of reflection in his authorial voice. In the passage above, the unreliable narration consists of Frankie's misreading (of the power of their prayers, of the meaning of death) and of his misregarding (of the appropriateness of what happens to Mickey); furthermore, over the course of the whole narrative McCourt employs all six kinds of unreliability. McCourt's frequent unreliable narration is one of the main means by which he repeatedly shows his audience, to use McDonnell's phrase, "how awful life was," with little explicit and almost no detailed reflection from his authorial perspective on that awfulness. Yet, as the responses of countless readers, the Pulitzer Prize, and other critical acclaim for *Angela's Ashes* indicate, McCourt's strategy has not at all impeded the success of his narrative.

In general terms, the gap between Gornick and McDonnell, on the one hand, and McCourt, on the other, exists because Gornick and McDonnell conceive of memoir writing as involving an art of direct telling from author to audience and McCourt in *Angela's Ashes* conceives of it as an art of indirection. Rather than speaking in his own voice at the time of the telling, McCourt uses the historical present tense and speaks in the voice of his former self, whom I'll call Frankie, at the time of the action. The gap between Fludernik and Cohn, on one side, and McCourt, on the other, is only slightly different. As accomplished narratologists, Fludernik and Cohn are always aware of the potential difference between an author and a narrator, but each of them is interested in finding formal features that distinguish fiction from nonfiction. Consequently, they describe the standard case of nonfiction narrative and overlook the nonstandard case represented by *Angela's Ashes* and other autobiographical narratives such as Dave Eggers's celebrated *A Heartbreaking Work of Staggering Genius*. My point is not to chide any of the theorists (let the theorist who has never overgeneralized cast the first stone), but to highlight the distinctive quality of the nonstandard technique.

The one theoretical generalization I would offer is that there is no one-to-one correspondence between any specific formal feature of a narrative and any effect, including the placement of a narrative along the fiction/nonfiction spectrum. Effects, whether cognitive, emotive, or ethical, always have multiple causes because effects always depend on both microlevel (e.g., diction and syntax) and macrolevel features (e.g., the pattern of the progression, the genre of the narrative). In other words, I agree with Cohn and Fludernik that distinguishing between fiction and nonfiction remains a worthwhile activity, but I do not believe—and Mc-Court's practice supports this belief—that we can make the distinction on the basis of techniques that are either sure markers of fiction or nonfiction or that appear exclusively in one. As soon as such techniques get identified, some narrative artist will use them for unanticipated effects.[1]

The gap between theory and McCourt's practice also exists within academic autobiography studies, a field now deeply informed by contemporary critical theory, especially feminist and poststructuralist theory. The gap is evident, among other places, in the discussion of the autobiographical "I" by Sidonie Smith and Julia Watson in their learned and accessible overview, *Reading Autobiography: A Guide for Interpreting Life Narratives* (2001). Announcing that they want to get beyond traditional discussions that identify only an I-now and an I-then (a narrating-I and an experiencing-I), they distinguish among four different autobiographical "I"s:

1. The real or historical I, who is "unknown and unknowable by readers and is not the I we gain access to in autobiographical narrative" (59). In my terms this "I" is the flesh-and-blood author.
2. The narrating I, who is "available to readers," who "tells the autobiographical narrative" (59), and whose voices may be multiple.
3. The narrated I, who is "the object 'I,' the protagonist" (60), or, in other words, the character whose experiences constitute the events of the narrative.
4. The ideological I, who is "the concept of personhood culturally available to the narrator" (61).

The gap in the schema is the absence of the implied authorial I. If we accept the claims that the historical I is unknown and inaccessible, and

1. At the end of chapter 4, I will return to this general point as I discuss the relation between technical flaws and ethical deficiencies in character narration.

that the narrating I may adopt multiple voices, we also must recognize that there is another, knowable agent involved: the one who determines which voices the narrator adopts on which occasions—and the one who also provides some guidance about how we should respond to those voices. That agent, as I argued in the previous chapter, is the implied author. Once we add this "I" to the others, then we are well positioned to account for the art of indirection in nonfictional narrative as practiced through unreliable narration. In *Angela's Ashes*, the implied McCourt, through the use of the historical present tense, gives the same vision to both the narrating-I and the narrated-I (that is, to the narrator and the character), even as he uses the narration itself to communicate a very different vision from Frankie's. Furthermore, as we can see with a detailed look at the narration about Mickey Spellacy and his family, the figure of the implied author is crucial to the ethical dimension of the narrative.

I'm nine years old and I have a pal, Mickey Spellacy, whose relations are dropping one by one of the galloping consumption. I envy Mickey because every time someone dies in his family he gets a week off from school and his mother stitches a black diamond patch on his sleeve so that he can wander from lane to lane and street to street and people will know he has the grief and pat his head and give him money and sweets for his sorrow.

But this summer Mickey is worried. His sister, Brenda, is wasting away with the consumption and it's only August and if she dies before September he won't get his week off from school because you can't get a week off from school when there's no school. He comes to Billy Campbell and me to ask if we'll go around the corner to St. Joseph's Church and pray for Brenda to hang on till September.

What's in it for us, Mickey, if we go around the corner praying?

Well, if Brenda hangs on and I get me week off ye can come to the wake and have ham and cheese and cake and sherry and lemonade and everything and ye can listen to the songs and stories all night.

Who could say no to that? There's nothing like a wake for having a good time. We trot around to the church where they have statues of St. Joseph himself as well as the Sacred Heart of Jesus, the Virgin Mary and St. Therese of Liseux, the Little Flower. I pray to the Little Flower because she died of the consumption herself and she'd understand.

One of our prayers must have been powerful because Brenda stays alive and doesn't die till the second day of school. We tell Mickey we're sorry for his troubles but he's delighted with his week off and he gets the black diamond patch which will bring the money and sweets.

My mouth is watering at the thought of the feast at Brenda's wake. Billy knocks on the door and there's Mickey's aunt. Well?

We came to say a prayer for Brenda and Mickey said we could come to the wake.

She yells, Mickey!

What?

Come here. Did you tell this gang they could come to your sister's wake?

No.

But, Mickey, you promised . . .

She slams the door in our faces. We don't know what to do till Billy Campbell says, We'll go back to St. Joseph's and pray that from now on everyone in Mickey Spellacy's family will die in the middle of the summer and he'll never get a day off from school for the rest of his life.

One of our prayers is surely powerful because next summer Mickey himself is carried off by the galloping consumption and he doesn't get a day off from school and that will surely teach him a lesson. (171–72)

The complex effects of this passage depend largely on the interactions between its unreliability on the axes of understanding and of values, and then, in turn, on the consequences of that interaction for our emotional and ethical response. As a self-interested nine-year-old, Frankie neither understands the significance of the events he reports nor is able to evaluate properly the behavior of Mickey, Billy, or himself. The implied McCourt lets Frankie's straightforward reporting, including the recording of other voices, guide us to inferences way beyond anything Frankie is himself aware of. We infer, first, that the characters' behavior clearly leaves much to be desired: Mickey Spellacy is more concerned about his days off from school than about the death of his sister; Billy Campbell and Frankie are more concerned about what they will get in return for praying than with what they are praying for; Mickey breaks his promise to Billy and Frankie; Billy and Frankie seek a revenge out of all proportion to this offense; above all, Frankie is too self-absorbed to register the horrifying toll tuberculosis is taking on the Spellacy family.

The emotional effects of the passage become most powerful at the end, as the misreading and misregarding reach their peaks in Frankie's narration of Mickey's death. The unreliability includes the following discrepancies between the implied McCourt and Frankie. (1) Where Frankie sees a causal connection between his and Billy's prayers and Mickey's death, the implied McCourt and his audience do not. (2) Where Frankie clings to the concepts of days off from school and getting taught a lesson, McCourt and his audience recognize that Mickey's death renders these concepts irrelevant. (3) Thus, where Frankie sees punishment and a lesson in Mickey's death during school vacation, the implied McCourt and his audience see sorrow and loss in Mickey's death from tuberculosis. Furthermore, McCourt and his audience see the grim and painful consequences of the poverty that is, in a larger sense, the cause of the disease and that makes death so common in Limerick that Mickey, Billy, and Frankie treat it as an occasion for self-advantage rather than for yet more mourning. As a result, the juxtaposition of Frankie's explicit interpretations and evaluations and McCourt's implicit ones here creates a striking combination of comedy and pathos: we laugh at how much Frankie's self-absorption distorts his understanding and evaluation, but we also recognize the horror of the conditions that lead to so many members of a family being killed by tuberculosis and to these three nine-year-olds being inured to that horror.

We can see more of the connection between the emotional and ethical effects of the passage by attending to the implied McCourt's shaping of it. The implied McCourt conveys his respect and confidence in his audience by relying solely on Frankie's own narration to convey his own different views; he does not, for example, introduce, as he sometimes does, the voice of another character who articulates his views. He trusts that we will at the very least intuit if not consciously register the signs of his tacit but careful control behind Frankie's naïve narration. These signs include his structuring and pacing of the anecdote so that there's a steady buildup to the longer dramatic scene at Mickey's house, which functions as a peripeteia. After the turning point, the implied McCourt very quickly brings us to the simultaneous climax and resolution (Mickey's death) and then ends with the ironic coda. The signs of the implied author's control also include the parallel phrasings in the descriptions of the prayers' effects ("One of our prayers must have been powerful" and "One of our prayers is surely powerful") and the use of the voices of other characters both to dramatize the scene and carefully attribute agency and motive—for example, it's Billy Campbell, not Frankie, who suggests that they pray for the members of Mickey's family to die. These signs of control suggest that, however naïve and self-absorbed Frankie is, the implied author is sophisticated and clear-visioned, able to guide his audience to an understanding of his former self with both a sense of humor and a sense of the horrible reality that Frankie remains oblivious to.

The emotional and ethical effects of the passage also depend on our awareness that we are reading memoir rather than fiction. This awareness leads us to read with the tacit knowledge that the naïve, fallible, destitute Frankie has evolved into the skillful, clear-visioned, and good-humored implied author. Thus, regardless of what happens to Frankie as character and regardless of what happens to his interpretive and evaluative abilities as narrator, we know that none of these things can be totally catastrophic because he has survived to become the man and the artist capable of writing *Angela's Ashes*.

## General Consequences

Attending to the unreliable narration and the implied author in *Angela's Ashes* helps us understand how the narrative works with other key elements identified by autobiography theorists, particularly experience, memory, truth, identity, and design.[2] McCourt's central technique of narrating from the vision and in the voice of his younger self is, in one sense, an effort to remove memory and its effect on truth as an issue in the narrative and to focus on Frankie's experience. But of course the technique shows that McCourt is more concerned with the *illusion* of truth-telling than with literal truth itself, since the effort to eliminate memory as an issue depends on the illusion that he has a flawless memory of characters, facts, and events, including who said what to whom on which occasion. The technique paradoxically and simultaneously heightens the mimetic component of Frankie as character and of the larger narrative and foregrounds the synthetic component of each. The mimetic gets heightened because the technique erases any temporal distance between Frankie the narrator and Frankie the character: we see Frankie's experience as it happens and through his own eyes. At the same time, however, this hypermimetic quality of the narrative also calls attention to its synthetic component. McCourt is obviously constructing Frankie to serve certain purposes, and he is obviously filling in gaps in memory, even refashioning events and inventing dialogue to serve the same purposes.

---

2. Timothy Dow Adams offers a fine discussion of the importance of design and truth, while Smith and Watson identify experience, memory, and identity as central issues. Leigh Gilmore has written persuasively about the complex interactions of all these issues in works that do not fit neatly into the traditional category of autobiography. Smith and Watson also point to the importance of two other issues, embodiment and the ideological-I, and I would not disagree with them about the relevance of these issues to *Angela's Ashes*. My rhetorical approach, however, leads me to give more prominence to other issues.

The unreliable narration is itself one of the means of heightening the mimetic component of the narrative: the gap between the child's understanding and evaluation of events and those of the mature author is crucial to McCourt's construction of Frankie as a plausible nonfictional character. Strikingly, McCourt pushes the technique to the point that even Frankie's reporting will sometimes be off the mark. However, because McCourt is writing a certain kind of memoir, one in which the actual events carry considerable weight, there is one important restriction on Frankie's unreliable reporting: *whenever Frankie is unreliable on the axis of facts, characters, and events, he must be unreliable on at least one of the other axes and be unreliable in such a way that the authorial audience can still infer an accurate understanding of the events.* As we saw in the previous chapter, in fictional narrative it is typical to have misreporting accompanied by at least one other kind of unreliability, but in McCourt's memoir that accompaniment becomes a necessity. That accompaniment allows McCourt simultaneously to provide an implicit explanation for the misreporting and an invitation to look for clues to a proper understanding of the events. Indeed, much of his skill involves his ability to provide those clues—and thus his own report, interpretation, and evaluation of events—while restricting himself to Frankie's vision.

As for truth, I have already indicated that McCourt's technique itself signals that his narrative cannot be literally true in all its particulars, but, as autobiography theory has repeatedly shown, subjective truth is far more important to memoir than literal truth. Subjective truth matters because it is crucial to the autobiographer's ability to give shape and meaning to experience, and, indeed, conveying the truth as the autobiographer perceives it is one important purpose of writing the autobiography. Nevertheless, subjective truth must also be accountable to some extent to facts, people, and events that have an existence independent of the autobiographer's perception. Thus, in *Angela's Ashes,* it does not matter whether every detail of the Mickey Spellacy story is literally true, but it does matter whether the McCourts were poor, whether Frankie's father was an alcoholic who failed to provide for his family, and whether three of Frankie's siblings died in infancy.

This approach to the issue of truth has consequences for our understanding of Frankie's reliability along the axis of facts, characters, and events. The first relevant question about Frankie's reliability is not, "Did these events happen to these people in just this way?," but rather, "Does the implied McCourt expect us to take this report as accurate within the context of his narrative?" If we answer the question affirmatively, then we need to make an additional judgment about the implied McCourt's use of the past. Thus, for example, when McCourt has the mature Frank report, in the opening pages, the dialogue of people during events he never witnessed such as the birth of his mother, the presence of the dialogue is not a sign of unreliable reporting but a sign of the license with literal truth McCourt takes throughout the book. To take another example, in the Mickey Spellacy anecdote, Frankie's narration is reliable on the axis of facts, characters, and events, and, indeed, McCourt builds all the other effects of the passage on the accuracy of Frankie's reporting. If, however, we were to decide that the ironies of the anecdote are too neat to be credible, we would be deciding not that Frankie's narration is unreliable but that the implied McCourt is cheating because he has taken too great a license with the events of the past.[3] Our judgment of the narration, in other words, would apply to the implied McCourt himself, not to his evolving character narrator, and the judgment would be simultaneously an ethical and aesthetic one.

Another way to make this point is to note that nonfiction narratives may contest each other about characters, facts, and events in ways that fictional narratives cannot. That is, a fictional narrator, even one who is unreliable on the axis of facts, character, and events, will almost always succeed in stipulating certain fundamentals of the narrative world. However unreliable Stevens is as a reporter, we do not doubt the existence of Darlington Hall, his father, Miss Kenton, and Mr. Benn, do not doubt that he takes a journey, do not doubt that Miss Kenton married Mr. Benn, and so on. If another author were to write a novel called *The True Adventures of Mr. Stevens*, which stipulated an alternative set of fundamentals about Mr. Stevens's narrative world, we would not ask, "What really happened to Mr. Stevens?" but instead understand that the author of *The True Adventures* wanted to contest other elements of Ishiguro's

---

3. Many residents of Limerick have contended that the memoir misrepresents life in Limerick because it seriously overstates its hardships; some, including the late actor Richard Harris, who was McCourt's contemporary, have also claimed that McCourt's account of Angela's sexual relationship with Laman Griffin is a fabrication. The first contention comes down to a refusal to accept McCourt's subjective truth, and so those who make it will never be able to falsify McCourt's account. The second contention involves something that, in principle, could be proven true or false, though it is not likely that anything definitive will emerge. On the basis of internal evidence—that is, McCourt's representation of Angela, Laman Griffin, and the situation in which their involvement occurs—I would judge McCourt's account as accurate. But of course internal evidence cannot be decisive.

narrative. If, however, William Campbell were to write an account of "The Life and Death of Mickey Spellacy" that gave no credence to McCourt's account, we would ask, "What really happened to Mickey?" and, if we decided that Campbell's narrative was the more accurate account, we would also conclude that McCourt is cheating.

Identity and design are closely related in *Angela's Ashes,* in part because of the technique. In one respect, the design of the narrative is a combination of memoir and Bildungsroman, as Smith and Watson define these terms in *Reading Autobiography.* Memoir, they write, is "a mode of life narrative that historically situates the subject in a social environment, as either observer or participant; the memoir directs attention more toward the lives and actions of others than to the narrator" (198). Bildungsroman is a narrative of "development and social formation," traditionally with a young man as protagonist, and often involving his escape from a repressive family or environment into the larger world.

The narrative traces Frankie's life from his birth in New York in 1931 through his childhood and adolescence in Limerick to his return to New York at the age of nineteen in 1950. The bulk of the narrative (approximately 300 of its 363 pages) is devoted to his life from age three, the time of his earliest memories, to age fourteen, when he stops attending Leamy's school and begins working as a delivery boy for the Limerick telegraph office. This stretch of the narrative conforms largely to the mode of memoir as Frankie reports tellable episodes in the life of his family and friends, episodes that include but are not restricted to significant events in his own growth. The last section of the narrative moves into the mode of Bildungsroman as it focuses on the events in Frankie's life that enable him to carry out his plan to escape Limerick for the United States. Throughout all sections of the memoir, McCourt deals with a set of recurrent issues: the poverty and hardship of his family, including the deplorable living conditions in Limerick; his father's alcoholism and its terrible consequences for his mother, himself, and his siblings; his mother's efforts to make ends meet; the presence of the Catholic Church and its teachings in their lives.

McCourt's technique provides the linchpin between design and identity because that technique, first, requires that he represent the evolving vision and voice of Frankie as he matures, and, second, because the strong presence of the implied McCourt right from the beginning of the narrative shows the endpoint of the evolution. Indeed, for both these reasons we can see that one of the important precursor texts for *Angela's Ashes* is *A Portrait of the Artist as a Young Man.* Though working completely within what Northrop Frye would call the low mimetic mode, McCourt pays homage to Joyce by adapting the techniques and some of the structural elements of *Portrait*. Where Joyce uses internal focalization to represent the evolving consciousness of Stephen Dedalus, McCourt uses character narration.[4] Where Joyce shows Stephen leaving Dublin to forge in the smithy of his consciousness a new conscience for his race, McCourt shows Frankie leaving Limerick and arriving in New York to explore what one of his traveling companions calls a "great country altogether" (362). Furthermore, where Joyce is explicit about Stephen's ambition to become a great artist and, indeed, almost explicit about Stephen as a version of his former self, McCourt's construction of himself as implied author subtly invites us to regard him as the artist that the naïve, destitute Frankie has almost miraculously become.

## Initial Reliability: The Vision and Voice of the Mature Narrator

While the dominant mode of McCourt's narration is to use the vision and voice of the young Frankie, he begins the narrative following the principles enunciated by the theorists quoted at the outset of this chapter. That is, he uses the vision and voice of his mature self—there is no distance between implied author and narrator—and he reflects on his life. As a result, the opening passage provides a filter through which we can read the subsequent unreliable narration, and it provides an excellent introduction to the man whose childhood will be the main subject of the book.

> My father and mother should have stayed in New York where they met and married and where I was born. Instead, they returned to Ireland when I was four, my brother, Malachy, three, the twins, Oliver and Eugene, barely one, and my sister, Margaret, dead and gone.
>
> When I look back on my childhood I wonder how I survived at all. It was, of course, a miserable childhood: the happy childhood is hardly worth your while. Worse than the ordinary miserable childhood is the miserable Irish childhood, and worse yet is the miserable Irish Catholic childhood.
>
> People everywhere brag and whimper about the woes of their early

4. McCourt has also clearly learned a lot from the tradition of implied authors using naïve narrators, a tradition whose greatest example is *Adventures of Huckleberry Finn*. I believe that a comparison of Twain's techniques with McCourt's could be highly illuminating, though such an extended study is beyond the scope of this chapter.

years, but nothing can compare with the Irish version: the poverty; the shiftless, loquacious alcoholic father; the pious defeated mother moaning by the fire; pompous priests; bullying schoolmasters; the English and the terrible things they did to us for eight hundred long years.

Above all—we were wet.

Out in the Atlantic Ocean great sheets of rain gathered to drift slowly up the River Shannon and settle forever in Limerick. . . .

From October to April the walls of Limerick glistened with the damp. Clothes never dried: tweed and woolen coats housed living things, sometimes sprouted mysterious vegetations. In pubs, steam rose from damp bodies and garments to be inhaled with cigarette and pipe smoke laced with the stale fumes of spilled stout and whiskey and tinged with the odor of piss wafting in from the outdoor jakes where many a man puked up his week's wages.

The rain drove us into the church—our refuge, our strength, our only dry place. At Mass, Benediction, novenas, we huddled in great damp clumps, dozing through priest drone, while steam rose again from our clothes to mingle with the sweetness of incense, flowers and candles.

Limerick gained a reputation for piety, but we knew it was only the rain. (11–12)

This opening divides cleanly into two main parts, the summary judgment of his parents' choice and its consequences for his childhood, and the designation of the constant rain and dampness as the overriding condition of that childhood. The voice is that of a hardheaded, down-to-earth, humorous and, above all, safe (and dry) survivor. He is sufficiently hardheaded to criticize the choices that led to his miserable childhood and to detail without flinching such features of that childhood as the poverty, the alcoholic father, and the defeated mother. At the same time, he is sufficiently humorous and safe to joke about the act of narration he has begun: in claiming pride of place for the misery of his Irish Catholic childhood, he also implicitly acknowledges that he is about to engage in the most egregious bragging and whimpering of anyone who complains about his or her childhood. The humor also creeps into his list of the features of the miserable childhood in the hyperbolic reference to "the English and the terrible things they did to us for eight hundred years." McCourt further emphasizes his safe survival, his current distance from the hardships of his childhood, by folding them into the larger pattern of the Irish Catholic childhood. That distance allows him to see that his miserable childhood is not his alone but one shared by a whole culture.

In the second half of this opening, the voice and vision remain that of the mature narrator until the final sentence, when the vision shifts to that of the collective "we" located in the past. The description of the rain forming on the Atlantic and the iterative narration of the rain's effects begin to show the seriousness implicit in the claims about the miserable childhood: there's an unflinching quality to these unpleasant descriptions and even some clear evidence of McCourt's effort to underline rather than downplay the overall misery. In his description of the smells in the pubs, he might have written something like "laced with the stale fumes of spilled stout and whiskey not to mention the odor of urine from the outdoor jakes." But he heightens and elaborates: "laced" is balanced by "tinged," and he chooses the colloquial "piss" and modifies "jakes" not with further direct comment on smell but rather with the information about "puking up his week's wages."

In the final paragraph, the humorous tone returns, and it is shared between the mature narrator's perspective and that of the collective "we," a sharing that is evident in the relation between the phrase "our refuge, our strength, our only dry place" and the final acknowledgment that "we knew it was only the rain." With the first phrase, the humor arises from the adaptation of Psalm 46, "God is our refuge and our strength, a very present help in trouble," as McCourt moves from echoing the metaphorical sublimity of the Psalm ("our refuge and our strength") to insisting on the literal practicality of being in the church building: "our only dry place." With "we knew," McCourt shifts to the perspective of the collective we and cuts to the truth of Limerick's reputation for piety: it was only the rain. This variation in the technique nicely conveys that the citizens of Limerick, including of course McCourt himself, maintained their humor in the face of the miserable conditions of their lives.

More generally, then, after reading the opening we infer that the implied author is a hardheaded, realistic, and humorous guide to his past, one given to plain speaking and at times a quiet eloquence. In constructing this filter, McCourt is also signaling that he is not going to be telling us a traumatic narrative in the sense that the term has come to mean.[5] He does not regard the past as unspeakable, does not regard himself as still recovering, does not need to tell the story for therapeutic reasons. This point further underlines the usefulness of the distinction between the flesh-and-blood author and the implied author. The flesh-and-blood McCourt may very well have found it therapeutic to write this narrative, but the narrative itself does not make McCourt's relation to

5. For an excellent discussion of traumatic narrative, see Caruth.

his past one of the instabilities or tensions. Instead, the opening suggests that the implied McCourt, in the tradition of good Irish storytellers, is going to tell his tale because it is full of tellable incidents, and he is going to use his telling to enhance its tellability.

## Restricted Narration and Unreliable Narration

Now let's look at the first instance of the dominant technique:

> I'm in a playground on Classon Avenue in Brooklyn with my brother Malachy. He's two, I'm three. We're on the seesaw.
>
> Up, down, up, down.
>
> Malachy goes up.
>
> I get off.
>
> Malachy goes down. Seesaw hits the ground. He screams. His hand is on his mouth and there's blood.
>
> Oh, God. Blood is bad. My mother will kill me.
>
> And here she is, trying to run across the playground. Her big belly slows her.
>
> She says, What did you do? What did you do to the child?
>
> I don't know what to say. I don't know what I did.
>
> She pulls my ear. Go home. Go to bed.
>
> Bed? In the middle of the day?
>
> She pushes me toward the playground gate. Go.
>
> She picks up Malachy and waddles off. (19–20)

After the careful exposition of the first sentence, which marks the mature narrator's adoption of the historical present tense, the passage shifts to the vision of the three-year-old Frankie and its diction indicates that McCourt wants to adopt a voice in keeping with that perspective. The passage implicitly addresses a generalized rather than specifically characterized narratee, one who does not have much prior knowledge of Frankie and his family, though one who is close at hand ("here she is"). By constructing a generalized narratee, McCourt requires Frankie to do a certain amount of exposition, though by adopting Frankie's vision and voice, McCourt necessarily also takes on serious perceptual limitations and thus provides the grounds for his frequent unreliability on the axes of reading and regarding. The perceptual limitations also lead to some brief violations of the restrictions McCourt sets up for Frankie, violations justified by the principle that disclosure functions ultimately trump narrator functions. In this passage, for example, McCourt needs his audience to know that Angela is pregnant and that Frankie doesn't realize it, so he stretches the limitation on voice he has set up and puts the word "waddles" in Frankie's mouth.

The passage also provides a fine example of another kind of character narration, what I will call *restricted narration*, a technique marked by an implied author's limiting a narrator to only one axis of communication while requiring the authorial audience to make inferences about communication along at least one of the other axes as well. I have touched on one example in my discussion of the first passage of under-reading from *The Remains of the Day*. McCourt's use of the technique provides a more typical case, and one that allows us to see its relation to unreliable narration.

For much, though not all, of the passage McCourt restricts Frankie's narration to the reporting function, to the axis of facts, characters, and events, but he accompanies that restriction with invitations to his audience to interpret and evaluate as well. I distinguish restricted narration from unreliable narration on the basis of their different rhetorical dynamics. With unreliability, the implied author asks us to reconfigure what the narrator reports, interprets, or evaluates; with restricted narration, the implied author, in effect, limits the narrator's agency to only one of the three axes of communication—and the narrator's discourse may or may not be unreliable on that axis. If the narration is reliable, the authorial audience does not need to reconfigure it but does need to supplement it by inferring what the implied author wants to convey along the restricted axes.

With naïve narrators such as Frankie, the most common restriction will be to the axis of facts, characters, and events, and that restricted narration will most commonly be reliable. But the authorial communication will depend on the audience interpreting and perhaps even evaluating the naïve narrator's report in ways that the narrator would never even attempt. In this passage, for example, McCourt invites us to interpret Frankie's family situation without Frankie having any idea that his narration contains such an invitation. The first inference we're invited to make is that, because the brothers are playing without close supervision, the accident is not at all surprising. The second, related inference is that Angela is overwhelmed by the work of taking care of her two-year-old and three-year-old boys while in an advanced stage of pregnancy (we learn shortly that the twins, Eugene and Oliver, are born even before Malachy's tongue heals). This dimension of the situation comes through most clearly in the gap between Frankie's self-centered confusion and Angela's efforts just to respond to the immediate crisis: she needs him to go home to bed so she can take Malachy to the hospital, but, as already noted, Frankie isn't even sure what he has done. By guiding us to inferences such as these, McCourt is taking the limits he has set for his narration and turning it into an advantage.

When McCourt moves away from the restricted narration, he aligns the authorial audience's emotions with Frankie. Although he has injured Malachy by jumping off the seesaw, our participation in his vision and his acts of reading and interpreting lead us to sympathize with him. The participation in the vision, which allows us to see his confusion, also leads us to infer that Frankie jumps not out of malice but out of curiosity. This inference and the sympathy that follows from it are reinforced by the sentences that break from the mode of restricted narration: "Oh God. Blood is bad. My mother will kill me. . . . I don't know what to say. I don't know what I did. . . . Bed? In the middle of the day?" The questions about bed are nicely ambiguous: does Frankie actually ask Angela these questions or are they just his own thoughts? It is not possible to tell, but the ambiguity serves to highlight Frankie's sense of confusion.

As the narrative progresses, McCourt continues to turn Frankie's limited vision to his own advantage by using unreliable and restricted narration in tandem. Consider, for example, this communication about Angela's miscarriage shortly after the family settles in Limerick:

> Mam is moaning in the bed, her face pure white. Dad has Malachy and the twins out of the bed and sitting on the floor by the dead fire. I run across the street and knock on Aunt Aggie's door till Uncle Pat Keating comes coughing and grumbling, What's up? What's up?
>
> My mother is moaning in the bed. I think she's sick.
>
> Now Aunt Aggie comes grumbling. Ye are nothing but trouble since ye came from America.
>
> Leave him alone, Aggie, he's only a child doing what he's told.
>
> She tells Uncle Pa to go back to bed, that he has to go to work in the morning not like some from the North that she won't mention. He says, No, no, I'm coming. There's something wrong with Angela.
>
> Dad tells me sit over there with my brothers. I don't know what's up with Mam because everyone is whispering and I can barely hear Aunt Aggie telling Uncle Pa the child is lost run for the ambulance and Uncle Pa is out the door, Aunt Aggie telling Mam you can say what you like about Limerick but the ambulance is fast. She doesn't talk to my father, never looks at him.

> Malachy says, Dad, is Mammy sick?
>
> Och, she'll be all right, son. She has to see the doctor.
>
> I wonder what child is lost because we're all here, one two three four of us, not a lost child anywhere and why can't they tell me what's wrong with my mother. Uncle Pa comes back and the ambulance is right behind him. A man comes in with a stretcher and after they carry Mam away there are blood spots on the floor by the bed. Malachy bit his tongue and there was blood and the dog on the street had blood and he died. I want to ask Dad to tell me if Mam will be gone forever like my sister Margaret but he's going with Mam and there's no use asking Aunt Aggie anything for fear she'd bite your head off. She wipes away the blood spots and tells us to get back into bed and stay there till Dad comes home. (62)

The first half of the passage—down to the last line of dialogue—is an extended stretch of reliable restricted narration along the axis of reporting. Frankie records Angela's moaning and the movements and speech of the other characters, and through that recording McCourt communicates more to us than Frankie realizes, especially about Aunt Aggie, Uncle Pa, and Frankie's father, Malachy. Frankie's report of Aunt Aggie's behavior, for example, leads us to interpret and evaluate it in ways that he does not. Her comments to Frankie and to Uncle Pa show that she is helping grudgingly, out of familial obligation rather than any spirit of love or generosity; similarly, her refusal to talk to Malachy works to convey both her ongoing disapproval and the tension between them even at this moment of family crisis. Consequently, we recognize that McCourt is inviting us to judge her negatively, at least until things are at their worst, when she does try to offer her sister some hope.

In the second half of the passage McCourt removes the restriction and employs underreading and misreading to heighten the effect of the miscarriage on Frankie. Frankie does not understand either Aggie's "the child is lost," or the significance of the blood spots on the floor. The first misreading underlines Frankie's confusion, and the second, which leads him to the association between blood and death, underlines his fear. In sum, McCourt turns the restricted and the unreliable narration to his advantage here because he successfully (a) conveys the unfolding drama of this latest family hardship; (b) gives us a vivid sense of Frankie's feelings amidst the larger family hardship, and, thus, adds a dimension to that hardship that a straight report focused on the miscarriage might have omitted; and (c) does both things without complaining, whining, or otherwise directly commenting on the misery of their situation.

## Deviations from the Dominant Technique

There are moments in the narrative, however, when McCourt moves away from his reliance on unreliable and restricted narration, and allows Frankie to narrate perceptions that he could not have had. These instances demonstrate the principle that disclosure functions ultimately trump narrator functions.

> When he's not looking for work Dad goes for long walks, miles into the country. He asks farmers if they need any help, that he grew up on a farm and can do anything. If they hire him he goes to work right away with his cap on and his collar and tie. *He works so hard and long the farmers have to tell him to stop. They wonder how a man can work through a long hot day with no thought of food or drink. Dad smiles.* He never brings home the money he earns on farms. That money seems to be different from the dole, which is supposed to be brought home. He takes the farm money to the pub and drinks it. (94–95, emphasis mine)

The italicized sentences are a straightforward case of what Genette calls paralepsis, the narrator telling more than he could have known. It is possible to naturalize this passage as Frankie's reconstruction of his father's labor, the farmers' response to it, and his father's reply based on his father's report of those days. But this hypothesis must deal with the recalcitrant evidence that Malachy always "takes the farm money to the pub and drinks it" (95); the recalcitrance resides in the unlikelihood that Malachy would be telling his oldest son how he funded the drunkenness that left the family starving. In any case, the implied McCourt characteristically does not give a source for Frankie's knowledge but has him report the events authoritatively. The technique works because McCourt needs to tell his audience about Malachy's farm labor in order to round out his portrait of Malachy and the consequences of Malachy's alcoholism for the family.

A different example is the scene in which Nora Molloy exposes Mrs. McGrath's manipulation of her grocery scale:

> I think there was a little accident there the way your hip was pressed against that paper and you didn't even know the paper was pulled down a bit. Oh, God, no. A woman like you that's forever on her knees before the Virgin Mary is an inspiration to us all and is that your money I see on the floor there?
>
> Mrs. McGrath steps back quickly and the needle on the scale jumps

and quivers. What money? she says, *till she looks at Nora and knows.
Nora smiles.* Must be a trick of the shadows, she says, and smiles at the
scale. There was a mistake right enough for that shows barely half a
pound of flour. (67, emphasis mine)

This scene is different from the one about his father's farm labor because here Frankie is actually an eyewitness, and because the break in
the mimetic illusion of keeping to Frankie's vision is so brief. Nevertheless, the break is major and again instructive about the relation between disclosure functions and narrator functions. The only way Frankie
can legitimately report that Mrs. McGrath "knows," the only way for
him to be in a position to make it clear that Mrs. McGrath and Nora
share their knowledge of each other's intentions, and the only way he
can do both in such a way that the narratee will also share that knowledge is for him to know at least as much as the two women. That is, since
Mrs. McGrath's knowledge is registered only in her look, and Nora's only
in her smile, he must know the significance of that look and that smile
in order to report that "Mrs. McGrath knows." Furthermore, once he
knows that much, his straightforward report, "Nora smiles," contains
the same understanding of its meaning that McCourt's audience has. At
this juncture of the narrative Frankie is only six years old, too young to
be cognizant of Nora's trick and the women's shared understandings.
Again, however, because the effect of the scene for the authorial audience is better if McCourt allows his audience to infer the meanings in
the silent exchange between Mrs. McGrath and Nora, he needs to violate briefly the restrictions of narrating from Frankie's six-year-old perspective. As a result, once again the disclosure functions trump the
narrator functions with the blessing of McCourt's audience.

McCourt also occasionally breaks from the limitations of Frankie's
perspective by explicitly shifting to the voice of the mature narrator of
the opening pages, and these shifts often have important consequences
for the ethical dimension of the narrative. The report of the death of his
brother Eugene provides the most dramatic shift:

> Malachy and I play with [Eugene]. We try to make him laugh. We make
> funny faces. We put pots on our heads and pretend to let them fall off.
> We run across the room and pretend to fall down. We take him to the
> People's Park to see the lovely flowers, play with dogs, roll in the grass.
>
> He sees small children with fair hair like Oliver. He doesn't say Ollie
> anymore. He only points.

Dad says Eugene is lucky to have brothers like Malachy and me because we help him forget and soon, with God's help, he'll have no memory of Oliver at all.

*He died anyway.*
    *Six months after Oliver went, we woke on a mean November morn-
ing and there was Eugene, cold in the bed beside us.* (81–82, emphasis
mine)

The shift from Frankie's vision and voice to the mature Frank's is
sharp, sudden, and extremely effective. McCourt signals the shift by the
white space, the three-word paragraph set flush left, and the move to past
tense. He underlines the shift by reference to the interval between
Oliver's death and Eugene's: Frankie's narration to this point has not yet
shown any similar awareness of time's passage. The shift is even more
strongly underlined by the bitterness in the mature Frank's voice: that
November morning was "mean," Eugene's body was "*cold in the bed* beside us." Even "anyway" is colored by this tone, since it looks back at
the collective naïveté of his father, his brother, and himself for thinking
and hoping that playing with Eugene would keep him alive.

The shift is effective both emotionally and ethically because it sends
the signal that, as he has to narrate the death of a sibling for the third
time, McCourt can no longer sustain the artifice involved in restricting
himself to Frankie's perspective. Indeed, he cannot follow his previous
practice of narrating the last days or hours of the child's life but feels
compelled simply to report the brute fact of Eugene's death. As a result,
McCourt's audience feels the shock and finality of the child's death along
with the bitterness in Frank's voice. Furthermore, although McCourt
soon returns to Frankie's perspective as he reports on Doctor Troy's visit,
he eschews his frequent practice of using unreliability either to generate humor that buffers the pain associated with the events or to communicate indirectly the pain he and others feel. Instead, he has Frankie
report Doctor Troy's grim view of the situation, including his comment
that "God was asking too much, too damn much" (82). We know from
the shift in the narrative technique that Doctor Troy is giving voice to
the implied McCourt's view of the situation, and that view seems not
just understandable but entirely appropriate.

## Moments of Reflection

Now consider a somewhat different passage:

> I think my father is like the Holy Trinity with three people in him,
> the one in the morning with the paper, the one at night with the stories
> and the prayers, and then the one who does the bad thing and comes
> home with the smell of whiskey and wants us to die for Ireland.
>
> I feel sad over the bad thing but I can't back away from him because
> the one in the morning is my real father and if I were in America I could
> say, I love you, Dad, the way they do in the films, but you can't say that
> in Limerick for fear you might be laughed at. You're allowed to say you
> love God and babies and horses that win but anything else is a softness
> in the head. (210)

In this passage McCourt engages in the kind of reflection that Mc-
Donnell calls for, with the important difference that the reflection is
restricted to Frankie's perspective as an eleven-year-old. The analogy between his father and the Holy Trinity is telling more for its existence
than for its aptness: which manifestation of God "does the bad thing"?
But the larger point is clear: Malachy is like a God to Frankie, even if
there is one part of him that "does the bad thing." The unreliability in
the passage exists on all three axes, and it includes underreporting, misreading, and underregarding. Furthermore, the three kinds of unreliability are interrelated. Frankie's description of the "bad thing" focuses on
what is arguably the most innocuous part of Malachy's alcoholism: not
the failure to support the family, not the spending of the wages or dole
money on drink when Angela and the children are starving, but simply
the coming home smelling of whiskey and asking the boys to pledge that
they'll die for Ireland. Frankie's assertion that "the one in the morning
is my real father" misreads the situation, since the implied McCourt
wants us to recognize that all parts of his father are "real." Indeed, by
this point in the narrative, we have had almost two hundred pages devoted to the very real consequences of Malachy's alcoholism. Ultimately, then, Frankie's assertion is also a form of underregarding: by
downplaying the third part of his father's personality and overplaying the
first, he ultimately misjudges his father.

McCourt adds another twist to this passage with Frankie's wish to be
in America so that he could say "I love you, Dad" without being thought
soft in the head. Besides once again hitting the note of Frankie's desire

to be in America and once again showing his misreading (his wish is based on the naïve assumption that American films are an accurate representation of American life), this wish also turns away from the direct expression of Frankie's emotion and to his humorous comment about the ways of Limerick. This turn allows McCourt to have it both ways— to have Frankie express his love and then move on; to fit, in a sense, both his idea of an American son and his idea of a Limerick one. Frankie's reflections remain moving in ways that I'll discuss in a minute, even as the humor provides some emotional relief for McCourt's audience.

Again, the emotional effect of the passage is tied to both the unreliability and the ethics of that unreliability. If we ask why the eleven-year-old Frankie is unreliable in just these ways, we can answer by considering together the first two ethical positions, that of Frankie in relation to his father and that of Frankie in relation to his audience. By this point in his life—and in the narrative—Frankie must admit his father's weakness and failure. Indeed, his remark that "I can't back away from him" suggests that he is aware that he has grounds for backing away. But as an eleven-year-old who still loves his father, he wants to minimize that side of his father's character and maximize his father's good qualities—qualities of which McCourt has previously given us ample evidence. More generally, we recognize that the denial that fuels Frankie's underreporting, misreading, and underregarding arises from his love for his father and his desire that his father were different. As a result, the unreliability, for McCourt's audience, is marked as much by Frankie's generosity and gratitude as by his error. At the same time, however, we can't help but recognize that Frankie's generosity, gratitude, and error leave him wide open for further pain and disappointment, and this recognition makes his unreliable reflection deeply moving.

Turning to the implied McCourt's ethical position toward Frankie, Malachy, and his audience, we can recognize, first, a communication through McCourt's agency rather than Frankie's about Malachy. Because McCourt has had Frankie include ample evidence of Malachy's good qualities, he underlines here an additional painful element of Malachy's alcoholism. If Malachy could have stayed sober, he could have been an extraordinary father—someone that his son might well have continued to think of as like a God. The revelation, however, is gentle rather than bitter: the implied McCourt here still shares some of Frankie's feelings for his father. McCourt again comes across as the successful survivor, able to look back with a combination of clarity and sympathy on both actors here.

But now compare this passage with a much shorter one, just eleven
pages later, after Frankie reports on his father's move to England to find
work during World War II:

> We sit around the fire and drink our tea and cry because we have no
> father, till Mam says, Don't cry, don't cry. Now that your father is gone
> to England surely our troubles will be over.
>     Surely. (221)

With that second "surely" McCourt leaves Frankie's vision and offers
the survivor's perspective on his father's leaving. The cynical irony of
that perspective is in marked contrast to the eleven-year-old boy's
comparison between his father and the Holy Trinity. But the break is effective both formally and ethically. Malachy's behavior warrants the survivor's cynical irony: the moment he left for England was the moment
he all but abandoned the family. Once again he drank his wages rather
than sending them home, and the result was several years of even greater
difficulty for his family. The mature Frank's ironic "surely" allows Mc-
Court to communicate a clear, candid, and fit judgment of his father's
behavior and to do it without belaboring the obvious. But this "surely,"
following just a few pages after Frankie's comparison between Malachy
and the Holy Trinity, also builds on the effects of that comparison. It
shows how much Frank's feelings have changed, and in doing that,
it deftly and unobtrusively points to the pain associated with those
changed feelings. This sequence of revelations about McCourt's feelings
toward his father and the techniques by which he makes the revelations
significantly contribute to our respect for the implied McCourt as artist
and as ethical being.

## The Maturing Vision and Voice

As Frankie gets older, McCourt not only shows the evolution of his vision and voice but also naturally represents him in more complex ethical situations. McCourt's treatment of these situations remains subtle
and sure-footed, as this account of his visits to Theresa Carmody shows.

> For weeks after that I deliver the telegram. Sometimes we have the ex-
> citement on the sofa but there are other days she has the cough and you
> can see the weakness on her. She never tells me she has the weakness.

> She never tells me she has the consumption. The boys at the post office
> say I must be having a great time with the shilling tip and Theresa Car-
> mody. I never tell them I stopped taking the shilling tip. I never tell them
> of the green sofa and the excitement. I never tell them about the pain
> that comes when she opens the door and I can see the weakness on her
> and all I want to do then is make tea for her and sit with my arms around
> her on the green sofa. (324)

Frankie is just fourteen when he meets Theresa and has his first experience of sexual intercourse, and, as this passage shows, his first experience of heterosexual love, events that, even more than his dropping
out of school and taking a full-time job, mark his crossing from childhood to young adulthood. Frankie has told us about his raging hormones
and his frequent masturbation, and has told us that the other, older telegraph boys don't want to take the telegrams to the Carmodys because
Theresa has tuberculosis. He has also told us of the fantasy-like event of
delivering the telegram to Theresa and being seduced by her. Though he
does not directly comment on Theresa's motivation, he implies that her
knowledge of her impending death leads her to seize the day by seizing
him. In this passage, Frankie reliably reports on the all-too-real situation
of continuing to deliver the telegrams and visit with Theresa as she
moves closer to death. McCourt's treatment of the situation underlines
its ethical significance in Frankie's life, and the indirection of the communication reinforces his own admirable ethical stance.

First, the use of the iterative rather than the singulative helps reinforce
the point that Frankie and Theresa have a relationship that continues
"for weeks." Second, the first few sentences are a skillful use of restricted narration as Frankie simply reports his behavior and Theresa's.
We need to supplement the restriction here by noting the connection between Theresa's never telling about having the weakness and the days
that they don't have what Frankie calls the excitement. Theresa never
tells not only because she is courageous but also because she doesn't
have to: Frankie is sensitive enough to see that she is too weak. Third,
the movement from what Theresa never tells to what Frankie never tells
emphasizes their shared secret love. He knows what she doesn't tell, but
he makes sure that the other boys don't know what has happened between him and Theresa: his not telling the others partakes of the same
spirit as Donne's claim in "A Valediction: Forbidding Mourning":
"'Twere profanation of our joys / to tell the laity our love" (ll. 7–8),
with the important difference that their joy is significantly alloyed by

Theresa's suffering. But there is more to his declaration in this part of
the passage: Frankie's pain when he perceives Theresa's pain is empathetic and unselfish. Frankie won't tell the other boys because he cannot trust them to be similarly empathetic. The fact that he does tell the
narratee and, thus, the authorial audience, means that he and McCourt
are trusting us to be empathetic in our turn. In this way, McCourt's ethically admirable handling of Frankie's narration puts ethical demands on
us.

   The emotional and ethical effects of this passage are significant for the
working out of Frankie's continued maturation. When Theresa dies, he
feels guilty because he believes that she has gone to hell because of the
way the two of them "tumbled naked and wild on the green sofa" (325).
Because of this passage, we recognize Frankie's self-evaluation as another instance of misregarding and feel almost as much relief as he does
when he finally confesses to a priest and the priest tells him that Theresa
is "surely in heaven" because she "suffered like the martyrs in olden
times and God knows that's penance enough" (343).

   Frankie's experience with Theresa Carmody also provides a telling
contrast with one of the last events of the narrative, Frankie's sexual encounter with Frieda of Poughkeepsie, New York, during a rest stop by
the *Irish Oak* on his first night in the United States. This encounter occurs with a priest standing right outside the bedroom door:

> She pulls out my excitement climbs up on me slides up and down up
> and down Jesus I'm in heaven and there's a knock on the door the priest
> Frank are you in there Frieda putting her finger to her lips and her eyes
> rolling to heaven Frank are in you in there Father would you ever take a
> good running jump for yourself and oh God oh Theresa do you see what's
> happening to me at long last I don't give a fiddler's fart if the Pope him-
> self knocked on this door and the College of Cardinals gathered gawk-
> ing at the windows oh God the whole inside of me is gone into her and
> she collapses on me and tells me I'm wonderful and would I ever con-
> sider settling in Poughkeepsie. (361)

   The contrast of course is that Frankie, at the age of nineteen and away
from Ireland, has also escaped the Church's judgments about sex outside
of marriage. McCourt underscores the point not only through the explicit address to Theresa—"do you see what's happening to me at long
last"—but also through the cadence of the sentence. The headlong pace
of the narration conveys Frankie's movement toward climax and the mo-

ments right before climax are the ones when he most strongly announces his independence from the Church's views on sex outside marriage: "I don't give a fiddler's fart if the Pope himself knocked on this door and the College of Cardinals gathered gawking at the windows."

If there are any doubts about the implied McCourt's endorsement of Frankie's new independence, the concluding comment of the narrative should erase them. Back on board the *Irish Oak*, the Wireless Officer, who has just enjoyed his own encounter with another woman of Pough-keepsie, comments to Frankie "My God, that was a lovely night" and then asks the rhetorical question, "Isn't this a great country altogether?" (362). At this point, McCourt ends the chapter, thereby putting his one-word answer by itself in the final chapter: "'Tis" (363). Through the chapter break and the answer to a rhetorical question, McCourt invites us to recognize that both the vision and voice are doubled here. That is, the vision and voice belong simultaneously to Frankie at the time of the action and to the implied Frank McCourt at the time of the telling. The answer to the Wireless Officer's rhetorical question is both what Frankie thought on that "lovely night" and what he thinks about the country now as he finishes telling the story of his childhood. Furthermore, the doubled vision and voice confirm that the break from Church-induced guilt about sex is not temporary but permanent, and, thus, the one-word conclusion strongly signals a clean break from the past and a new beginning. Furthermore, with the presence of the vision and voice of the mature Frank in that word the narrative returns at its end to the voice and vision of its beginning. Though we don't know the rest of the story at this point, the continuity between the opening and closing voices suggests that the most important events for the transformation of Frankie into Frank have already occurred. Isn't it great ending altogether?

## The Ethics of *'Tis* and the Implied McCourt Once More

McCourt's sequel *'Tis* inevitably disrupts the neat closure of *Angela's Ashes* because it focuses on a new set of instabilities, those arising from Frankie's struggle to find his way in the United States from the time of his arrival in 1950 until 1986, the year that his father died; it ends with his narration of the 1985 trip that he and his brothers took to Limerick to scatter Angela's ashes in their final resting place, the cemetery at-tached to Mungret Abbey outside of Limerick. Frankie's struggle in-cludes his working as a houseman at the Biltmore Hotel and at other menial jobs; his finding his way into the College of Education at New York University; his own complicated relationship with alcohol; his courtship and marriage to Alberta Small, a marriage that leads to the birth of their daughter, Maggie, but eventually to their divorce; his teaching first at McKee Vocational School, then at New York Technical College, and finally at Stuyvesant High School. Parts of 'Tis are simply stunning: McCourt's narration of his experiences in the American military in Europe in the 1950s, and his account of his responses to the deaths of his parents are as formally accomplished, as emotionally moving, and as ethically powerful as any part of Angela's Ashes. However, for my purposes here, the most salient feature of 'Tis is that, at other moments, the ethical position of McCourt as implied author seems deficient. I would like to explore that deficiency and then consider its consequences for the way we think about both books.

As Frankie McCourt matures into Frank McCourt, the gaps between the character narrator and the mature implied author that so strongly mark Angela's Ashes are not as immediately apparent. (For this reason, I will from this point forward refer to the narrator of 'Tis as Frank.) Consequently, even as McCourt's continued use of the historical present and his continued interweaving of voices through direct and indirect discourse allow him sometimes to convey distance between the character narrator and the implied author, the burden on the narration shifts. As character, Frank has greater ethical responsibilities, and the character narration needs to reflect that greater responsibility. Rather than the audience having to infer the implied author's values through the carefully controlled unreliability of the naïve narrator, those values need to come through more clearly in Frank's narration itself. Sometimes what comes through is unimpressive.

At the end of chapter 47, Frank tells an anecdote about how he came to teach Shakespeare to his students at McKee Vocational School, when he was supposed to be teaching The Scarlet Letter, an anecdote that ends with his report of the school administrators taking the course away from him. Here are passages from the beginning and end of this mini-narrative:

> I told the class, It's Shakespeare or The Scarlet Letter, kings and lovers or a woman having a baby in Boston. If we read Shakespeare we'll act out the plays. If we read The Scarlet Letter we'll sit here and discuss the deeper meaning and I'll give you the big exam they keep in the department office.

Oh no, not the deeper meaning. English teachers always be going on about the deeper meaning.

All right. It's Shakespeare, no deeper meaning and no exams except what you decide. (310)

Mr. Sorola came to observe me with the new head of the Academic Department, Mrs. Popp. They smiled and didn't complain about this Shakespeare book not being on the syllabus though the next term Mrs. Popp took this class away from me. I lodged a grievance and had a hearing before the superintendent. I said that was my class. I had started them reading Shakespeare and I wanted to continue in the next term. The superintendent ruled against me on the grounds that my attendance record was spotty and erratic.

My Shakespeare students were probably lucky in having the head of the department as their teacher. She was surely more organized than I and more likely to discover deeper meanings. (312)

In between these two passages is a well-managed story of triumph, a story of how the students find Shakespeare so engaging that their intellectual curiosity becomes activated and they want to learn. The mini-narrative, in other words, fits the pattern of one in which an unconventional but successful teacher is thwarted by the school administration, and one in which the audience is invited to feel some indignation at his defeat. However, McCourt's handling of the narration, which is now in the past tense, creating the important effect of having the final paragraph focalized through his perspective after the event, suffers from two problems that unintentionally block that effect. The first involves the attendance record, and, more specifically, Frank's withholding of the information about it. The problem, in other words, is less in his behavior as character than in his action as narrator, because his withholding means that he has not treated his narratee—and McCourt has not treated the authorial audience—with the proper respect. Furthermore, the implied McCourt does not seem at all aware of this problem. Although Frank has previously acknowledged that he sometimes succumbs to the temptation to stay drinking with his fellow teachers on Friday nights instead of going home to Alberta, he has not previously acknowledged his attendance problems. The previous acknowledgment of his drinking, however, now gives credence to the superintendent's finding, especially since McCourt gives no indication that the charges are trumped up. But the most significant problem with the sudden revelation is how it changes our understanding of the mini-narrative. Prior to this revelation,

Frank has presented himself as the engaged teacher trying to find a way
to reach his students. But this revelation about his attendance record
suggests that his own engagement flags to the point where he just doesn't
show up.

The second problem is that Frank's concluding comment is not just a
witticism but also a cheap shot at Mrs. Popp, since the set-up of the mini-
narrative associates the activity of discovering deeper meanings with
alienating students. Frank's labeling of the students as "lucky" then
clearly becomes ironic, and when we note that the labeling comes from
his perspective after the event, the result is that McCourt unintentionally makes Frank the narrator look bad. After having Frank reveal that
he loses his appeal on grounds related to his own performance, he does
not have Frank accept the judgment with good grace but instead has him
turn to sniping at Mrs. Popp under the guise of exercising his wit—and
he does nothing to signal his own distance from that sniping. Underneath Frank's wit, then, there is a distasteful nastiness that never appears
in *Angela's Ashes*.

More significant ethical problems emerge in the implied McCourt's
handling of Frank's relationship with Alberta, which is too often treated
only in terms of abstractions: she is the Irish immigrant's dream, the
blond, blue-eyed, middle-class WASP American, a sort of Daisy Buchanan
to Frank's Jay Gatsby, rather than a fully mimetic character who is more
than these abstractions. This problem and others are evident in Frank's
narration of his final exit from the marriage.

> Mornings with Maggie were as golden or pink or green as the morn-
> ings I had with my father in Limerick. Till he went away I had him to
> myself. Till everything fell apart I had Maggie.
>
> Weekdays I'd walk her to school and take the train to my classes at
> Stuyvesant High School. My teenage students wrestled with hormones
> or struggled with family problems, divorces, custody battles, money,
> drugs, the death of faith. I felt sorry for them and their parents. I had the
> perfect little girl and I'd never have their problems.
>
> I did and Maggie did. The marriage crumbled. Slum-reared Irish
> Catholics have nothing in common with nice girls from New England
> who had little curtains at their bedroom windows, who wore white
> gloves right up to their elbows and went to proms with nice boys, who
> studied etiquette with French nuns and were told, Girls, your virtue is
> like a dropped vase. You may repair the break but the crack will always
> be there. Slum-reared Irish Catholics might have recalled what their fa-
> thers said, After a full belly all is poetry.

The old Irish had told me, and my mother had warned me, Stick with your own. Marry your own. The devil you know is better than the devil you don't know.

When Maggie was five I walked out and stayed with a friend. It didn't last. I wanted my mornings with my daughter. I wanted to sit on the floor before the fire, tell her stories, listen to "Sergeant Pepper's Lonely Hearts Club Band." Surely, after all these years, I could work on this marriage, wear a tie, escort Maggie to birthday parties around Brooklyn Heights, charm wives, play squash, pretend an interest in antiques.

I walked Maggie to school. I carried her bookbag, she toted her Barbie lunchbox. Around her eighth year she announced, Look, Dad, I want to go to school with my friends. Of course, she was pulling away, going independent, saving herself. She must have known her family was disintegrating, that her father would soon leave forever as his father had long ago and I left for good a week before her eighth birthday. (352)

As Frank describes his problems in his marriage he takes little responsibility for them, preferring to see everything in terms of the gap between "slum-reared Irish Catholics" and "nice girls from New England," and his description of that gap implies the superiority of the lessons of the slums to the lessons of a New England girlhood. The combination of the assumed superiority and the failure to take any responsibility makes both Frank and McCourt, who seems unaware of these problems, unappealing.

As Frank narrates his move back into the family, he says nothing directly about Alberta as an actor, as he focuses on Maggie and on himself. The oblique references to Alberta, in the list of activities he will do as part of working on the marriage, stack the deck against her: Alberta is concerned with superficial things, with keeping up middle-class appearances, while he, though above all that, will pretend an interest for the sake of his daughter. Frank's withholding of information about his and Alberta's actions toward each other is not an example of underreporting because the vision of the passage from the time of the telling marks it as reliable narration. There is, I submit, an ethical deficiency here, not in the lack of detail about who said what when but in the continued evasion of responsibility and agency and in the stacking of the deck against Alberta. Let me be clear: I don't see the ethical problem as Frank's decision to leave but rather as McCourt's relation to the authorial audience. McCourt/Frank is narrating a crucial incident in his life, one in which his own agency must go beyond the playing out of the cultural stereotypes he identifies in this passage, but he never gets beyond those stereotypes.

Furthermore, with respect to agency, Frank's focus on Maggie works as a kind of smokescreen behind which McCourt avoids the discussion of the marriage, and then, in the last paragraph, he barely stops short of giving the final agency in the breakup to Maggie: once Maggie no longer wanted to be walked to school, I left. But then, at the very end of the passage, McCourt finds a way to give a powerful twist to his telling when he not only asserts his agency but also reveals his guilt by associating his own leaving with that of his father. It is striking, however, that the guilt remains tied to his relation with Maggie and never extends to his relation with Alberta.

The twist is a result of the progression of focalization and of agency in that last sentence: "She must have known her family was disintegrating, that her father would soon leave forever as his father had long ago and I left for good a week before her eighth birthday." McCourt starts by focalizing the narration through Maggie, albeit in the subjunctive mode ("she must have known"), and ends by focalizing through "I." The transition occurs in the middle of the sentence after "that her father would soon leave forever" with the clause "as his father had long ago." Is the focalization here Maggie's or Frank's—or to acknowledge the subjunctive, does Frank imagine that Maggie is aware of the similarity between her grandfather and her father? Even if we say that he does, we need to remember that in adopting the subjunctive and telling us what Maggie "must have known" Frank is, at some level, sharing her vision. In other words, the ambiguity of focalization here does not interfere with our recognition that McCourt is associating his leaving with his father's.

As the beginning of the passage and other markers throughout 'Tis indicate, the authorial audience of this memoir is one that also knows Angela's Ashes. Just as McCourt's invocation of his mornings with his father in Limerick at the beginning of the passage calls up the pleasure of their early father-son bond, so too the invocation of his father's leaving at the end calls up the pain and suffering that departure inflicted on his family. By associating his leaving with that of his father, McCourt acknowledges the pain and suffering he must have caused Maggie— though again Alberta is significantly absent from this paragraph. Thus, the turn at the end partially—but only partially—redeems the passage.

In this account of McCourt's two narratives, then, we have two different ethical evaluations of the implied author. In Angela's Ashes, the implied McCourt fulfills Wayne Booth's ideal of an ethically admirable guide to the narrative world, one who is, in all probability, a superior version of the flesh-and-blood author, while in 'Tis the implied McCourt is less consistently admirable and even at times deficient. It is, I believe, no accident that most readers of both books prefer *Angela's Ashes* because the ethical and the aesthetic are inextricably interwoven: *Angela's Ashes* is a better book because McCourt has succeeded in matching his technique with his ethical vision of his Limerick childhood, and *'Tis*, though often remarkable, is a lesser achievement because the ethical vision is cloudier and the technique suffers along with it.

This difference also raises another question: do the problems with *'Tis* detract from the achievement of *Angela's Ashes*? Consider the case of two different fictions by the same author about different characters and situations, one of which is ethically admirable and the other ethically problematic. In such a case, there is no interactive effect—the problems with the second narrative do not detract from the achievement of the first, just as the success of the first does not erase or even mitigate the problems of the second. If this account is correct, then it also provides additional support for the concept of the implied author and of the career author: the two fictions have the same flesh-and-blood author but that author has two different presences in the two narratives—or to put it more efficiently, the implied authors of the two narratives are notably different from each other. At the same time, there is an interactive effect on our overall evaluation of the author's body of work, and this effect is nicely explained by Booth's concept of the career author.

*Angela's Ashes* and *'Tis*, however, are connected in ways that our two hypothetical fictions are not. Since the authorial audience of *'Tis* knows the narrative of *Angela's Ashes*, and since the two narratives have the same protagonist and many other continuing characters, they form a continuous autobiography with a single implied author. Thus, the problems with *'Tis* do detract from the achievements of *Angela's Ashes* just as the achievements of *Angela's Ashes* mitigate the effects of the problems with *'Tis*.

*Angela's Ashes* sharply delineates the perspectives of Frank and Frankie, but what happens in the case of a retrospective narrator who moves from sharing the perspective of his former self to questioning it or even condemning it? And what happens when the perspective of the former self is clearly ethically deficient? How might the unreliable narration change over the course of the narrative, and how will the implied author guide us to see the changes in the perspective of the character narrator? What are the ethical consequences of such a technique? Answering these questions in connection with Vladimir Nabokov's handing of his pedophile narrator's confession in *Lolita* will not only require further analysis of shifting reliability and unreliability but also a fresh look at the concept of focalization.

# 3 Dual Focalization, Discourse as Story, and Ethics

*Lolita*

*Lolita* and *The Kiss* are hot-button narratives, ones that evoke strong positive and negative reactions in their readers. These reactions involve both the subject matter of each book—pedophilia and incest, respectively—and its treatment: having the pedophile tell the story in Nabokov's case and having the incest victim confess to it in Harrison's. And the reactions are ultimately ethical: writing and reading these books is, for some, challenging, provocative, and valuable and, for others, dangerous, disgusting, and debasing. In the next two chapters, I will consider the relation between technique and ethics in these narratives, starting with *Lolita* and then turning to *The Kiss*. *Lolita* already has a complex critical history, one initially dominated by discussions of its aesthetics, while more recent work has brought the ethical issues to the foreground.[1] *Lolita* is nothing if not a deeply layered book, one in which

---

1. The history of criticism of *Lolita* itself makes an interesting narrative, with most of the early responses focusing on the novel's aesthetics; these responses not only counter the charge that it was pornographic but they also follow the lead offered by Nabokov in his "Afterword: On a Book Entitled *Lolita*" in which he talks about his interest in creating "aesthetic bliss." Lionel Trilling offered an early account of the novel as a love story. Alfred Appel Jr.'s appreciative work has contributed not only the very helpful *Annotated Lolita* but also considerable understanding of Nabokov's allusions and parodic techniques. The turn to an ethical criticism that finds significant fault with the novel is relatively recent, spurred primarily by Kauffman. For important later contributions see especially Wood and Patnoe. In my chapter on *Lolita* in a 1981 book on style, I, too, focus on the book's aesthetics, arguing, among other things, that during the davenport scene, readers simultaneously condemn Humbert's actions and admire his—and Nabokov's—virtuoso style. For a

Nabokov combines Humbert Humbert's realist confession of his treatment of Dolores Haze with elements of parody, satire, and metafiction. (In order to differentiate my own perspective from that of Humbert Humbert I shall refer to the girl whom he calls Lolita by her given name.)[2] The novel is also richly intertextual, full of allusions to works by writers from Sophocles to Shakespeare, from Poe to Stevenson, Baudelaire to Dostoevsky. In my view, however, these layers of the novel support rather than undermine the realist layer, serving largely to characterize Humbert and his situation.[3] Consequently, in this chapter, I will attend primarily to the realist layer because that is where the relation between technique and ethics is most vexed.

One of the most startling sequences in the novel occurs toward the end of part 1 when Humbert follows the account of his first sexual intercourse with Dolores Haze by describing the murals that he imagines painting in the dining room of the Enchanted Hunters Hotel. Here is the end of chapter 29, the final portion of Humbert's account of the intercourse:

> My life was handled by little Lo in an energetic, matter-of-fact manner as if it were an insensate gadget unconnected with me. While eager to impress me with the world of tough kids, she was not quite prepared for certain discrepancies between a kid's life and mine. Pride alone prevented her from giving up; for, in my strange predicament, I feigned supreme stupidity and had her have her way—at least while I could still bear it. But really these are irrelevant matters; I am not concerned with so-called "sex" at all. Anybody can imagine those elements of animality. A greater endeavor lures me on: to fix once for all the perilous magic of nymphets. (133–34)

Here is the description of the murals, which takes up almost the whole of chapter 30:

---

good sample of essays, see Bloom's collection, and for a fuller sense of the critical history from 1977 to 1995, see Jones.

2. John Ray Jr.'s introduction reveals that her last name only rhymes with "Haze," but it gives no reason to doubt that Dolores is her given name.

3. I would not, however, argue that all the strokes of the novel are fully integrated in support of the realist core. Nabokov's interest in play, parody, and satire sometimes means that he will go for local effects without much concern for making them serve another purpose. To take just one example, planting the anagram of his own name ("Vivian Darkbloom") in the excerpt Humbert quotes from the fictitious *Who's Who in the Limelight* is no more—and no less—than part of his game of peek-a-boo with the authorial audience.

Had I been a painter, had the management of The Enchanted Hunters
lost its mind one summer day and commissioned me to redecorate their
dining room with murals of my own making, this is what I might have
thought up, let me list some fragments:
   There would have been a lake. There would have been an arbor in
flame-flower. There would have been nature studies—a tiger pursuing a
bird of paradise, a choking snake sheathing whole the flayed trunk of a
shoat. There would have been a sultan, his face expressing great agony
(belied, as it were, by his molding caress), helping a callypygean slave
child to climb a column of onyx. There would have been those luminous
globules of gonadal glow that travel up the opalescent sides of juke
boxes. There would have been all kinds of camp activities on the part of
the intermediate group, Canoeing, Coranting, Combing Curls in the
lakeside sun. There would have been poplars, apples, a suburban Sunday. There would have been a fire opal dissolving within a ripple-ringed
pool, a last throb, a last dab of color, stinging red, smarting pink, a sigh,
a wincing child.[4] (134–35)

The sequence is startling because Humbert's narration in chapter 30 con-
tradicts his statements of purpose at the end of chapter 29. He says nothing about "the perilous magic of nymphets," opting instead to invite the
narratee to reflect on the "animality" of the scene of intercourse through
the images of predators and prey, and most remarkable of all, offering his
audience not only a reminder of his physical exertions ("a last throb," "a
sigh") but also a glimpse of Dolores's pain: "stinging red, smarting pink
. . . a wincing child."
   This chapter will seek to uncover (1) the role of the character narration in the narrative logic behind this sequence; (2) what that logic suggests about the design of the larger narrative; and (3) what ethical
consequences follow from that logic and that design. The role of the

---

4. There is one short intervening stretch of narration between the end of chapter 29 and
the passage I have just quoted from chapter 30, an address by Humbert to possible narratees: "I have to tread carefully. I have to speak in a whisper. Oh you, veteran crime reporter,
you grave old usher, you once popular policeman, now in solitary confinement after grac-
ing that school crossing for years, you wretched emeritus read to by a boy! It would never
do, would it, to have you fellows fall madly in love with my Lolita!" (134). This passage
clearly locates Humbert's perspective in the time of the narration, and it reveals, in the wake
of the narration of the intercourse, his lingering desire to possess Dolores himself and his
belief that other men harbor similar desires. The passage makes psychological sense, given
Humbert the narrator's awareness that Quilty was present at the Enchanted Hunters Hotel
on the night of the first intercourse. All these effects make the shift in Humbert's narration
in the rest of the chapter all the more striking.

character narration is heavily dependent on Nabokov's handling of the narrative perspective, what narratologists since Genette have called focalization. As we will see, narratologists after Genette have not reached consensus about focalization, and, in order to make my case about *Lolita*, I will propose a new way of thinking about this element of narrative discourse that will be the basis for my claim about a double narrative in the novel: the story of Humbert and Dolores, and the story of Humbert's struggle to tell that story.[5] Before I turn to Nabokov's technique, however, it will be helpful to consider the ongoing debate about the ethics of *Lolita*.

Although the debate can be found in the criticism of the novel, I choose to highlight its major features by reporting on two of my experiences in teaching it, once in a graduate seminar, once in an NEH Summer Seminar for College Teachers. People in both groups, especially those encountering the book for the first time, had very strong but very different reactions. Some thrilled to Humbert Humbert's cleverness, wit, fancy prose style, and ability, in the words of John Ray Jr., to use "his singing violin [to] conjure up a tendresse" (5). Others found the experience of reading the book painful and resented being required to read it. These readers found Humbert repulsive, regardless of his allegedly redeeming features and his (and Nabokov's) stylistic brilliance. Some of them also pointed out that what we know about the incidence of sexual abuse makes it likely that one or more members of any class would have experienced such abuse and that it was, therefore, irresponsible to require students to read it. Defenders of the book responded that the book's focus on illicit sexual desire raised important questions about desire in general and societal imperatives to restrict desire; these readers also contended that part of the book's value was to make us uncomfortable. Although neither class split neatly along gender lines, the arguments sometimes linked gender to response, with a few women saying "It's mostly you men who like the book and although you talk in class about its aesthetic qualities, what you really like is the way Humbert acts out male sexual fantasies." And a few men said, "It's mostly you feminists who don't like the book because it's definitely not PC and your politics prohibit you from getting past the surface story and appreciating Nabokov's transformation of his offensive subject matter into articulate art."

---

5. My perception of this element of the novel has been enhanced by Wayne C. Booth's essay on what he calls "struggle stories."

Strikingly, people on different sides of the debate sometimes took the same elements of the novel as evidence for their positions. Defenders would point to the shift in the purpose of Humbert's narration—from exonerating himself to condemning himself—to his heartfelt protestations of love for the adult Dolores, and to his wish to have his confession give her immortality. Nabokov, in their view, is attempting the difficult job of making Humbert's transformation plausible, and they argue that readers should recognize the artistry involved in that effort. Those who attacked the book countered that the shift in purpose is another effort on Humbert's part to manipulate his audience into sympathizing with him, that his love is impoverished because he still had no idea who Dolores was, and that his confession is another way of objectifying her. In their view, Humbert's transformation is very limited, if it occurs at all, and it redeems neither himself nor Nabokov's novel.

This debate is ultimately about the ethics of reading and about the relation between aesthetics and ethics. Readers and critics who defend the book along the lines expressed by my students and my NEH colleagues make two key ethical assumptions: (1) a literary work's overall treatment of its topic is more important than the topic itself and some individual aspects of its treatment; that is, we need to see Humbert's narration of his pedophilia as part of a larger narrative project that is worthy of defense; and (2) we ought to remain open to the possibility of reform—and even a modicum of redemption—in others, including those as reprehensible as Humbert Humbert. Both of these assumptions entail the principle that aesthetics and ethics are inextricably intertwined, though they tend to give pride of place to aesthetics.

Those readers and critics who object to the book along the lines expressed by my students and my NEH colleagues are making two different ethical assumptions: (1) the very act of representing some subjects from some perspectives—including pedophilia from the perspective of the pedophile—is ethically suspect and not capable of being defended on aesthetic grounds; that is, this topic and aspects of its treatment are so offensive as to seriously impair any larger narrative project Nabokov may be undertaking; (2) giving credence to Humbert's questionable claims about his new understanding of and feelings for Dolores puts the ethical emphasis in the wrong place: on Humbert the narrator rather than on Dolores and what Humbert the character has done to her. Both of these positions also regard aesthetics and ethics as interconnected, but they also entail the principle that ethics trumps aesthetics.

As a rhetorical theorist I see the ethical and the aesthetic as so deeply intertwined that any attempt to give one precedence over the other is misguided, but I also believe that recognizing this underlying issue in the debate about *Lolita* helps us understand why that debate can be so charged. Readers and critics get exercised about the novel not only because of the controversial subject matter and Nabokov's complex representation of Humbert Humbert but also because coming down for or against the book also implies a position about the purposes of literature. I shall return to this dimension of the ethical debate toward the end of the chapter. For now, I want to begin to analyze the link between technique and ethics by first considering how Humbert's narration is different from that of any of the other narrators we've seen in this book and then turning to the novel's famous davenport scene.

Mary Elizabeth Preston has developed a very useful set of terms and concepts to help identify a narrator's relation to the act of narration, terms and concepts that enable me to indicate what is distinctive about Humbert among our character narrators. *Authorial disposition* refers to the narrator's awareness of himself or herself as a storyteller. Thus, Stevens, who often remarks on the occasion of his writing, and Humbert, who on the very first page remarks that "you can always count on a murderer for a fancy prose style," share this authorial disposition, while Cisneros's child narrator and Frankie McCourt in *Angela's Ashes* do not. *Self-consciousness* refers to the narrator's awareness of his or her agency in crafting the effects of the narration. Cisneros's child narrator, Stevens, and Frankie lack this self-conscious craft, while the implied Nabokov makes it a large feature of Humbert's narration. As the example of Stevens suggests, not every narrator with an authorial disposition will be self-conscious; however, every self-conscious narrator will have an authorial disposition. Huck Finn, who refers to the act of writing at the beginning and end of his narrative, is another unself-conscious narrator with an authorial disposition. To put this point another way, an authorial disposition is a necessary but not a sufficient condition for self-consciousness.

Nabokov gives us several signals early in the narrative that point to Humbert's self-consciousness. John Ray Jr.'s introduction calls attention to Humbert's stylistic power, and Humbert's early remarks about his word choices and other narrative strategies underline his self-consciousness. Later, after Dolores reveals the name of the man she left Humbert for, he writes, "Quietly the fusion took place, and everything fell into order, into the pattern of branches that I have woven throughout this memoir with the express purpose of having the ripe fruit fall at the right moment . . . " (272). Most of the wit, the word play, and the allusions, detailed so extensively and helpfully by Alfred Appel Jr. in *The Annotated Lolita*, also point to Humbert's conscious crafting of the narrative. In *Lolita*, the stylistic virtuosity belongs both to implied author and narrator; by contrast, the different kind of stylistic virtuosity in *Angela's Ashes* belongs only to the implied McCourt.

*Aesthetic control* refers to the narrator's ability to achieve the effects he seeks and to have those effects endorsed by the implied author. Unself-conscious narrators such as Stevens and Frankie do not exercise aesthetic control, but self-conscious ones such as Humbert seek it. Humbert's aesthetic control is, however, far from complete. To the extent that he is unreliable on any axis, he loses aesthetic control. With this understanding of Humbert as a self-conscious narrator with an authorial disposition and only partial aesthetic control, let us turn to his narration of the famous davenport scene.

In this scene, Humbert contrives to bring himself to orgasm without Dolores's knowledge as he engages in various kinds of play with her. The scene, which runs for almost five pages, begins with an expression of Humbert's self-conscious effort to exercise aesthetic control: "I want my learned readers to participate in the scene I am about to replay; I want them to examine its every detail and see for themselves how careful, how chaste, the whole wine-sweet event is if viewed with what my lawyer has called, in a private talk we have had, 'impartial sympathy.' So, let us get started. I have a difficult job before me" (57). Humbert the narrator clearly wants to defend Humbert the character and so frames his account by interpreting his behavior ("careful" and "chaste"), by implicitly challenging his "learned readers" to adopt the right attitude ("impartial sympathy"), and by implicitly asking for their sympathy for his role as narrator ("I have a difficult job before me"). Humbert's rhetoric is very skillful, but let's turn to a sample from the account and see whether Humbert succeeds in exercising aesthetic control.

> . . . there was, I swear, a yellowish-violet bruise on her lovely nymphet thigh which my huge hairy hand massaged and slowly enveloped—and because of her very perfunctory underthings, there seemed to be nothing to prevent my muscular thumb from reaching the hot hollow of her groin—just as you might tickle and caress a giggling child—just that—and: "Oh it's nothing at all," she cried with a sudden shrill note in her voice, and she wiggled, and squirmed, and threw her head back, and her teeth rested on her glistening underlip as she half-turned away, and my

moaning mouth, gentlemen of the jury, almost reached her bare neck, while I crushed out against her left buttock the last throb of the longest ecstasy man or monster had ever known. (60–61)

The technique here is relatively straightforward: Humbert the narrator reports the scene primarily from the perspective of Humbert the character, though he occasionally switches to his perspective at the time of the narration ("I swear," "just as you might," and "gentlemen of the jury"). Furthermore, the voice of the narrator and the voice of the character are essentially the same. Although there are a few shifts in the temporal perspective, there are no corresponding shifts in the attitudes expressed: both Humbert the narrator and Humbert the character remain focused on how he manipulates the situation for his physical pleasure.

As a result of that focus, our ethical positioning in this passage—and throughout the scene—is both complicated and uncomfortable, as we can see by tracing the relations among the first three ethical situations. Despite Humbert's initial rhetoric, the ethical situation between the characters is easy to apprehend: Humbert treats the young and innocent Dolores as a sex object and uses her for his sexual gratification, transforming her from a child into a sexual toy. This position interacts with the second ethical situation, that between Humbert and his subject matter and audience. And here we must come to terms with Humbert's contention that he has been careful and chaste, and with his pride that because Dolores is "safely solipsized" (60), that is, unaware of what he is doing, his pleasure is innocent. Humbert's insistence on his innocence and his effort to sway, even seduce, the audience to adopt an attitude of "impartial sympathy" exacerbates the ethical deficiencies of his treatment of Dolores. Indeed, his designs on his audience are, in one sense, similar to his designs on Dolores: in both cases, he wants to use the other for his own selfish purposes. In this respect, then, Humbert is not entirely successful in exercising his aesthetic control.

This second ethical situation interacts, in turn, with the third, the implied Nabokov's relation to *his* audience and *his* subject matter, including Humbert. Because Nabokov has Humbert describe the action largely from his perspective as character, *Nabokov* not only invites but virtually commands us to "participate in the scene." This invitation/command means that we see the events through the filter of Humbert's attitudes: his pride in his cleverness, his eager anticipation of success, and his ultimate satisfaction. In other words, simply to read the scene is to take on Humbert's perspective, and to take on his perspective means to see his perverse desire from the inside. Furthermore, because Humbert's effort in narrating the scene is to sway us to adopt his attitudes, and because Nabokov gives Humbert formidable verbal skills and rhetorical power, the authorial audience can't help but feel the force of Humbert's appeal. Although Humbert's aesthetic control is far from complete, his efforts have genuine force.

At the same time, it is the implied Nabokov who guides our recognition that Humbert's aesthetic control is only partial, that we should resist Humbert's seduction, and that the line between solipsizing and molesting is paper thin—in short, our recognition that Humbert's use of Dolores for his pleasure is an ab-use of her. For example, Humbert's high-flown language and explicit address to "gentlemen of the jury" invite the authorial audience to put a little distance between Humbert and themselves. But the authorial audience's position is further complicated because some of these signals about Humbert's misregarding are themselves discomfiting. For example, Nabokov uses Humbert's acute awareness of what he might do with his "muscular thumb" both to underline the physical disparity between Humbert and Dolores and to suggest how close Humbert is to molesting her. While Humbert compares the possible motion of his thumb with caressing and tickling a giggling child, his references to her "perfunctory underthings" and the "hot hollow of her groin" actually conjure up a more explicit sexual act, one Nabokov expects his audience to find painful to contemplate.

In addition, Nabokov uses Humbert's description of Dolores's voice and movements to suggest that, at some level of consciousness, Humbert is imagining her not as an innocent, playful child but as a sexual partner: she cries out with "a sudden shrill note in her voice"; she wiggles and squirms and throws her head back. Humbert's desire once again seems far from being as innocent as he claims. Finally, with a bolder stroke, Nabokov invites us to see Humbert as a vampire: "*My moaning mouth* . . . almost reached *her bare neck,* while [I enjoyed] the longest ecstasy man or *monster* had ever known" (my emphasis).

Through these signals, Nabokov clearly communicates to the authorial audience Humbert's misregarding and hence his own distance from Humbert's attitudes. Yet because Nabokov's technique requires his audience to stand with Humbert and share his perspective before we can stand back and distance ourselves, the same signals that communicate the distance also require the participation in Humbert's perverse perspective. The ethical dynamics, then, can be described this way: Nabokov, through Humbert's narration, gives voice to pedophilic fantasies, guides his audience to participate in those fantasies and feel something of their appeal, even as he *simultaneously* signals the audience to reject both the fantasies and Humbert. It is no wonder that many flesh-and-blood readers find the novel to be so distasteful that they stop reading in part 1 and that many other readers who do finish the book find Humbert's protestations of love and remorse in part 2 to be unconvincing. But it is also no wonder that many flesh-and-blood readers find Nabokov's technique and Humbert's narrative offering a challenging reading experience, one that provides a window into the oft-times complicated workings of sexual desire. For my part, if Nabokov always restricted the perspective to that of Humbert at the time of the action, I would be among the ranks of those who would not teach the book. But it is precisely because Nabokov does other things with the narrative perspective as part of the novel's larger progression, including what happens in the sequence between chapter 29 and chapter 30 of part 1, that I find the book to be worth teaching and writing about. Before I move toward any conclusions about the ethical positioning in the narrative as a whole, including the relation between Nabokov and my own flesh-and-blood reader response, I want to consider what Nabokov does with Humbert's perspective in that sequence and how it helps us understand some significant elements of the novel's progression. In order to appreciate Nabokov's technique, I will first say more about the relation of Humbert's self-consciousness to his unreliability, and then consider Nabokov's handling of focalization.

As the analysis of the davenport scene suggests, despite all the artistry and cleverness of Humbert's telling, his control over the effects of his narration has significant limits, the most important of them involving his unreliability on the axis of ethics and evaluation. Other examples abound throughout the narrative, especially in part 1, and I will cite just a few of them here. Humbert is totally oblivious to the way his narration of his marriage to Valeria makes her look like a long-suffering saint and him like a cruel egotist. He also seems unaware, despite the lesson of Charlotte's reading, of the effect that the diary of his first weeks in the Haze household is likely to have on his audience. He introduces it as "Exhibit number two" (40), part of his defense, something that he apparently believes will work toward his exoneration much like exhibit number one, the story of his abortive love for Annabel Leigh, does. But what the diary details is the "Portrait of a Pedophile as a Lusting but Cautious Boarder."

The second dimension of Humbert's lack of control involves the larger design of the narrative, especially its trajectory from beginning to end, but I can address that dimension more easily after returning to what happens at the end of part 1, starting with the conclusion of chapter 29, which I will quote once again for ease of reference.

> My life was handled by little Lo in an energetic, matter-of-fact manner as if it were an insensate gadget unconnected with me. While eager to impress me with the world of tough kids, she was not quite prepared for certain discrepancies between a kid's life and mine. Pride alone prevented her from giving up; for, in my strange predicament, I feigned supreme stupidity and had her have her way—at least while I could still bear it. But really these are irrelevant matters; I am not concerned with so-called "sex" at all. Anybody can imagine those elements of animality. A greater endeavor lures me on: to fix once for all the perilous magic of nymphets. (133–34)

Humbert's narration here exhibits underreporting, misreporting, and misregarding. The underreporting is evident in the swerve the narration takes after his admission that he let her have her way "at least while I could still bear it." Prior to this move, Humbert has given many details about how Dolores suggested that he and she play the game Charlie Holmes taught her at camp, and he has begun his account of their game, complete with an acknowledgment of "certain discrepancies" between Dolores's expectations and his adult male body. Once Humbert becomes the main actor—after his lust conquers his patience—he stops reporting the behavioral details and goes so far as to claim that they are "irrelevant." The absence of any attention to the effect of his actions on Dolores is a conspicuous sign of underreporting that is also an instance of misregarding—indeed, it is a failure to regard at all. Humbert is misreporting because his own narration has repeatedly shown that he is concerned with sex and especially with his own sexual pleasure; to claim that the "perilous magic of nymphets" is separate from what, in his artful dodging, he labels "so-called 'sex'" is to misreport. In addition, he is misregarding when he resorts to the Nymphet Defense—a subtle but ultimately transparent way of blaming the victim.

The interaction of the unreliability with the self-consciousness is consistent with Humbert's main motive for telling during part 1. He wants to defend himself not only against a charge of murder but even more against the condemnation he knows his pedophilia would normally receive. In narrating the event of the first intercourse, he deliberately underreports his own actions so that he can maximize Dolores's role as the initiator, and he deliberately resorts to the Nymphet Defense to make himself seem more eccentric than perverse. Indeed, if his fancy prose style and attention to the magic of nymphets take in credulous ladies and gentlemen of the jury so much the better. What, then, is the narrative logic underlying his shift to the description of the murals he imagines himself painting?

> There would have been a lake. There would have been an arbor in flame-flower. There would have been nature studies—a tiger pursuing a bird of paradise, a choking snake sheathing whole the flayed trunk of a shoat. There would have been a sultan, his face expressing great agony (belied, as it were, by his molding caress), helping a callypygean slave child to climb a column of onyx. There would have been those luminous globules of gonadal glow that travel up the opalescent sides of juke boxes. There would have been all kinds of camp activities on the part of the intermediate group, Canoeing, Coranting, Combing Curls in the lakeside sun. There would have been poplars, apples, a suburban Sunday. There would have been a fire opal dissolving within a ripple-ringed pool, a last throb, a last dab of color, stinging red, smarting pink, a sigh, a wincing child. (134–35)

The differences from chapter 29 are remarkable. Where chapter 29 is riddled with unreliability, chapter 30 is utterly reliable. Where chapter 29 is dominated by Humbert's concern for how he comes across, and is very much a part of his self-conscious strategic defense, chapter 30 progresses toward the spontaneous overflow of powerful feeling. Furthermore, this powerful feeling belongs to Humbert the narrator, and it is so powerful as to be a major factor motivating Humbert to change the purpose of his narrative from exoneration to condemnation. Indeed, we begin to see the effects of that change very shortly, though perhaps most clearly in this passage at the end of chapter 3 of part 2, where Humbert clearly condemns himself:

> And so we rolled East, I more devastated than braced with the satisfaction of my passion, and she glowing with health, her bi-iliac garland still as brief as a lad's, although she had added two inches to her stature and eight pounds to her weight. We had been everywhere. We had really seen nothing. And I catch myself thinking today that our long journey had only defiled with a sinuous trail of slime the lovely, trustful, dreamy,

enormous country that by then, in retrospect, was no more to us than a collection of dog-eared maps, ruined tour books, old tires, and her sobs in the night—every night, every night—the moment I feigned sleep. (175–76)

Before I analyze the detailed workings of the technique here and in chapter 30 of part 1 ("Had I been a painter . . . ") I need to reconsider work on "focalization," the term Gérard Genette coined to refer to the way narrative discourse signals the perceiver of the events. This reconsideration will, for a time, necessarily broaden the scope of my discussion to both character narration and noncharacter narration. Part of my case will be that Genette's initial taxonomy of focalization, while helpful in many respects, is also flawed, especially in its ability to account for focalization in character narration. I will propose a revised taxonomy that, in my view, allows for a more adequate account of such focalization, but I do not propose to develop a comprehensive theory of focalization, because I regard that task as beyond the scope of this book.[6]

## A Tour through the Theory of Focalization

In *Narrative Discourse*, Genette uttered one of those simple but profound statements that sharpen perceptions and open up a whole subarea of scholarship, when he observed that point of view was a term that had conflated two concepts that need to be kept distinct, vision (who sees?, later amended to who perceives?) and voice (who speaks?). With voice, Genette retained the term and proposed his distinction between homodiegetic and heterodiegetic narrators. With vision, Genette proposed both a new term—focalization—and a short taxonomy of three kinds:

---

6. Such a comprehensive account would need, among other things, to work through the debate between Genette and Mieke Bal about the usefulness of expanding the theory, as Bal suggests, to include (a) a category not just of the "focalizer" but also of "the focalized" (the object perceived by the focalizer) and (b) degrees or levels of focalization (in which one character's focalization would be embedded within another's). See Bal's *Narratology* and Genette's *Narrative Discourse Revisited*, and the discussion of each of their positions in Manfred Jahn's excellent essay from a cognitivist perspective, "Windows of Focalization." My own views are closer to Bal's than Genette's, though in practice I find much more use for the category of focalizer than for that of the focalized.

Another useful comprehensive account of focalization is offered by David Fitzsimmons in his 2003 dissertation, "I See, He Says, Perhaps, On Time: Vision, Voice, Hypothetical Narration, and Temporality in William Faulkner's Fiction."

1. zero focalization (appropriately renamed "free focalization" by Nelles): noncharacter (or heterodiegetic) narration such as that in Fielding's *Tom Jones,* where the narrator perceives and knows more than any character;

2. internal focalization: center of consciousness narration such as we find in the fiction of Henry James, where the narrator perceives and knows only what the central consciousness perceives and knows; and

3. external focalization such as we find in the fiction of Dashiell Hammett, where the narrator perceives and knows less than the protagonist.[7]

To my vision, Genette was doing fine until he proposed this taxonomy, because it actually reproduces the problem he wanted to solve and because it has led the conversation about focalization among narratologists if not down some mean streets at least into some blind alleys. Although Genette's taxonomy does maintain the separation between "who sees" and "who speaks," it involves a different conflation, that between *"who sees"* and *"what (or how much) is seen."*[8] Genette would have done better, I believe—and I'll return to this point—by working out a typology of possible relations between speaker and perceiver.

What many other narratologists have focused on, however, is not Genette's failure to follow through on the logic of his initial distinction but rather on a difference between free and external focalization, on the one hand, and internal focalization, on the other. The focalizer in free and external focalization is the narrator, while the focalizer in internal focalization is the character.[9] Some narratologists, including Seymour

7. For an excellent exposition of the logic of Genette's position along with intelligent proposals for some slight modifications, see Nelles. Unlike Nelles, however, I think that conceiving of focalization as a relation of perception/knowledge among narrator and character muddies rather than clarifies the questions of who speaks and who perceives.

8. In order to be fair to Genette, I should also stress that his move fits the logic of his approach in *Narrative Discourse.* Genette sees focalization as part of the larger category "mood" (as opposed to either "tense" or "voice"), and under mood, he considers the *degrees* by which things are seen, reported, done, etc. His relational typology with its concerns about degrees of vision and knowledge and their role in conveying information is very consistent with this conception of "mood." This dimension of his thinking about "focalization" is even more explicit in his chapter "Focalizations" in *Narrative Discourse Revisited* (see esp. 77–78), where he argues that Bal's categories of focalizer and focalized are not necessary to get at the essence of focalization, which is concerned with the different ways a narrative restricts its conveyance of information.

9. In *Narrative Discourse Revisited,* Genette resists this inference about internal focalization, arguing that, if Bal's term *"focalizer* applies to anyone, it could only be the person who focalizes the narrative—that is, the narrator, or, if one wanted to go outside the conventions of fiction, the author himself, who delegates (or does not delegate) to the narrator his power of focalizing or not focalizing" (73). But at this point, Genette's emphasis on fo-

Chatman and Gerald Prince, resist the idea that both characters and narrators can be focalizers because that idea violates the logic of the story/discourse distinction, which locates characters in story and narrators in discourse and stipulates that never the twain shall meet. More specifically, the distinction says that characters perceive, think, act, and feel but narrators only report. Here's the way Chatman and Prince make their cases.

Chatman actually wants to get rid of the term *focalization* and replace it with two terms: "filter" to describe a character's perceptions, and "slant" to describe a narrator's angle of reporting. Chatman's illustrative example is the opening of Dickens's *Dombey and Son*: "Dombey sat in the corner of the darkened room in the great armchair by the bedside, and son lay tucked up warm in a little basket bedstead, carefully disposed on a low settee immediately in front of the fire and close to it, as if his constitution were analogous to that of a muffin, and it was essential to toast him brown while he was very new" (1). Chatman comments:

> the narrator is not to be imagined as literally *contemplating* the new baby and deciding, in that contemplation, that he resembles a muffin. . . . The narrator, in this case omniscient and unidentified, is a reporter, not an "observer" of the story world in the sense of literally witnessing it. It makes no sense to say that a story is told "through" the narrator's perception since he/she/it is precisely *narrating*, which is not an act of perception but of presentation or representation. (143)[10]

For Chatman, what is true of noncharacter (or heterodiegetic) narrators is ultimately true of character (or homodiegetic) narrators as well: "The heterodiegetic narrator *never* saw the events because he/she/it never occupied the story world. The homodiegetic or first-person narrator *did* see the events and objects at an earlier moment in the story, but his recountal is after the fact and thus a matter of memory, not of perception"

---

calization as an approach to the restrictions on the way a narrative can convey information runs counter to his fundamental insight about focalization being a way to talk about "who perceives." As we will see, much of the debate about focalization gives more weight to his fundamental insight than to his opposition to Bal, and so regards internal focalization as an instance in which a character is a focalizer.

10. Shaw also cites this example in his debate with Chatman, claiming that Dickens's "loose narrator" here "*imitat[es] the role* of someone who has happened upon the scene" (99, my emphasis). Like Shaw, I think that Chatman's account of the narrator as only a reporter is inadequate, but I don't think it's necessary to view him as imitating an observer. As I explain below, I think that the narrator's function of reporting necessarily entails a function of perceiving.

(145). Shortly after this passage, Chatman indicates why he is so insistent on the difference between perception and reporting: *"If we are to preserve the vital distinction between discourse and story,* we cannot lump together the separate behaviors of narrator and character under a single term" (145, my emphasis). Needless to say, the rhetoric of Chatman's sentence presupposes that we want to preserve the Vital Distinction. Thus, about the passage from chapter 3 of part 2 ("And so we rolled East . . ."), Chatman would say that Humbert the narrator remembers but does not perceive either Dolores or his former self. Instead, the narrating-I reports how the experiencing-I once saw her and how he now retrospectively thinks of the whole situation.[11]

Prince offers his own version of Chatman's position, and several new justifications for it. Prince wants to retain the term "focalization" but argues that characters can be focalizers and narrators cannot; he explicitly acknowledges that for him the term is "roughly equivalent" to Chatman's term "filter" (44). Prince introduces the concept of focalization by identifying the two ways in which a narrative reveals information about the narrated world: the narrator either reports what some entities in that world are perceiving—or does not. "Focalization obtains in the first case . . . but does not obtain in the second" (44). Prince reveals his own reliance upon and faith in the story/discourse distinction at a key point in the essay. Having proposed his definition, he acknowledges that

> cases of (fictional) anterior or simultaneous narration and cases of homo- or hetero-diegetic narration in real time . . . might provide counterexamples and so might passages like the following from *Malone Dies:* "For it is evening, even night, one of the darkest I can remember, I have a short memory. My little finger glides before my pencil across the page and gives warning, falling over the edge, that the end is near." (46)

But Prince dismisses these possible counterexamples with one fell swoop of the story/discourse distinction: "If the narrator is *never* a focalizer, it is because *qua* narrator and regardless of his or her (homo- or hetero-, intra- or extra-) diegetic status and narrational stance, s/he is

---

11. As Prince's summary of the debate indicates, this paragraph does not include all the proposals about how to understand focalization; see also Bal, Nelles, Edmiston, O'Neill, Ronen, and Herman ("Hypothetical" and *Story Logic*). Herman's and Ronen's suggestive work deserves a special mention here because they are concerned not just with the debate among narratologists but also with rethinking the concept of focalization in relation to other theoretical perspectives: possible-worlds theory for Ronen and cognitive theory for Herman. Herman's *Story Logic* is an excellent contribution to the cognitive approach to narrative.

never part of the diegesis s/he presents. *Qua* narrator, s/he is an element of discourse and not story (of the narrating and not the narrated) whereas focalization is an element of the latter" (46). Referring directly to Chatman, Prince adds that "with a verbal narrative . . . , the narrator is an instrument of presentation and not focalization" (46–47). In other words, Prince's point that narrators cannot be focalizers is based on the same logic as Chatman's point that narrators cannot perceive: the story/discourse distinction establishes boundaries that limit the powers of narrators. Thus, although Prince's terms would be different, he would agree in principle with Chatman's conclusions about the passage from chapter 3 of part 2 of *Lolita* ("And so we rolled East . . .").

## Why Narrators Can Be Focalizers

The great advantage of the Chatman/Prince position is its adherence to Occam's Razor: unlike Genette's typology, it uses a simple criterion to identify focalization (perception by a character in the story), and that simple criterion allows for greater clarity and economy in narratological theory. In my vision, though, the Chatman/Prince position is much like Genette's position in favor of eliminating the category of the implied author, an example of overcommitment to Occam—or to put it another way, of prizing the elegance of theory over the complexities of practice. To start with the most basic objection: their discussion of narrators inadequately captures the dynamics of narration as it is experienced by readers. If, as they contend, narrators cannot perceive the story world but only report on it with a given slant, then what happens to the perceptions of narratees, members of the authorial audience, and flesh-and-blood readers? Or, from the perspective of the audience is there any recognizable difference between a character's perceiving and a narrator's reporting with a slant? Since in each case the audience is presented with an angle of vision on the story world, it seems logical to acknowledge the similarity of the character's and the narrator's perceptual activity rather than to insist on their fundamental dissimilarity. We can of course signal that similarity by using the same term for that perception—and I see no need to coin a new one, since *focalization* has wide currency—and to indicate whether the character or the narrator is the focalizer.

Looking more closely at the reporting function of a narrator will help clarify these issues. Reporting itself performs two subfunctions: (1) stipulating elements of the narrative world and (2) providing some angle of vision, however wide or narrow, on what is reported. When George Orwell has his narrator open *1984* with the report that "it was a bright, cold day in April and the clocks were striking thirteen" (3), Orwell specifies a time of year for the action to follow as well as a location in a place that keeps time of day but not time of year differently from the way it is kept in his own England. To the extent that Chatman and Prince want to exclude this function of narrative reporting from the category of focalization, I am in full agreement,[12] since these fundamentals transcend any angle of vision in which they are expressed. At the same time, any report entails an act of perception.

To come at this point from another direction, the distinction between perceiving and reporting—or, in the case of character narrators, between perceiving and remembering—is ultimately impossible to maintain unless we reduce all narrators to reporting machines ("Hello, my name is HAL, and I will be your reporter for this narrative"). Happily, neither Chatman nor Prince is inclined to make that reduction (just as neither one of them nor I would insist that all narration must be understood as coming from a human agent). A human narrator, I submit, cannot report a coherent sequence of events without also revealing not just a set of attitudes (or slant) but also his or her angle of perception. The story/discourse distinction itself helps to explain why. From the perspective of story, the distinction implies that any coherent sequence of events can be reported in more than one way; from the perspective of discourse, it implies that any narration takes only one of many possible paths through the story world. Consequently, any path marked by the narrator's perspective (whether we call it "slant" or "focalization") will be not only a report on the story world but also a report from within a particular angle of vision, an angle that, in turn, influences how audiences perceive that world. In other words, as the narrator reports, the narrator cannot help but simultaneously function as a set of lenses through which the audience perceives the story world. Of course, the narrator's perceptions may be unreliable or partial, but just as a character cannot act without revealing something of him- or herself, a narrator cannot report without also revealing his or her perceptions.[13] If that's right, then

12. For a useful analysis of the relation between this stipulative function of narrative reporting and the concept of "omniscience," see Culler's essay on that concept.

13. Indeed, because Chatman and Prince see the narrator as doing something parallel in discourse space to what focalizing characters do in story space, they implicitly admit that the distinction between reporting and perceiving is impossible to maintain. Chatman does suggest that the parallel between the powers of narrators and those of characters is not ex-

narrators can be focalizers. But this is not to say, as Genette (*Narrative Discourse Revisited*, 73) and Patrick O'Neill (87) do,[14] that every passage of narration is ultimately focalized through the narrator: when the narration leaves the narrator's perspective for a character's, then the focalization shifts; the audience doffs the narrator's lenses and dons the character's.

To illustrate these points, let us return to the opening of *Dombey and Son*. I have no quarrel with Chatman's claim that the narrator is not literally in story space contemplating the baby and "deciding, in that contemplation, that he resembles a muffin" (141). But notice that Chatman assumes presence to be a necessary condition for perception. It is a plausible assumption, but the passage from *Dombey* suggests that it is not warranted. Even if we accept Chatman's description of the narrator as "omniscient," we need to recognize that he gives us an angle of vision that focuses on the scene in Dombey's room in particular ways: that perception makes Dombey the most important presence in the room, places him in the corner, and then moves on to "son." The striking quality of the muffin metaphor tellingly reveals the simultaneity of report and perception. The narrator is taking the muffin path through this scene rather than, say, the steak-and-kidney-pie path or the clay pot path—and his taking this path reflects his perception of the story world. Most important, the narrator's act of reporting/perceiving provides a perception for the narratee, the authorial audience, and the flesh-and-blood reader. The passage illustrates what Chatman's strictures about narrators lose sight of: the wonder of narrative (especially fictional narrative) is that, by convention, narrators can—and do—perceive, can and do act as our lenses on the story world, without being physically present in it.

In short, narrators can be focalizers. Determining focalization is just a matter of answering the question *who perceives?*[15] In both character

---

act when he introduces his distinction between "slant" and "filter": "I propose *slant* to name the narrator's attitudes and other mental nuances appropriate to the report function of discourse, and *filter* to name the much wider range of mental activity experienced by characters in the story world—perceptions, cognitions, attitudes, emotions, memories, fantasies, and the like" (143). But a little reflection on Tristram Shandy, Lucy Snowe, Pip, Humbert Humbert, and others will yield the conclusion that this range of mental activity has been shown by narrators as well.

14. Indeed, O'Neill goes on to suggest that it is the implied author who is "the ultimate locus of focalization" (96). I do not follow O'Neill here because, in my view, the implied author is not himself or herself part of the technique of a narrative but rather the agent who chooses those techniques.

15. Jahn's "Windows of Focalization" offers a very fine expansion of the notion that focalization is "just a matter of who perceives" by developing the metaphor of his title. Not

narration and noncharacter narration sometimes the answer to that question will be the narrator. The opening of *Dombey* is a passage in which the narrator is the perceiver and, thus, the focalizer; in the following passage, also quoted by Chatman, the character is: "[Mr Dombey] would have reasoned: That a matrimonial alliance with himself *must*, in the nature of things, be gratifying and honorable to any woman of common sense. That the hope of giving birth to a new partner in such a house, could not fail to awaken a glorious and stirring ambition in the breast of the least ambitious of her sex. That Mrs. Dombey had entered on that social contract of matrimony: almost necessarily part of a genteel and wealthy station, even without reference to the perpetuation of family firms: with her eyes fully open to these advantages" (2–3).[16]

## Why It Matters

The first consequence of recognizing that narrators can be focalizers is that we can develop a revised view of the possible vision/voice relationships in narrative discourse. In place of Genette's typology or revisions of it such as that offered by Nelles, I propose the following set of combinations:

1. narrator's focalization and voice, as in the first passage from *Dombey*;
2. character's focalization and narrator's voice, as in the first sentence of the passage from chapter 3 of part 2 of *Lolita*;
3. character's focalization and voice, as in stream of consciousness narration;
4. blends of narrator's focalization and voice with character's focalization and voice as in free indirect discourse or the middle sentences of the passage from *Lolita*;
5. narrator's focalization and character's voice, as when a naïve character narrator unwittingly takes on the voice of another character.

---

incidentally, Jahn also argues that Chatman's case about why narrators cannot be focalizers is ultimately unconvincing.

16. One can also ask and answer the question "who perceives" about so-called second-person narration. This narration is typically focalized through the "you," whether that "you" is a disguised form of "I" or a character external to the narrator. Its striking effects stem from the discourse's apparent (but not always real) insistence on merging the narratee, the authorial audience, and the flesh-and-blood audience with that "you."

Genette's typology cannot be easily mapped on to this one because, as noted above, Genette develops his on the basis of the answers to the questions, "Who perceives?" and "How much does s/he perceive?" But it is worth noting that combinations 2, 3, and 4 are all variations of what Genette calls "internal focalization." Indeed, while that term remains useful, the typology proposed here indicates that any example of internal focalization can be more precisely described by reference to the voice as well as the vision/perception of the passage.

Perhaps the most important consequence of revising our understanding of focalization emerges from a closer look at the last sentence of the passage from chapter 3, part 2 of *Lolita:* "And I catch myself thinking today that our long journey had only defiled with a sinuous trail of slime the lovely, trustful, dreamy, enormous country that by then, in retrospect, was no more to us than a collection of dog-eared maps, ruined tour books, old tires, and her sobs in the night—every night, every night—the moment I feigned sleep" (177–78).

The first part of the sentence is focalized through Humbert the narrator ("I catch myself thinking today . . ."). What is most striking about the sentence, though, is something that cannot be seen from the Prince/Chatman perspective with its interdiction on narrators as focalizers: when Humbert the character's focalization enters in the second half of the sentence ("by then, in retrospect, [the country] was no more to us") the narrator's focalization does not drop away. Instead, the narrator's focalization contains the character's. The source of this effect here can be found in the syntax, which clearly indicates that everything in the sentence is included in what Humbert catches himself "thinking today." The syntax is sufficient to produce the effect, but it is reinforced by the temporal ambiguity of the phrase "in retrospect," which can refer either to a retrospect from the character's present moment or to one from the narrator's.

Thus, although it is only the narrating-I who draws the conclusion that their journey had defiled the country, it is both the narrating-I and the experiencing-I who envision Lolita sobbing "every night, every night." Moreover, the narrating-I is also perceiving his former self's awareness of that sobbing. In other words, at the end of this sentence, we have the counterpart in focalization to what Mikhail Bakhtin has, in matters of voice, labeled double-voicing: dual vision or dual focalization (I avoid the term "double-vision," since its negative connotations are likely to make readers do a double-take). It is worth emphasizing that in cases of dual focalization generally and in this case in particular, story and discourse overlap: Humbert the narrator is perceiving the sobbing Lolita and his own former self—through the eyes of that self. If this analysis is on target, then it suggests that the story/discourse distinction has heuristic, not absolute value.[17]

Furthermore, if this analysis is on target, it also suggests that an author may use dual focalization as a key element of an implied second story in retrospective character narration: a story about the narrator's struggle to tell the story of what happened in the past. Chapter 30 of part I provides strong evidence that Nabokov uses dual focalization in just this way.

## The Shift in Humbert's Motive for Telling

In chapter 30 of part 1, the focalization begins with Humbert the narrator and then moves to include Humbert the character. The present tense ("this is what I might have thought up") immediately locates the focalization in Humbert the narrator, and it remains there for most of his catalog of what he would have painted. The catalog is notable for the contrast it forms with Humbert's unreliable claims at the end of chapter 29 about not being concerned with so-called sex. As noted above, the catalog includes metaphors of Humbert's predatory behavior toward Dolores that suggest something of the "animality" of that behavior: the "nature studies" are of "a tiger pursuing a bird of paradise, a choking snake sheathing whole the flayed trunk of a shoat." The next fragment reverts to Humbert's focus on his own desire even as its mini-allegory again underlines the difference in power and size between himself and Dolores: "a sultan, his face expressing great agony (belied, as it were, by his molding caress), helping a callypygean slave child to climb a column of onyx." The

17. This concept of "dual focalization" is different from Booth's concept of "dual focus," which refers to competing centers of attention in a narrative such as, for example, an unreliable observer narrator and a protagonist. See his discussion of Henry James's "Liar" in *The Rhetoric of Fiction* (347–54). Genette uses the term "double focalization" once in *Narrative Discourse* to refer not to the simultaneity of perception by character and narrator but to the coexistence of Marcel's focalization alongside that of another character; he describes the technique this way: "Two concurrent codes are functioning here on two planes of reality which oppose each other without colliding" (209). In *Narrative Discourse Revisited*, Genette says, "I do not believe the *focus* of the narrative can be at two points simultaneously" (76–77). My case is that in dual focalization we have such simultaneity. In this respect, it is closely related to Bal's concept of "levels of focalization," in which one focalizer contains another, though I believe that *Lolita* itself shows why we should regard dual focalization in character narration as a technique worthy of special attention.

focus on his own desire—and pleasure—continues in the next fragment: "those luminous globules of gonadal glow that travel up the opalescent sides of juke boxes." Furthermore, the catalog contains references to previous scenes of sex involving each of them: "all kinds of camp activities," an allusion to the game Dolores played with Charlie Holmes, "apples, a suburban Sunday," an allusion to the davenport scene.

Then a more dramatic shift occurs in the last sentence: "a fire opal dissolving within a ripple-ringed pool, a last throb, a last dab of color, stinging red, smarting pink, a sigh, a wincing child." First, Humbert abandons the pretense of listing only paintable images as the catalog expands to include "a last throb" and "a sigh." Second, Humbert's narration shifts to dual focalization. Humbert the narrator is perceiving (once again) what Humbert the character perceived and felt at the end of his intercourse with Dolores: his last throb (the phrase itself echoes the davenport scene and in so doing highlights the weakness of his claim for the innocence of his actions then) and his sigh intermingled with her "stinging," "smarting," "wincing" child's body. The rethinking of the event by Humbert the narrator as he develops his catalog of fragments has brought him to the point of re-seeing it. Consequently, Humbert obliquely rewrites the scene of the first intercourse, and in this revision, his selfish violence and Dolores's pain are foregrounded.[18]

In terms of ethical positioning, then, the dual focalization indicates significant changes in the character-character relations and in the narrator's relation to the told and the audience. Humbert, *through the very act of telling his story, the effort of perceiving and reperceiving himself and Dolores,* is changing his relation to the story as well as to himself, to Dolores, and to his audience. That the focalization is dual is crucial: during the first intercourse, he has seen her wincing, stinging, and smarting, and during his two years with her, he has seen the kind of suffering that led to her sobs in the night, but during these years he refused to let those sights affect his behavior. Emmanuel Levinas's concept of Facing is especially apt here. The first time Humbert gives the account of the intercourse, he succeeds in keeping his eyes averted from Dolores's pain. But chapter 30 suggests that the act of telling leads him to begin to face much of what he had previously turned away from. The more he allows

18. Patnoe argues that Humbert's narration is so unreliable and ambiguous in chapter 29 that we have reason to doubt that Dolores makes the first move. Although I don't see the ambiguity in Humbert's account of Dolores's suggestion, I have been influenced by Patnoe's argument that, even if we regard Dolores as the initiator, she does not really know what sex with an adult male means, and so Humbert cruelly and selfishly inflicts himself upon her.

himself to see, the less he can pursue his exoneration, and so the motive for his telling shifts.

It is significant, however, that chapter 30 does not mark a total break with Humbert's original motive or his unreliability. In chapter 31, Humbert the narrator begins to shift back to the sensibility governing the end of chapter 29 as his narration returns to the nature of "nymphet love." "I am trying to describe these things not to relive them in my present boundless misery, but to sort out the portion of hell and the portion of heaven in that strange, awful, maddening world—nymphet love. The beastly and beautiful merged at one point, and it is that borderline I would like to fix, and I feel I fail to do so utterly" (135). Yet even here Humbert's emphasis on the "portion of hell" and "the beastly" imply, however indirectly, a new willingness to admit the horror of his behavior. But then the next paragraph reverts to the kind of rationalization that Humbert has engaged in before, as he cites legal precedents for adult-child sexual relations ("The stipulation of the Roman law, according to which a girl may marry at twelve, was adopted by the Church, and is still preserved, rather tacitly, in some of the United States"), and claims "I have but followed nature. I am nature's faithful hound" (135). In the very next sentence, though, there is another shift as Humbert suggests that even he finds such protestations to be an inadequate defense: "Why then this horror that I cannot shake off?" The end of chapter 30 has provided an answer, but Humbert the narrator is not yet ready to deal with its consequences, and so he moves back toward exoneration: "Did I deprive her of her flower? Sensitive gentlewomen of the jury, I was not even her first lover" (135).

In terms of the third ethical position, then—Nabokov's relation to the telling, the told, and his authorial audience—this sequence and especially the technique of dual focalization indicate, first, that Nabokov is using Humbert's act of telling as itself part of the represented action of the novel, a present-tense story running parallel to the past-tense story of Humbert and Dolores. Nabokov uses the technique of dual focalization to invite us to notice the ways in which the autobiographical act affects Humbert the narrator's development. More specifically, Nabokov uses this present-tense story and the technique of dual focalization to add a significant layer to the whole narrative: the ethical struggle of Humbert the narrator. The struggle, at the most general level, is about whether he will continue to justify and exonerate himself or shift to admitting his guilt and accepting his punishment. The struggle is also one about vision or Facing: whether he will continue to turn away from what he has done to Dolores as he focuses upon himself or whether he will al-

low himself, as he begins to do at the end of chapter 30, to look upon Dolores and what he has done to her.

The distinction between narrator functions and disclosure functions
further illuminates Nabokov's complex communication. Humbert does
not directly communicate to his narratee the events of the second story;
instead Nabokov, through the representation of Humbert's telling, discloses that story to the narrative audience. The one place where the narrator functions and the disclosure functions converge in the telling of the
second story is in the short chapter 26 of part 1, where Humbert, approaching the task of narrating the events of their night at the Enchanted
Hunters Hotel, writes, "Have written more than a hundred pages and not
got anywhere yet. . . . Don't think I can go on. heart, head—everything.
Lolita, Lolita, Lolita, Lolita, Lolita, Lolita, Lolita, Lolita, Lolita. Repeat
till the page is full, printer" (109). In this chapter, for the first and last
time, Humbert the narrator acknowledges some struggle with the storytelling, but the exact nature of that struggle remains unclear. Furthermore, Humbert's difficulty appears to be very brief; the instruction to the
printer at the end of the passage indicates that Humbert has regained his
wit and his willingness to go on with the telling. Thus, while the convergence of narrator and disclosure functions in chapter 30 alert the
authorial audience to the potential for a second story, the narrator functions directly contribute very little to that story. From chapter 30 on-
ward, however, Nabokov skillfully uses the disclosure functions to
communicate that story.

One important effect of this layer of the narrative—and Humbert's
move toward seeing more—is to make Humbert the narrator more sympathetic and Humbert the character more odious. It makes the narrating-I more sympathetic because it shows him taking responsibility for
what he has done, but it makes the experiencing-I more odious because
the narration now more clearly reveals the horror of his actions: he was
aware of Dolores's pain at the time of the action but refused to attend to
it long enough for it to make any difference in his behavior. Similarly, in
the authorial audience, we find Nabokov's communication both more
remarkable and more difficult to take in: Humbert's struggle becomes a
significant part of our interest, even as it becomes increasingly painful
to see what he sees about his past behavior. To put this point in terms
of ethical positioning, this layer of the narrative affects the character-
character relations one way and the narrator-audience relations in a very
different way: the ethical dimension of Humbert's relation to Dolores is
even more clearly exposed as deficient, while his relation to his audience

improves as his reliability improves. I will return to this double movement and its relation to the other ethical situations after further discussion of part 2.

After chapter 3 of part 2, Nabokov continues to let the struggle show in Humbert's narration in various ways, especially through shifting focalization and modulations in Humbert's reliability. Consider this passage from chapter 7 of part 2, part of Humbert's confession that, over time, he began to pay Dolores for sex.

> O Reader! Laugh not, as you imagine me, on the very rack of joy noisily emitting dimes and quarters, and great big silver dollars like some sonorous, jingly and wholly demented machine vomiting riches; and in the margin of that leaping epilepsy she would firmly clutch a handful of coins in her little fist, which, anyway, I used to pry open afterwards unless she gave me the slip, scrambling away to hide her loot. And just as every other day I would cruise all around the school area and on comatose feet visit drugstores, and peer into foggy lanes, and listen to receding girl laughter in between my heart throbs and the falling leaves, so every now and then I would burgle her room and scrutinize torn papers in the wastebasket with the painted roses, and look under the pillow of the virginal bed I had just made myself. Once I found eight one-dollar notes in one of her books (fittingly—*Treasure Island*), and once a hole in the wall behind Whistler's Mother yielded as much as twenty-four dollars and some change—say twenty-four sixty—which I quietly removed, upon which, next day, she accused, to my face, honest Mrs. Holigan of being a filthy thief. Eventually, she lived up to her I.Q. by finding a safer hoarding place which I never discovered; but by that time I had brought prices down drastically by having her earn the hard and nauseous way permission to participate in the school's theatrical program; because what I feared most was not that she might ruin me, but that she might accumulate sufficient cash to run away. I believe the poor fierce-eyed child had figured out that with a mere fifty dollars in her purse she might somehow reach Broadway or Hollywood—or the foul kitchen of a diner (Help Wanted) in a dismal ex-prairie state, with the wind blowing, and the stars blinking, and the cars, and the bars, and the barmen, and everything soiled, torn, dead. (184–85)

The first sentence contains a trace of Humbert's narrative style in part 1: he focuses more on himself than on Dolores, and with the injunction to "laugh not," he engages in a brief misdirection. That injunction suggests that something comic is about to follow, but the image of Humbert as a noisy, bouncing cash machine is far from laughable as it turns his ideal of "nymphet love" into a reality consisting of equal parts torture, bribery, mechanization, and disease ("rack of joy"; "emitting dimes and quarters and great big silver dollars"; "machine vomiting riches"; "leaping epilepsy"). The focalization here belongs to Humbert the narrator: he can offer this image of himself to the narratee only after imagining himself that way, and the present tense signals that he can engage in this imaginative act only at the time of narration. Indeed, as we have seen before, it is only through the act of narration that he acquires the necessary distance to see himself this way.

As the passage continues, Nabokov continues to focalize the narration through the perspective of Humbert the narrator. The iterative narration of the second sentence ("every other day I would cruise," etc.) depends on Humbert's being able to perceive and report on the pattern as he narrates. The singulative narration in sentence three about Humbert's theft of Dolores's money includes comments that slide easily into the present tense ("fittingly—*Treasure Island*"; "say twenty-four sixty") or subtly reinforce Humbert's perspective as narrator ("once," "once," "eventually"). The descriptions in the iterative narration of the second sentence carry sufficient negative connotation ("I would cruise"; "I would burgle"; "I would . . . scrutinize torn papers") to convey both Humbert the character's domineering possessiveness of Dolores and Humbert the narrator's awareness of it. But in the third sentence, with the move to singulative narration, Humbert the narrator slips back into unreliability on the axes of perception and of evaluation: "Next day, she accused, *to my face*, honest Mrs. Holigan of being a filthy thief" (my emphasis). The sentence has the appearance of revealing Dolores's bad behavior and insisting on Humbert's innocence (compare "Stevens lied to Miss Kenton's face"), when of course the passage makes it clear that Humbert is the thief—and worse. Furthermore, this sentence and the beginning of the next ("Eventually she lived up to her I.Q.") suggest that Humbert perceives the crucial matter to be not his theft of Dolores's money but her intelligence in concealing it.

Even more remarkably, the second half of the fourth sentence returns to direct, reliable reporting along the axes of perception and of evaluation even as Nabokov maintains the focalization through Humbert the narrator: "but by that time I had brought prices down drastically by having her earn the hard and nauseous way." The fluctuation in the reliability signals Humbert's struggle with the narration as he perceives his former behavior. At this stage, he still occasionally departs from reliable reporting as he seeks to exonerate himself or win the narratee's sympathy, but the focalization from his perspective as narrator increasingly leads him to a direct report of his despicable behavior.

The next move of the passage is to dual focalization, which begins with the phrase "because what I feared most" and continues through the dash in the final sentence, when Nabokov returns to Humbert the narrator's focalization. Initially, as Humbert reperceives his fear of Dolores's departure, he also explains—and to some extent seeks to justify—his effort to bring prices down ("she might accumulate sufficient cash to run away"). But as the dual focalization continues in the final sentence, Humbert characterizes Dolores in a way that implicates him—"the poor fierce-eyed child"—and this characterization leads to the sharp break in the perspective. The first half of the sentence reports what he believes the child had figured out, but the second half, though syntactically parallel to the first, leaves Dolores's perspective entirely. It is not she and not Humbert the character who imagines "the foul kitchen of a diner in some dismal ex-prairie state" but only Humbert the narrator. And the movement toward that image, which culminates in his description of "everything soiled, torn, dead," conveys his sorrow, his loss, and his awareness of responsibility for such a fate. Furthermore, Humbert's reinvocation of the lines from the popular song that he and then Dolores sang during the davenport scene ("the stars and the cars and the bars and the barmen") subtly indicates how much the act of telling has changed his perception of himself and of Dolores.

By the end of that telling, of course, Humbert has ceased seeking exoneration and moved toward condemning himself. The most oft-quoted passage from part 2 of the novel, placed in the fifth paragraph from the end, clearly expresses his final attitude. Waiting to be taken from the car by police after he has killed Quilty, Humbert reports that he "evoked a last mirage of wonder and hopelessness," a memory of a scene he came upon after he had pulled to the side of a mountain road when searching for Dolores after she had run away. He describes the colors he can see below and then comments on the sounds:

> Reader! What I heard was but the melody of children at play, nothing but that, and so limpid was the air that within this vapor of blended voices, majestic and minute, remote and magically near, frank and divinely enigmatic—one could hear now and then, as if released, an almost articulate spurt of vivid laughter, or the crack of a bat, or the clatter of a toy wagon, but it was all really too far for the eye to distinguish any

movement in the lightly etched streets. I stood listening to that musi-
cal vibration from my lofty slope, to those flashes of separate cries with
a kind of demure murmur for background, and then I knew that the
hopelessly poignant thing was not Lolita's absence from my side, but the
absence of her voice from that concord. (308)

Nabokov's emphasis on what Humbert hears provides a link—and a
sharp contrast—with the passage from chapter 3 of part 2: there he re-
heard her nightly sobs, while here he is aware that her voice is missing
from the melody of children at play. Here, too, Nabokov employs dual
focalization: as Humbert narrates his action of standing and listening, he
rehears the children's sounds and reaffirms the hopeless poignance of the
absence of Dolores's voice. But this dual focalization is different from
that in the earlier passage, because here the narrator's vision does not
subsume or otherwise complicate the character's. Instead, the two perceptions are in total accord. Indeed, we can plausibly locate the begin-
nings of the transformation in Humbert the character at this moment
after Dolores's disappearance and the end of that transformation at this
moment in Humbert the narrator's telling. That is, the passage indicates
that even before he began his narration Humbert had begun to admit that
he'd robbed Dolores of her childhood. That admission combines with his
explicit claims to love her (claims to which I will soon return) to make
him ready to see the past in a new way as he revisits it in his narration.
Although his self-interest initially overpowers his recognition, regret,
and love, the more his narration leads him to re-see the past the more
these feelings dominate his self-interest until we get to this passage,
which is the most Dolores-centric one in his narration. Just two paragraphs after this passage, he confesses that if he were his own judge, he
would have given himself "at least thirty-five years for rape" (308), a
word that he has never before applied to his behavior.[19]

---

19. That Humbert so readily dismisses the murder of Quilty indicates one of the continuing limitations of his present-tense perspective. Indeed, the murder scene is so gro-
tesque not only because both principals are drunk but also because Humbert the narrator
continues to think of Quilty in the same terms that Humbert the character has: as the Evil
Force that stole his nymphet. Humbert is aware that Quilty is his double, and very aware
that the satisfaction he expected to receive by killing him has never arrived. But he never
achieves the kind of perspective on Quilty and the murder that he achieves about Dolores
and her childhood. Although Nabokov carefully characterizes Quilty as an ethically
deficient man, he expects us to recognize Humbert's attitude toward him as the extreme
version of his attitudes toward Valeria and toward Charlotte before her death.

After Humbert moves from self-defense to self-condemnation, he articulates another purpose for his narrative: transforming his despicable behavior into art. There are two key statements of this purpose, one at the end of chapter 31, the other in the novel's final paragraph, the conclusion of his farewell address to Dolores:

> Unless it can be proven to me—to me as I am now, today, with my heart and my beard, and my putrefaction—that, in the infinite run it does not matter a jot that a North American girl-child named Dolores Haze had been deprived of her childhood by a maniac, unless this can be proven (and if it can, then life is a joke), I see nothing for the treatment of my misery but the melancholy and very local palliative of articulate art. (283)

> And do not pity C. Q. One had to choose between him and H. H., and one wanted H. H. to exist at least a couple of months longer, so as to have him make you live in the minds of later generations. I am thinking of aurochs and angels, the secret of durable pigments, prophetic sonnets, the refuge of art. And this is the only immortality you and I may share, my Lolita. (309)

In both cases, the narration is focalized through Humbert the narrator, but the emphases within the statements are very different. In the first, the pursuit of articulate art is less a statement of redeeming purpose than a statement of cold comfort. Humbert emphasizes the gravity of his crime, his new awareness of its seriousness, and, thus, his irredeemable misery. In this context, pursuing "articulate art" is a "melancholy and very local palliative." By contrast, the final passage is a statement of noble purpose: Humbert sees the shaping of his narrative into a work of art as a sign of his remorse and an effort to atone for what he has done to Dolores: though he has stolen her youth, he can strive to give her immortality. Furthermore, the very last line shows that he harbors no illusions about his own redemption: the implication of where he expects to spend eternity—in contrast to where he expects Dolores to spend it—is very clear.

Humbert's concluding statement of purpose is also an implicit expression of what he has explicitly expressed previously: his love for Dolores. Nabokov's technique indicates that Humbert is sincere in his claim—even if Nabokov also gives us cause to question the adequacy of that love. Humbert is most insistent during his narration of his final scene with Dolores, during which she tells him about Quilty and rejects his offer to come away with him:[20]

> You may jeer at me, and threaten to clear the court, but until I am gagged and half-throttled, I will shout my poor truth. I insist the world know how much I loved my Lolita, *this* Lolita, pale and polluted, and big with another's child, but still sooty-lashed, still auburn and almond, still Carmencita, still mine. . . . even if those eyes of hers would fade to myopic fish, and her nipples swell and crack, and her lovely young delicate velvety delta be tainted and torn—even then I would go mad with tenderness at the mere sight of your dear wan face, at the mere sound of your raucous young voice, my Lolita. (278)

Humbert's expression of his "poor truth" here itself indicates something of the nature of this love—and its limitations. Nabokov again focalizes the passage through Humbert the narrator, then moves to dual focalization as he describes "this Lolita," and then moves back to single focalization through the narrator as he turns, at the end of the passage, to address Dolores directly. The concluding part of the passage does show Humbert with a different set of emotions toward her, the dominant one being lust's opposite number, tenderness. This tenderness, furthermore, would be triggered not by touch but rather by sight and sound—of her "dear wan face" and of her "raucous young voice." It is this voice, we will soon learn, whose absence Humbert felt so poignantly after Do-

---

20. Leona Toker, building on an essay by Christina Tikener entitled "Time in *Lolita*," argues that Nabokov wants us to infer that this scene, like the murder of Quilty, occurs only in Humbert's imagination while he is in jail for his molestation of Dolores. This reading is based on the impossibility of Humbert doing everything he claims to have done between the time of receiving Dolores's letter asking for money and the time of his death as given by John Ray Jr. Tikener and especially Toker offer a very intriguing analysis, one that deserves serious consideration. I am not, however, finally persuaded, because Nabokov does include the murder of Quilty in the screenplay he wrote for the Kubrick film version (though Toker tries to address this objection) and because, finally, it does not make sense that Nabokov would bury the clues to this reading so deeply that it would escape the attention of most readers. In addition, Toker is motivated to adopt this reading because she finds it troubling that Humbert the character claims to love Dolores but Humbert's narration does not show that love in the beginning and the middle of the tale. But that objection can be met: Humbert does give indications of his love in many of his present-tense interjections during the beginning and the middle; since Humbert begins writing so soon after his incarceration, he has not yet realized the incompatibility of exonerating himself with his love for Dolores; and, finally, as we saw in chapter 1, one of "the lessons of Weymouth" is that a character narrator need not have his narration informed by the character's realizations until the narrator reports on the event that produces those realizations.

lores's disappearance and whose absence he would feel again as he waits to be arrested after killing Quilty. But the earlier part of the passage indicates that Humbert, to some extent, still regards Dolores as primarily a sexual object that he wants to possess. The attention to Dolores's body—as run down and beautiful both—dominates the first half of the passage, and the phrase "still mine" carries ominous overtones. Humbert sincerely loves Dolores, but he does not yet comprehend what a mature love entails.

At the end of his act of telling, then, Humbert is in very different situation from the one he occupied when he began. While he started out self-absorbed and focused on his own defense, he ends up far more concerned about Dolores than himself. He loves her, however imperfectly, and he has admitted to himself and articulated for his audience how deeply and irredeemably he has hurt her. Furthermore, he recognizes that he cannot do anything to ameliorate his situation or Dolores's; all he can do is to tell the story. The primary agents of Humbert's transformation are his genuine feeling for Dolores and the act of telling itself.

## Limits of the Transformation and Further Ethical Consequences

This analysis of technique and progression has several important consequences for our ethical positioning. First, as noted above, there are countervailing movements in the character-character relations, on the one hand, and the narrator-audience relations on the other. The more clear-sighted Humbert the narrator becomes about his past self, the more clearly does his violence against Dolores come through: he was "a pentapod monster," who offered a twelve-year-old girl who suddenly lost her mother only "a parody of incest" as he repeatedly coerced her into "hard and nauseous" acts of sexual intercourse. By the end of Humbert's narrative, he and Nabokov both want us to see that Dolores's life with him was a horror and that Humbert was the agent of that horror. At the same time, the story of Humbert's gradual move toward greater clear-sightedness is a move to greater reliability along the axis of evaluation, and it indicates a greater respect for his audience. By the end of the narrative he has stopped trying to hoodwink both himself and his audience and has instead confessed to his crimes against Dolores and condemned himself for them.

These countervailing movements have consequences for the third ethical position, that of Nabokov in relation to his subject matter and his audience. On the one hand, as Nabokov traces Humbert's gradual recognition of his violence against Dolores, Nabokov himself emphasizes the horror of that violence—and moves away from the relation with his audience that I noted in the davenport scene. On the other hand, Nabokov's attention remains resolutely on Humbert, and, indeed, the second story told via the disclosure functions runs the risk of doing on the authorial level what Humbert does on the narratorial level for most of part 1: subordinate Dolores and her pain to Humbert and his concerns. As Linda Kauffman and Peter J. Rabinowitz point out in different ways, whatever else we might say about the complexities of Nabokov's technique, he never moves in the direction of giving Dolores a significant voice in the narrative: it is Humbert the criminal and his response to his crimes as he writes about them that dominate the narrative first, last, and always. Dolores matters for Nabokov—Humbert cannot be clear-sighted about the crimes unless Nabokov is too—but finally she matters less than Humbert.[21] To read the novel in the authorial audience, as I have tried to do here, is to adopt that perspective.

As flesh-and-blood reader, I find that perspective to have significant strengths and major problems. On the one hand, Nabokov is doing something extraordinary, however distasteful: occupying the perspective of a pedophile, asking us to take that perspective seriously, and, indeed, through the second story, asking us, at least to some extent, to sympathize with him. In this respect, the ethics of the novel involves performing one of the best functions of art: extending the perceptions and feelings of its dominant audience, doing so in ways that challenge preconceptions even if the challenge makes us uncomfortable and even likely to turn against the artist.

But even after all the analysis that leads me to this conclusion, I remain disturbed. In part, this is a novel in which the initial character-character relations—particularly Humbert's repeated abuse of Dolores—are so distasteful that Humbert's later recognition of his crimes against her is almost beside the point. But the problems are also part and parcel of the technique. Because the attention Nabokov and the authorial audience give to Humbert's perspective comes at the expense of Dolores's, Nabokov's very construction of the novel mirrors Humbert's dominance

---

21. Toker does a nice job, though, of pointing out how Nabokov's construction of Dolores's dialogue allows the audience to see significant elements of her character that Humbert remains blind to.

of Dolores at the level of action. Furthermore, this recognition means that if my rhetorical analysis stopped with the reconstruction of the authorial audience's position, it, too, would mirror that dominance.

But I want to end not just with this call for a balanced view of the ethics but also with another significant dimension of my flesh-and-blood response to the implied Nabokov. The author who created this book is someone to be admired but also someone to be wary of. Nabokov's narrative project is enormously difficult—showing us the horror of Humbert in word, deed, and consequence and then asking us to find him worthy of sympathy—and executed with stunning skill. At the same time, my sense of Nabokov's success with his project does not obliterate my sense of distance from and distrust of his ethics. In writing this book, Nabokov, like Dolores, enters umber and black Humberland; but unlike her, he does not survey it with a shrug of amused distaste, but rather lives there with a kind of perverse relish. That, to my vision, is the inescapable ethical dark side of this book.[22]

How would the aesthetic and ethical dimensions of *Lolita* be different if Dolores were the narrator? And how would they be different if Dolores were a real person rather than a fictional character? And what if she were twenty years old rather than twelve? Because these questions are about a hypothetical rather than an actual narrative, any answers we offer would be speculative and likely to say more about Nabokov's narrative than this hypothetical one. But Kathryn Harrison's *Kiss*, her memoir about her incestuous affair with her father, does raise a set of similar questions, and it is to them and their answers that I turn next.

22. For an intriguing case that Nabokov's creation of Humbert comes out of more than a fertile imagination, see Centerwall.

# 4 Suppressed Narration in Confessional Memoir

*The Kiss*

*The Kiss*, Kathryn Harrison's account of her four-year incestuous affair with her father that began when she was twenty, generated considerable debate upon its publication in 1997, at the height of the so-called memoir boom. Indeed, the book became the chief example in discussions of whether contemporary memoirists were going too far, telling too much, and, in effect, trying to convert past trauma to present treasure. Like the debates about *Lolita* discussed in the previous chapter, the ones about *The Kiss* are implicitly about the relation between ethics and aesthetics—but here because Harrison is writing memoir rather than fiction the question of "truth" is added to the mix. Is Harrison, as reviewers such as Jonathan Yardley alleged, telling a sensational, trashy story with the cynical motive of cashing in on the market for the memoir—and cashing in on her failure to resist her father in the past? Or is she, as others such as Tobias Wolff maintained, combining both personal courage and considerable artistry in revisiting her traumatic past through a compelling narrative? Or does the very artistry of the telling, as Christopher Lehmann-Haupt suggested, call into question her veracity?[1]

Academic critics have been especially interested in the negative responses to *The Kiss*, though they move from those responses in different directions. Paul John Eakin uses them to launch a discussion of the

1. In addition to Yardley, Wolff, and Lehmann-Haupt, see also Crossen, Powers, and Pogrebin.

ethics of making the private public, especially when the memoirist is writing about people who are still alive. In fact, he contrasts Harrison, who writes while her father lives, with McCourt, who insists that he could not have written about Angela's affair with Laman Griffin while she was still alive. Laura Frost relates the negative responses to some specifics of the narrative itself, particularly Harrison's representation of her agency in the affair and her violation of genre boundaries. Harrison, Frost points out, does not stay within the usual boundaries of the incest narrative, which call for "an adult predator and a child innocent," and she blurs the boundaries between fiction and nonfiction by taking events that she had fictionalized in her novel *Thicker Than Water*[2] and presenting them as historical. Furthermore, *The Kiss* is a kind of confession, but it does not contain the standard confessional features of a clear admission of guilt or request for repentance. Frost herself questions Harrison's "silences around the four-year affair" and concludes with a comment on the ethical dimension of Harrison's presentation of her own agency: "Agency and sexual pleasure are two empowerments for which women have fought hard in the last forty years, but *The Kiss* represents a kind of female agency that no one wants to claim" (66). Leigh Gilmore uses the trope of jurisdiction to shed light on the negative reception, defining jurisdiction as "a forum of judgment" and understanding both the narrative itself and "the public sphere it enters" as such a forum ("Jurisdictions," 697). Gilmore gives more of her attention to that public sphere than to the narrative itself, offering an astute analysis of the gender politics operating in the negative reviews and contending that the negative reviewers are put off by Harrison's transgressive act of telling her story not as a victim but as a woman "coming to terms more with the mystery of her agency than her injury" (713).

In this chapter, I will attempt, in a sense, to come to terms with Harrison's coming to terms, especially with the ways in which the character narration reveals the underlying rhetorical logic and ethical consequences of Harrison's effort.[3] And like Eakin, I will also consider the ethics of Harrison's telling this story while her father remains alive. For

2. Before writing *The Kiss*, Harrison addressed her experiences with her father in her fiction. Harrison has said that she found the move to the more direct treatment of memoir both necessary and liberating. In addition to *Thicker Than Water*, see also *Exposure*.

3. Both Gilmore and Frost pay some attention to Harrison's technique but neither gives it the kind of detailed analysis I offer here. Frost's comparisons of parallel scenes in *The Kiss* and *Thicker Than Water* are astute and helpful, and Gilmore is very good on the way Harrison draws on both the myth of Oedipus and Antigone and on conventions of the fairy tale.

reasons that will become clear after a fuller account of the overall shape
of Harrison's narrative, I will pay special attention to how Harrison treats
what Gilmore calls "the mystery" of Kathryn's agency, and to Harrison's
decision to place her audience in the role of silent therapist. To distinguish between the narrating-I and the experiencing-I, I will refer to the
narrator as Harrison and to the character as Kathryn. I will also refer to
the implied author as Harrison because, in this memoir, unlike *Angela's
Ashes*, there is virtually no *evaluative or perceptual* distance between
the narrator and the implied author. Nevertheless, the distinction between the implied author and the narrator remains relevant because Harrison the implied author is the agent responsible for such choices as
when to use scene and when to use summary, when to use the historical present tense and when to switch to the past.

## Harrison's Story and Suppressed Narration

I start with an account of the main events Harrison narrates in the
seventeen sections of her memoir so that we can better appreciate the
rhetorical choices she makes in her treatment of those events.[4] Kathryn's parents meet when they are both seventeen. They become infatu-
ated with each other and get married when Kathryn's mother becomes
pregnant with her. Kathryn's maternal grandparents, however, dislike
her father because he is poor and Christian and they are wealthy and Jew-
ish. When Kathryn is only six months old, they succeed in eliminating
him from the family. They win Kathryn's mother's consent by persuad-
ing her that Kathryn's father will not be able to support her and her
daughter properly, and they tell him that he no longer has any obligations, financial or otherwise, for Kathryn and her mother. Kathryn and
her mother live with Kathryn's maternal grandparents until she is six,
when her mother moves to a different house in the same neighborhood.
Like any child, Kathryn craves her mother's love and attention, but her
mother, dealing with her own unhappiness, gives Kathryn very little of
either. Despite their divorce, Kathryn's parents remain fixated on each

4. I have not tried to construct this account to correspond precisely with the narrative's
fabula—that is, its events in their chronological order with no attention to their treatment.
Instead, I want to identify the main events as they emerge in Harrison's interpretation, since
such an account will allow me to proceed more efficiently with my rhetorical analysis. For
some excellent work that focuses on relations between fabula and sjuzhet, see the two essays by Kafalenos in the Works Cited.

other, even though Kathryn's father remarries and her mother has relationships with other men.

Kathryn's father visits when she is five, when she is ten, and again when she is twenty. During the first two visits, he is primarily concerned with her mother, but during the third, he takes new notice of Kathryn, and she, in turn, is fascinated with him. This mutual fascination is clearly fueled by each one's anger with Kathryn's mother: her father for the divorce; Kathryn for her neglect. In saying good-bye at the airport, Kathryn's father gives her the kiss referred to in the book's title: a French kiss that conveys not fatherly affection but sexual desire. Kathryn knows that the kiss "is wrong" and must therefore remain "a secret" (69), and she comes to regard it as a scorpion's "sting" that her father "administers in order that he might consume me. That I might desire to be consumed" (70). Even as Kathryn is disturbed by the kiss, she wants to reconnect with her father, and soon her interest in him becomes all-consuming—a response that matches his interest in her. After a time, the relationship becomes sexual at her father's insistence, and Kathryn even moves to the house where her father lives with his second wife and other children. (This wife knows about the incestuous relationship but looks the other way.) As the affair progresses, however, Kathryn feels increasingly unhappy and trapped, but her father uses various arguments to keep the relationship going. Kathryn begins to get the courage to escape when her grandfather's death gives her a new awareness of the finiteness of life, and she escapes for good—four years after the kiss—when her mother dies. Without her mother's presence, her father's hold over her is broken. The memoir ends with Harrison's account of a dream in which Kathryn and her mother reconcile.

As this summary indicates, *The Kiss* is, in part, an inverted version of *Lolita*: a nonfictional tale of incest, this time involving a biological father, told by the Dolores figure rather than the Humbert figure. Not surprisingly, though, Harrison's nonfictional narrative is not a perfect inversion of Nabokov's fictional one, and some of the discrepancies are very significant: Kathryn's mother was alive throughout the affair, and Kathryn was twenty rather than twelve years old and more sexually experienced than Dolores when the incest began. (Harrison tells us that Kathryn lost her virginity at seventeen, because she knew that was her parents' age when they met and lost their virginity.) *Lolita* and *The Kiss* are also similar and different in how they treat the relation of the telling of the tale to the represented action. Like Nabokov, Harrison makes the telling part of the action, but she does not dramatize any struggle to tell the tale. Instead, as I will discuss at greater length below, she implies that it is the telling that makes possible her psychological reconciliation with her mother.

Comparing *The Kiss* with *Angela's Ashes* also helps illuminate features of Harrison's technique. Like McCourt, Harrison employs the historical present tense, but, unlike McCourt, she does not typically restrict the vision or the voice to the experiencing-I. Instead, she employs either her vision and voice at the time of the narration or that voice in conjunction with a dual focalization in which her vision at the time of the action is contained within her vision at the time of the telling. In addition, unlike the implied McCourt, the implied Harrison does not establish any distance between herself and her narrator. In other words, despite following McCourt's practice of using the historical present tense, Harrison conforms to the pattern prescribed by Gornick, McDonnell, Fludernik, and Cohn. These points and others will emerge more clearly in a close look at the way Harrison frames Kathryn's experience in the first of the memoir's seventeen sections.

> We meet at airports. We meet in cities where we've never been before. We meet where no one will recognize us.
>
> One of us flies, the other brings a car, and in it we set out for some destination. Increasingly, the places we go are unreal places: the Petrified Forest, Monument Valley, the Grand Canyon—places as stark and beautiful and deadly as those revealed in satellite photographs of distant planets. Airless, burning, inhuman.
>
> Against such backdrops, my father takes my face in his hands. He tips it up and kisses my closed eyes, my throat. I feel his fingers in the hair at the nape of my neck. I feel his hot breath on my eyelids.
>
> We quarrel sometimes, and sometimes we weep. The road always stretches endlessly ahead and behind us, so that we are out of time as well as out of place. We go to Muir Woods in northern California, so shrouded in blue fog that the road is lost; and we drive down the Natchez Trace into deep, green Mississippi summer. The trees bear blossoms as big as my head; their ivory petals drift to the ground and cover our tracks.
>
> Separated from family and from the flow of time, from work and from school; standing against a sheer face of red rock one thousand feet high; kneeling in a cave dwelling two thousand years old; watching as a million bats stream from the mouth of Carlsbad Caverns into the purple dusk—these nowheres and notimes are the only home we have. (3–4)

The use of the iterative historical present marks this section as Harrison's summary of the affair at its height, even as it clearly locates both vision and voice in the narrating-I: it is only *after* all these meetings have occurred that the narrator can summarize them this way. To be sure, there are passages of dual focalization here, such as "I feel his fingers in the hair at the nape of my neck. I feel his hot breath on my eyelids," in which the narrating-I's perception includes the experiencing-I's perception, and, indeed, in which the experiencing-I's perception is foregrounded, but Harrison never departs from the narrator's vision. The reflection expressed in the last paragraph further underscores the important presence of the vision and voice of the narrating-I.

This opening section establishes several interrelated motifs that Harrison works with throughout the narrative. First, there is no pleasure to be found in the affair—even at its height. Harrison reports that Kathryn and her father sometimes quarrel and sometimes weep but not that they sometimes laugh or feel joy, excitement, or any other positive emotion in each other's presence. In addition, the places they visit, though some of the most beautiful to be found in the United States—indeed, ones whose beauty Ishiguro's Stevens would regard as displaying an "unseemly demonstrativeness" (29)—are breathtaking not because of that beauty but rather because they are "stark" and "deadly," "airless, burning, inhuman." Thus, their beauty is connected with the second major motif: the experience feels unreal because place and time are not just out of joint but no longer connected to Kathryn's experience. Behind this motif is Harrison's implicit point that the cause of this unreality is not the places themselves, which, after all, are real enough to be identifiable by their names alone, but rather what Kathryn and her father do in them. This point becomes clearer when we seek the causes for the feeling that they are living out of time. The only named cause is connected as much with place as with time and even more with a psychological state: "The road always stretches endlessly ahead and behind us."

What Kathryn and her father do in these places is represented through synecdoche: Harrison describes Kathryn's father kissing her in a way that invites us to infer that kissing as a sign of deeper physical intimacy. And the force of the synecdoche is greater because Harrison defers revealing the identity of the initial "we" until she introduces the trope. The synecdoche itself and what it signifies bring us to the third motif: what I will call Harrison's suppressed report about Kathryn's agency in the affair. On the one hand, Kathryn is very much a part of the "we" who meet, set out for a destination, quarrel, weep, and exist out of time and out of place. On the other hand, Kathryn is only the passive recipient of her father's active physical advances: he "takes my face in his hands. He tips it up and kisses my closed eyes, my throat." Kathryn "feels" his fingers and his breath, but Harrison suppresses any other narration about Kathryn's agency in these moments or even about her response.

I use the term "suppress" advisedly because the juxtaposition of the "we" who do things together and the "I" who is the passive recipient implies that Kathryn must at the very least have responses Harrison chooses not to tell about. *Suppressed narration* omits significant information that the narrative itself otherwise indicates is relevant to the character, situation, or event being reported on, thereby creating either a gap in the text that cannot be filled or a discrepancy between what is reported in one place and not reported in another. Suppressed narration is different from elliptical narration of the kind we find in Stevens's not reporting that he is crying, because the gap created by elliptical narration can be readily filled. We identify suppressed narration not by comparing what the narrator reports with some external standard of what such a narrator should say on such an occasion, but by comparing what the narrator conspicuously does not say on that occasion with what the narrator does say on other occasions.

Suppressed narration is also different from restricted narration; restricted narration guides us to fill in the authorial communication along the axes that the narrator is not using, while suppressed narration blocks any clear inferences about what has not been said. Suppressed narration, unlike restricted narration, points to a significant gap in the disclosure functions: the narrator's suppression is matched by the implied author's. To put this point another way, although suppressed narration has surface similarities to underreporting, it is fundamentally different because it is presented by the implied author as reliable narration. Consequently, as I shall argue about *The Kiss*, recognizing suppressed narration ultimately leads us to a judgment about *the implied author's* handling of both the aesthetics and the ethics of the narrative. A closer look at the passage will further clarify the concept of suppressed narration.

Although the second motif of this frame, the emphasis on the sense of the unreal, suggests that Kathryn has entered a zone beyond normal feeling, the first part of Harrison's treatment of Kathryn's agency indicates that Harrison is deliberately withholding information about Kathryn's responses to and involvement in the sexual dimension of the affair. Since Kathryn is part of the "we" who quarrel and weep, and since the report of the quarreling and weeping follows the synecdoche about physical intimacy, the narrative itself contains signals that Kathryn feels more than Harrison reveals. Our response to the suppressed narration is connected to our assumption that we are reading nonfiction rather than fiction, and especially to the inference that Harrison the implied author has constructed a narrator who speaks directly for her. If we were reading fiction, we would be inclined to interpret the suppressed narration as unreliable on the axis of characters and events, as, that is, underreporting. Furthermore, we would be inclined to interpret the underreporting as motivated by the narrator's self-interest in minimizing her agency, and, thus, in the absence of other mitigating evidence, we would regard the implied author as offering a negative judgment of the narrator on the axis of evaluation. But because we are reading memoir employing reliable narration, we do not make such a judgment of Harrison the narrator. Instead we make that negative judgment about Harrison the implied author—and thus about her book.

At this point in the narrative it is too early to reject the whole enterprise: this may be an isolated example, and Harrison may even be able to do something later in the narrative that leads us to reevaluate the suppressed narration here. At the same time, because the suppressed narration here and later in the memoir, including during the report of the kiss that gives the book its title, is so closely connected with Harrison's representation of Kathryn's agency and with the issue of her memoir's truth, it clearly merits further examination.

## Harrison's Purpose and Its Ethical Dimensions

The contrast between section 2 and section 17 provides substantial evidence of Harrison's purpose. In the second section, Harrison shows that as a young child Kathryn craves her neglectful mother's gaze, but her mother's habit is to sleep as late as possible. "Her eyes closed and hidden behind a satin sleep mask, her face as flat and white as the mask is flat and black: this terrifies me. Sleep makes my mother's face itself into a mask, one mask under another. . . . I make any noise I can that might rouse my mother but that can't be judged as a direct and purposeful assault on the fortress of her sleeping. *Because for as long as my mother refuses consciousness, she refuses consciousness of me: I do not exist"* (7–8, my emphasis). But waking her mother does not produce the desired effect: "If I wake her, she doesn't talk to me. She stalks around her room as if enraged, a wild and astonished look on her face. I make myself small; I back into the corner by the door, and often she doesn't seem to know I'm there. . . . Her eyes, when they turn at last toward me, are like two empty mirrors. I can't find myself in them" (8–9).

The psychological dynamics are easily understood here. In order to feel that she exists, Kathryn needs to feel that her mother values her existence, and so she desires her mother's welcoming gaze. And the more her mother withholds that gaze, the more Kathryn desires it. But the more Kathryn tries to force her mother to look, the more self-defeating her actions. As Harrison lays out these dynamics, she also guides her audience's ethical judgments and emotional responses: Kathryn's mother is seriously deficient and Kathryn herself deserving of great sympathy.[5] But more than that, the passage highlights the unhealthiness of their relationship. Each one contributes to the misery of the other—though of course Kathryn's mother is more culpable because she is the adult.

In the seventeenth and last section of the narrative, Harrison records a dream that Kathryn has about her now dead mother. The narration of the dream involves not only the alignment of Harrison the implied author and Harrison the narrator but also that of Kathryn the protagonist: the events of the dream happen to Kathryn but the perspective on the events is shared by all three. Harrison gives the date of the dream, the only full date she gives in the narrative: February 7, 1995. The dream is very different from the nightmares she usually has about her mother. In this one, "my mother finds me in my kitchen" (205); Kathryn wants to show her mother her children but is afraid of breaking the spell that has brought her mother's ghost to her. In the dream,

> My mother and I look closely at each other. We look into each other's eyes more deeply than we ever did in life, and for much longer. Our eyes don't move or blink, they are no more than a few inches apart. As we look, all that we have ever felt but have never said is manifest. Her youth and selfishness and misery, my youth and selfishness and misery. Our loneliness. The ways we betrayed each other. (206–7)

And then, finally, the breakthrough in the narrative's last paragraph: "In this dream, I feel that at last she knows me, and I her. I feel us stop hoping for a different daughter and a different mother" (207).

This narration, with its emphasis on the mutual gazing of mother and daughter and on all that is communicated in that gazing, obviously provides a clear contrast to the scene in the second section. Not only has Kathryn now been granted as an adult (albeit in a dream) what she so

---

5. Paul John Eakin suggests that Harrison's account is so focused on the description of the family dynamics that it does not offer judgments of the characters or events. I agree that the judgments are often not explicit, but, as this passage and others I will analyze suggest, the narration is filled with implicit judgments, and these judgments are a crucial element of the ethical dimension of the narrative.

deeply desired as a child but she also has the power to look at her mother as an equal. This power allows her to give as well as receive, allows her to grant forgiveness, acceptance, and peace. By including the date of the dream, Harrison signals her audience that her mother has been dead for ten years and underlines the temporal jump in the narrative: the penultimate section has reported on her mother's death and the end of the affair with her father. That temporal jump, in turn, invites us to infer the reason why Kathryn would have the dream at this point in her life, especially since she has not recounted any significant events in relation to her mother during this ten-year period.

After Kathryn's father kisses her erotically for the first time, she comments: "I am frightened by the kiss. I know it is wrong, and its wrongness is what lets me know, too, that it is a secret" (69). Of course the very act of narrating Kathryn's knowledge shows us that Harrison no longer believes it necessary to keep the secret; now in section 17, Harrison shows us that the consequence of breaking her silence is her coming to forgive and accept her mother—and to believe that her mother would be willing to forgive and accept her. In other words, the placement of the dream suggests that it results from Harrison's willingness to tell her story. That placement presents the dream as the culmination of what Harrison has worked through in breaking the secret, her reward for her effort to come to terms with what Gilmore calls "the mystery of her agency." I do not mean to suggest the literal interpretation that Harrison has this dream in February 1995 because by that point she has written the first sixteen sections of the narrative.[6] But I do mean to suggest that the decision to tell her story and her working through its details are crucial background for her claim that she achieves this resolution with her mother—and, indeed, for her audience to find the claim at all plausible.

The link between the act of telling and the dream becomes even clearer when we focus on the phenomenon of the reconciliation occurring in a dream. Although Harrison emphasizes the clarity of the dream and her confidence that she will always remember it vividly, she never suggests that she is actually seeing her mother's ghost, never suggests that the events she reports are anything more than a dream. The implication, then, is that everything occurs within Harrison's psyche, and,

---

6. At the same time, the date of the dream, February 1995, suggests that it is very likely Harrison has already decided to write the memoir. Her previous book, the novel *Poison*, was about to appear in April 1995, and *The Kiss* itself appeared in March 1997, approximately two years after the dream. But these dates finally are less important than the internal logic of *The Kiss*, which situates the dream as the culmination of the previous narration.

thus, that her mother's forgiveness and acceptance is ultimately a sign that she finally forgives and accepts herself. The placement of the dream and the overall logic of the narrative lead us to infer that telling the story has made this self-forgiveness and self-acceptance possible, even as the dream remains an effective and efficient way to convey Harrison's corresponding forgiveness and acceptance of her mother.

The dream also validates the somewhat surprising conclusion of section 16, which in turn takes us back to the dedication page of the book. Harrison highlights the importance of this conclusion by switching for the only time to past-tense narration, as she reports Kathryn's regret that she did not include any inscription under the dates on the headstone for her mother's grave:

> I left the space below the dates empty, because on that afternoon the only word that I could imagine carved in that blank struck me as one I didn't deserve to use, rather than the truth that it was. Is.
> Beloved. (203–4)

The tense shift from historical present to past and then, in the very last verb of this passage, back to the present of the telling, underlines Harrison's claim not only for the once and continuing truth contained in the word "Beloved" but also for how much her relation to that truth has changed since she picked out the headstone. The dedication page of the memoir prints the word "Beloved" above the dates of her mother's life, 1942–1985, but it is not until the end of section 16 that we know its referent, and it is not until the end of section 17 that we know its full meaning for Harrison.

Following these links between sections 2, 17, 16, and the dedication leads us to an understanding of Harrison's purpose: to tell the story with honesty and understanding and through that telling to achieve a psychological reconciliation with her mother that includes her self-forgiveness and self-acceptance. Furthermore, the logic of these connections indicates that Kathryn's dream has been made possible by the previous narration even as it enacts the final steps of the reconciliation. In that sense, then, Harrison's telling is itself a significant part of the narrative's represented action.

Again I find it helpful to compare Harrison's nonfictional narrative and Nabokov's fictional one. Where Humbert's narration functions as a means by which Nabokov initially reveals Humbert's unreliability and then dramatizes his struggle with his telling, Harrison's narration functions as a means toward her own therapeutic ends. Furthermore, our ethical relation to Nabokov, like our ethical relation to most other implied authors, is based on the principle of reciprocity, but that principle works somewhat differently in *The Kiss*. In general, an implied author asks for our time and attention and implicitly promises that there will be some repayment for them in the act of reading itself: a heightened emotional experience, an opportunity to contemplate beauty, the bestowal of new knowledge or increased understanding, the chance for a sharpened ethical sense, various combinations of these things, among others. The key point is that the author gains by having an audience, and the audience gains by attending to the author's narrative. *Lolita* is an ethically difficult work in part because the returns it offers for our investment of time and attention are not always ones that we welcome, but the narrative still relies on the principle of reciprocity. *Angela's Ashes* is a more straightforward case. Frank McCourt gains by shaping the details of his "miserable Irish Catholic childhood" into a narrative for an external audience, because that shaping leads him to articulate a coherent understanding of his diverse experiences—and perhaps even to achieve closure on some of the more painful ones. At the same time, his audience gains because the experience of reading the tale provides the pleasure of McCourt's humor, the satisfaction of watching Frankie achieve his goal of coming to America, and the positive ethical engagements I analyzed in chapter 2.

Reciprocity works differently in *The Kiss* because Harrison is dependent on her audience in a way that Nabokov, McCourt, and most other authors are not: she needs an audience to whom she can break her silence and before whom she can work through her relation to her mother. In this sense, Harrison casts her audience in the role of silent therapist. In return, Harrison offers us the satisfaction of seeing her achieve her psychological resolution, a resolution which allows us to believe that she is what she portrays herself to be by the end of the narrative: a woman who, though affected by her past, is no longer controlled by it, a woman who has managed to come to terms with her past and so be free to construct a healthy family life of her own. In other words, Harrison's purpose is both aesthetic and therapeutic, and the two purposes are interdependent. What Harrison offers her readers is a tale of pain, error, courage, and healing. Strikingly, however, the courage is to be found less in the events than in Harrison's willingness to tell the tale, and the healing occurs primarily because of that telling. Consequently, our ethical estimation of the tale will be greatly dependent on our assessment of how courageously Harrison tells it, and our estimation of its courage is crucially dependent on our estimation of its honesty. And any such estimation must come to terms with Harrison's representation of her agency, including her use of suppressed narration.


## Harrison's Suppressed Narration

Harrison does not narrate the event that gives the book its title until section 6, using the preceding sections to contextualize it. Harrison's effort is to explain the kiss less as a matter of illicit sexual desire between father and grown daughter and more as a consequence of the complex dysfunctional psychodynamics of her family. Indeed, the narration insists that the kiss has more to do with Kathryn's and her father's feelings of anger toward her mother than with their feelings about each other. Harrison does not stay with a straight chronological account of Kathryn's life, but jumps around among significant events of her childhood and even to different periods of her adulthood, including to moments when she is twenty and has begun the affair and to moments after her mother's death. Coupled with the frame provided by the opening section, this treatment of time keeps Kathryn's affair with her father at the center of the narrative. In addition, it invites us to read the scenes of childhood as clues to the causes of the affair and the scenes of adulthood as its effects. In giving us these causes, Harrison develops another significant motif in the whole narrative, one that we have already seen in the comparison between sections 2 and 17, a motif involving the trope of vision, of seeing and being seen.

I have already noted how, in the iterative report from section 2 about Kathryn's watching her sleeping mother, Harrison emphasizes her mother's deficiency. In other places, however, Harrison mitigates her negative judgment by emphasizing her mother's own suffering, and sometimes calls additional attention to these passages by breaking the chronological order of her narration. In the third section of the memoir, after reporting that Kathryn's mother and father met when they were seventeen, Harrison reveals Kathryn's responses to viewing her mother's photo in her high school yearbook "years after her death." Consistent with Harrison's attention to the trope of vision, Kathryn focuses on her mother's eyes and how they affect her overall expression in the photo: "They are dangerous, those eyes in the picture, unplumbed pools of sorrow into which I can tumble and drown. My mother's expression is one that betrays the kind of fear and vulnerability I associate with orphans or refugees, people who have lost everything" (17). As a result of the chronological break and the deep empathy Harrison expresses here, the passage accomplishes more than mitigating Harrison's previous negative judgments of her mother. It provides a tension in the narrative about this new feeling on the older Kathryn's part, a tension that is not resolved until the reconciliation reported in the narrative's final pages.

Later in section 3, Harrison adds her father to the triangle of gazing. During the visit when Kathryn is five, Harrison emphasizes that Kathryn watches him while worrying primarily about his effect on her mother: "What frightens me most about him is the way he fascinates my mother. I am sure, watching as they pack up the beach equipment and walk toward the car, that if I didn't follow, they wouldn't notice I was missing" (26). During the visit when Kathryn is ten, things have changed only a little: "I sense that my father regards me with some curiosity— his child, after all—and little pleasure. I am, as I have been from my birth, the inevitable compromise of my parents' privacy" (27).

In section 4, Harrison uses a scene from her childhood to lead into general reflections from her perspective as adult narrator. The scene occurs in Kathryn's grandmother's bedroom when Kathryn is "six, maybe seven" (34), and it provides a sharp contrast with Harrison's iterative report of Kathryn's waiting for her mother to wake up. Her grandmother welcomes Kathryn's attention and invites her to tickle her neck. Pleased, Kathryn says, "Do you know . . . I love you more than anyone else in the world. I love you more than Mommy." Her grandmother is clearly taken aback: she removes Kathryn's hand from her neck and tells her, "No. You don't. . . . You love your mother best. That's the way it is for every child, and that's the way it is for you, too" (35). Harrison the narrator articulates the larger significance of the scene:

> That afternoon, I begin to learn the wisdom of keeping my feelings to myself, a lesson reinforced often during a childhood of female warfare and tricky, shifting alliances, so often that my genius for evasion at last approaches that of my mother. . . . Rebuked by my grandmother, sitting in silence beside her, I begin to teach myself to define what I really feel toward my mother—a desperate, fearful anger over her having abandoned me, an anger that has left me stricken with asthma and rashes— as *love*. (36).

Although Harrison's style indicates that Kathryn is the active subject ("I begin to learn"; "I begin to teach myself"), other elements of the treatment, particularly the contrast with the scene in section 2, her childlike trust of her grandmother's word, and her reference to a "lesson reinforced often . . . so often" indicate that Harrison wants us to see Kathryn's secrecy and her equation of anger with love as behavior less chosen than forced upon her. As a result, Harrison implies that the consequences of that behavior are not Kathryn's responsibility but her mother's and grandmother's.

Harrison's treatment of her father's visit when Kathryn is twenty, the visit that ends with the kiss referred to in the title, again depends heavily on the motif of vision. Kathryn's mother is so nervous about the visit that she sends Kathryn to the airport alone to meet her father's plane. Here is Harrison's report: While still in the terminal, he says, "Don't move. Just let me look at you." She emphasizes how his gaze felt to Kathryn: "My father looks at me, then, as no one has ever looked at me before. His hot eyes consume me—eyes that I will discover later are always just this bloodshot. I almost feel their touch. He takes my hands, one in each of his, and turns them over, stares at my palms. He does not actually kiss them, but his look is one that ravishes" (51). From the start, then, Harrison underlines the change in her father's attitude and the charged, erotic quality underlying his gaze. Furthermore, Harrison limits her report of Kathryn's response by initially focusing almost exclusively on her father's actions and keeping Kathryn in the role of passive recipient of the gaze. Then, when Harrison turns to describe Kathryn's response, she emphasizes the power of her father's gaze over her. After Harrison reports a comment he makes about her long hair, she tells us, "I nod. I don't speak. His eyes rob me of words, they seem to draw the air from my mouth so that I can barely breathe" (51). The description suggests that this airport terminal is the first of the "airless" meeting places between father and daughter that Harrison describes in the very first section.[7] But more than that, the description suggests that Kathryn's father has so much power over her that his look not only renders her speechless but also sucks the air out of her environment.

Later in the section, Harrison shows that the erotic quality of her father's gaze mingles with something more basic, something that Harrison contrasts with Kathryn's unfulfilled desire for her mother's gaze.

---

7. At the end of the section, Harrison echoes her description in the first section of the places Kathryn and her father met as "burning," when she describes photographs her father took of Kathryn and her mother with a fire in the background: "In certain of the poses the fire looks as if it comes from our clothes themselves, as if the anguished expression we each wear is not the smile we intended but the first rictus of pain. As if what my father caught with his camera was the moment when suddenly we knew we'd begun to burn" (55).

I don't know it yet, not consciously, but I feel it: my father, holding himself so still and staring at me, has somehow begun to *see* me into being. His look gives me to myself, his gaze reflects the life my mother's willfully shut eyes denied. Looking at him looking at me, I cannot help but fall painfully, precipitously in love. And my loving him is inseparable from a piercing sense of loss. Whenever I am alone—in my bedroom, the bathroom—I find myself crying, sometimes even sinking to my knees. How am I to endure this new despair? How can it be that I'm twenty years old, that I've had to grow up without a father, only to meet him now when it's too late, when childhood is over, lost? (63)

Harrison here emphasizes not the erotic desire expressed in her father's gaze but its parental power to affirm and value Kathryn's existence. Given this frame, Harrison encourages us to view Kathryn's response as involuntary in the way that a child's response to a parent's loving look is involuntary: "Looking at him looking at me, I cannot help but fall painfully, precipitously in love." The falling is precipitous because the look has come suddenly and unexpectedly after twenty years, and the falling is painful because (a) she now understands more clearly what her mother withheld from her and (b) she now understands something of the difference between having and not having a father in one's life. The pain in turn generates a desire to fill the void, make up for the lack, overcome the lost twenty years.

Having shown her mother's neglect and Kathryn's equation of anger with love and having shown the gap between her father's erotic desire and Kathryn's desire to reclaim her lost parent, Harrison is ready to represent the kiss:

A voice over the public-address system announces the final boarding call for my father's flight. As I pull away, feeling the resistance of his hand behind my head, how tightly he holds me to him, the kiss changes. It is no longer a chaste, closed-lipped kiss.

My father pushes his tongue deep into my mouth: wet, insistent, exploring, then withdrawn. He picks up his camera case, and, smiling brightly, he joins the end of the line of passengers disappearing into the airplane. . . .

I am frightened by the kiss. I know it is wrong, and its wrongness is what lets me know, too, that it is a secret.

In years to come, I'll think of the kiss as a kind of transforming sting, like that of a scorpion: a narcotic that spreads from my mouth to my

brain. The kiss is the point at which I begin, slowly, inexorably, to fall
asleep, to surrender volition, to become paralyzed. It's the drug my father administers in order that he might consume me. That I might desire to be consumed. (68–70)

This account is clearly consistent with Harrison's preparation for it;
Kathryn's father is the willing initiator of the transgression: he is not
just unfazed about violating the norm but also very pleased—"smiling
brightly, he joins" the other passengers. Kathryn, for her part, is the passive recipient. But the passage is also an instance of suppressed narration, and the suppression involves both the report of Kathryn's response
to the kiss and the metaphor of the scorpion's sting. The narration implies that during the kiss itself Kathryn does not react to her father's
boldness either by resisting him or responding in kind. I see no evidence
in the narrative to question that implication and so do not regard it as
part of the suppressed narration. The suppression begins with Harrison's
withholding of any report of Kathryn's physical response to the kiss,
since such a report is relevant to the emotional and ethical responses
that Harrison does report. If Kathryn feels violated and repulsed by the
kiss, then we will read her fear, her sense that it is wrong and must be
kept secret very differently than we will if she feels physical pleasure in
the kiss, some awakening of her own physical desire that goes along with
her feelings of love. And of course it is possible that Kathryn's response
actually includes both desire and repulsion. The problem, however, is
that the suppressed narration does not allow us to know just how we
should interpret Kathryn's emotional and ethical responses. To suppress
Kathryn's agency at this key moment is, it seems to me, both an aesthetic and an ethical deficiency.

The metaphor of the scorpion's sting not only completes the pattern
of narration that portrays Kathryn as acting at the behest of forces beyond her control, but it also places the blame for everything that happens after the kiss on her father. The transforming sting causes her to
"fall asleep, to surrender volition, to become paralyzed," leaving her
powerless against her father's horrible desire to consume her. The force
of the metaphor is heightened by Harrison's calling attention to it as the
narrator's and implied author's interpretation of the event: this interpretation is not one Kathryn makes at the time but one that she arrives
at "in years to come." The problem is that the narrative has already given
us evidence and will subsequently give us even more that the metaphor
is at best a partial truth and one that Harrison can articulate here only

through suppressed narration. Let me be clear: I do not mean to argue that the metaphor is fundamentally dishonest in the sense that Harrison is engaging in an act of deception. Despite the suppression, the narrative does not contain enough evidence to support such a judgment, and without such evidence, I am willing to accept the metaphor as Harrison's subjective truth. However, the narrative also gives us other evidence that this subjective truth is only a partial truth, one that Harrison can utter at this critical juncture of her telling only by suppressing other significant relevant information. Since Harrison clearly would not want her silent therapist to infer that she is suppressing this information, the suppressed narration is both an aesthetic and an ethical problem for her narrative.

The suppression is evident if we recall the first section's report of the frequent quarreling and weeping, activities that involve an agent who has not surrendered volition. But it is even more evident in light of some later reports. In section 7, Harrison describes the frequent phone calls she exchanges with her father: "We talk for hours every night: a courtship encouraged by the paradoxical intimacy of long-distance calls, the telephone's invitation to say anything, to be *more forthcoming, passionate, reckless* in ways we might not be if we were meeting face-to-face" (78, my emphasis). This description provides a marked contrast with the one in which she describes her falling in love with her father as parent.

In section 10, during a visit to her father's father, Harrison recounts this event:

> At the motel, a squat sprawl of units built around a dusty courtyard, we share one room in which two twin beds are pushed together and covered with the same king-sized spread. Half asleep, I let my father kiss me the way he wants to, and *I kiss him back.*
>
> Early in the quiet morning, I wake as suddenly as if I've been roused by a loud alarm, my heart pounding as I remember *the heat of the kisses.* What I feel is not so much guilt as dislocation. I look around the dim room in confusion, not knowing, for a moment, where I am. In the bed beside mine, my father sleeps, the air whistling faintly in his nose as he breathes.
>
> I shower. I sit on the floor of the bathtub and let the hot water rain on me for an hour or more. My heartbeat doesn't slow. I watch the water curl down the drain, a yellow scum of soap at its edge. (123–24, my emphasis)

Even more telling is this report in section 14 after Kathryn has moved into her father's house: "*The heat of our early kisses* was lost long ago on the highways; the weight of him has smothered *the passion I once felt;* and the workaday drudgery of our contact flattens me to the point that each time I am more still, more silent, more lifeless. We fight about this. 'I hate it that you tolerate me!' my father yells, and I put my face in my hands, I cover my eyes. 'What do you think that does to me! How do you think it makes me feel!'" (166, my emphasis).

What is striking in each of the last two reports is that Harrison reveals something of Kathryn's "heat and passion" while emphasizing other matters. As a result these revelations appear to be inadvertent, unintended consequences of her communication about her suffering and her father's dominance. In the motel scene, Harrison emphasizes Kathryn's distance from her father, her sense of dislocation and unhappiness now that the affair has begun. In the scene from section 14, Harrison emphasizes her lack of pleasure and responsiveness during sex and her father's anger. But because these reports also reveal that Kathryn herself initially brought heat and passion to the affair, they are very difficult to reconcile with her report of the kiss and her metaphor of the scorpion's sting. These reports also affect our response to Harrison's narration of the act to which the kiss has just been prelude:

> When I give up, it's almost a relief, the way it must be for someone who, holding tight to a ledge, at last lets go. After the agony of resistance, when for so long it's been clear that a fall is imminent, plummeting is a kind of fulfillment. I plunge without knowing how fast I fall or how far, how hard the bottom will be when I hit. . . .
>
> The sight of him naked: at that point I fall completely asleep. I arrive at the state promised by the narcotic kiss in the airport. In years to come, I won't be able to remember even one instance of our lying together. I'll have a composite, generic memory. I'll know that he was always on top and that I always lay still, as still as if I had, in truth, fallen from a great height. . . . I'll remember every tiny thing about him. . . . But I won't be able to remember what it felt like. No matter how hard I try, pushing myself to inhabit my past, I'll recoil from what will always seem impossible. (136–37)

When we first come upon this passage in section 11 of the narrative, it does not seem to be an instance of suppressed narration but rather Harrison's honest account of the psychological feeling of the first intercourse and of her inability to remember more about "what it felt like." It is plausible both that Harrison would feel that consenting to the act of intercourse was like falling off a cliff and that she would want to forget how it felt—indeed, that her psychological health would be partially dependent on this forgetfulness. But when we come to her comment in section 14 that "the weight of him has smothered *the passion I once felt,"* we can't help but wonder whether Harrison has again suppressed something in her account. Again, let me be clear about my claim: I do not see the reports about Kathryn's heat and passion as containing the real truth about Kathryn's agency and the reports about the kiss and the act of intercourse as Harrison's deliberate efforts to deceive her audience (and perhaps herself). Instead, I see the reports about her greater agency as complicating her representation of herself as acting only in response to forces beyond her control, and especially as only her father's victim. The evidence of the suppressed narration renders these representations only partial truths. Similarly, I do not see the reports about Kathryn's agency as suggesting that she ever had a power equal to her father's. On the contrary, her own account of the psychodynamics of the family, of why she is attracted to her father, and of his power over her seems to me persuasive. But again the suppressed narration indicates that she has not fully disclosed the dynamics of the affair.

This analysis of the suppressed narration suggests that Harrison, despite her careful arrangement of incidents, her skillful use of the historical present tense, and her well-managed style, has not achieved sufficient aesthetic control over her material. The inadvertent quality of her revelations about Kathryn's own heat and passion and the incompatibility of this information with the dominant representation of her agency produce a troubling incoherence in the narrative. In order to explore this aesthetic problem further as well as its corresponding ethical consequences, I turn now to consider what motivates Harrison's suppressions.

## The Connections between Aesthetics and Ethics

The task of representing Kathryn's agency presents Harrison with her most difficult rhetorical challenge. The more Harrison shows Kathryn to be a willing collaborator in the affair the more likely it will be that she would lose the sympathy of her audience. Such a representation would, to adopt Frost's helpful terms, display an agency that no one would want to claim—and thus an agency that everyone would want to distance himself or herself from. Perhaps even more important, the more Harrison presents Kathryn as an active collaborator the more difficult it will be to achieve her psychological reconciliation with her mother and, ultimately, her own self-acceptance. In section 12, shortly after her account of sleeping with her father, Harrison refers to Kathryn and her mother as "the betrayer and the person betrayed" (140). Representing Kathryn as a more active collaborator would mean representing her betrayal as deeper and more treacherous. The worse the betrayal and the more she regards her mother as "Beloved" the more difficult it will be for her to forgive and accept herself. In short, the motivation for Harrison to represent herself as more sinned against than sinning, as more of a victim than a collaborator, is strong. On the other hand, if Harrison shows herself only as a passive victim of her father, as someone who has done wrong only by being wronged herself, then she has two other problems. Such a representation almost invites her audience to doubt her veracity, given her age and sexual experience at the time the affair began and given that it lasts for four years. Similarly, if that is her only self-representation, she is less likely to achieve her self-forgiveness and self-acceptance, since she will know that she has suppressed all signs of her agency from the tale. In light of these considerations, we can understand, even if we do not endorse, Harrison's use of suppressed narration.

This analysis also sheds light on a memorable set piece in the memoir, Harrison's narration of the eleven-year-old Kathryn's treatment of a litter of Persian kittens, creatures that her grandmother had told her not to touch.

> It was one day after school that I did it. I didn't know why, I only knew that I couldn't stop myself. I couldn't bear to see their always sleeping faces, their tiny eyes that never woke to me. For a week, longer, I'd held their beating, blind life in my hands, and I'd felt my heart squeezed in my chest. I'd felt as if I were dying.
>
> I laid one in my lap and, with one thumb on the upper lid, the other on the lower, I carefully pulled its eyes open, separating one delicate membrane of flesh from the other. My heart was pounding and I was sweating with fear, but I accomplished the violation gently. The kitten made no sound, it did not struggle. What I did hadn't seemed to cause it any pain. . . .
>
> Within a day [the kittens'] eyes were swollen shut, tightly resealed under lids that showed red beneath the fine white fur. I picked one up and tried to brush away the yellow crust that had formed in the corner of one

of its eyes. A worm of pus shot out, and, shocked, I dropped the kit-
ten. . . .

The veterinarian kept the cat and the kittens for a week. When they
returned, their eyes were open and clean, a pale icy blue: disdainful, dis-
interested. (89–91)

Harrison places the scene in section 8, after the report of the kiss and
shortly after Kathryn's mother tells her that her father was the only man
she enjoyed sex with, prompting Harrison's comment that her mother
was "innocent of how I, and my father, will come to use [this informa-
tion]" (84). In this context and with the reference to Kathryn's desire
when she stands before a sleeping face, the scene functions as a covert
admission of Kathryn's agency in the affair with her father. Kathryn
could not force her mother's eyes open, but she could force the kittens'
eyes open. When presented with the chance to force her mother's eyes
open in another sense, Kathryn seizes it. When presented with that
chance, her knowledge of the violence done to the kittens seems to spur
her on rather than cause her to hold back. Again, given the challenges of
representing her agency we can understand, if not approve, Harrison's
choice to communicate covertly here.[8] And of course the inclusion of
the scene adds to the incoherence of the narrative: Harrison's covert admission of her active role does not fit with the metaphor of the scorpion.

Finally, the effort to understand Harrison's motives for the suppressed
narration does not alter the conclusion that the technique points to a
genuine aesthetic and ethical limitation of the book. Since Harrison's
achievement of her purpose depends on her willingness to confront the
past openly and honestly, the evidence that she has suppressed important information about her own behavior and motives at crucial junc-
tures of the story indicates that she, finally, is not as honest as she needs
to be and, indeed, seems to be too easy on herself. Harrison is willing to
dig deep into the motives of her mother and father, able to analyze them
with a ruthless honesty, but the suppressed narration indicates that she
does not give herself that same treatment. Instead, she gives us partial
truths that mitigate her responsibility and glimpses of more complex
truths that suggest a responsibility she is not quite ready to claim.

A related ethical issue is raised by Eakin, who, as noted earlier, asks
about the consequences of telling the tale while her father is alive. Part

8. Frost offers an insightful comparison between this scene in *The Kiss* and a similar
scene in *Thicker Than Water*. Frost also sees the scene as an admission of Kathryn's agency.

of Harrison's achieving reconciliation with her dead mother involves exposing her living father to public denunciation. Indeed, although Harrison never gives her maiden name or refers to her father by name, Warren
St. John, a reporter for the *New York Observer*, tracked him down and
asked him to comment on Harrison's narrative. (He claimed not to know
about the book, saying, "Kathy writes fiction," but he stopped short of
denying the affair.) To the extent that the story is a fair representation
and that Harrison's father hasn't changed, she does not owe him any pro-
tection. To the extent, however, that Harrison's suppressed narration has
misrepresented her own role in the affair and exaggerated her father's,
the publication of the memoir while her father is alive magnifies the ethical problem. Furthermore, if Harrison's father has himself come to recognize and repent his heavy responsibility for the affair and its negative
effects on his daughter, then Harrison's representation of his discarded
private self is even more troubling. Harrison may be denying him the
kind of peace she herself is seeking. As my use of the subjunctive mood
suggests, at this point our inquiry into the ethics of Harrison's narration
goes beyond what we can now know.

By way of conclusion, I would like to return to the negative reviewers.
Although I have emphasized what seem to me the problems with Harrison's narrative, I see no reason to condemn it, or to regard it as a sensational or cynical effort to cash in on the market for memoir. Such a view
seems not only churlish but also to misunderstand Harrison's project of
using her telling to bring about her self-forgiveness and self-acceptance.
What she is undertaking in this narrative is arguably more difficult than
what any of the other implied authors considered in this book have at-
tempted. At the same time, recognizing that difficulty does not eliminate the problems, and so my analysis does negatively affect my response
to Harrison as implied author. Although I have no regrets about giving
her my time and attention, and although I acknowledge both the difficulty and the value of what she tries to do, I find aesthetic and ethical
flaws in her execution. Most telling, my analysis of the memoir's ethics
affects my assessment of Harrison's final chapter. I now have reason to
doubt the depth and thoroughness of the final reconciliation, and, thus,
the success of Harrison's self-forgiveness and self-acceptance. Since these
matters depend on the partial truths in her narrative, they now appear
too easily achieved and thus not entirely secure.

Finally, working through the aesthetics and ethics of Harrison's narrative induces me to take one more step in the analysis and reflect on

my conclusions. To say that Harrison has been too easy on herself is to invite a similar response to one's analysis, particularly on the grounds that it misregards two key elements of Harrison's telling: the courage it took to go public with this narrative that will inevitably put her in a bad light; and the achievement involved in her working through her horrible experiences to the extent that she did. To say that Harrison has been too easy on herself also gives me pause because I worry that it puts me on the side of the negative reviewers, whom I regard as too easy in their attacks on *The Kiss*. But I keep returning to the point that the suppressed narration interferes with Harrison's purpose of achieving psychic reconciliation, and, thus, to my assessment that the suppressed narration makes the narrative flawed on its own terms.

Having now offered a series of ethical engagements with narratives that represent a spectrum from admiration to some disapprobation, I would like to step back and consider the general question of the relation between technique and ethics. We have seen considerable evidence of the interdependence of the two, but it is worth probing their relation further. Is the interdependence so great that we can conclude that there is a kind of one-to-one correspondence between them such that an author's technical deficiency will always entail an ethical deficiency and an author's technical mastery ensure an admirable ethical achievement? The answer, I believe, is "no, but" with each part of the answer deserving emphasis. Although technique always has an ethical dimension, there is no one-to-one correspondence between a technical deficiency and an ethical deficiency or technical mastery and ethical achievement because there are other factors affecting our ethical response, primarily our assessment of the underlying value structure of the narrative. An author who is technically clumsy need not write ethically deficient narratives, just as an author who is technically brilliant need not write ethically admirable ones.

At the same time, because narrative's capacity to explore the realm of ethics depends on its concrete particularity, and because that concrete particularity in turn is intimately tied to its techniques, we must add the "but" to our "no." The technically clumsy author may not write ethically deficient narratives, but his technical clumsiness will put a limit on the quality and depth of his ethical explorations. The technically proficient author may write a narrative that is ethically deficient, but that technical proficiency is likely either to mitigate or to exacerbate that deficiency by either opening up the complexity of the unsatisfactorily resolved ethical issues or inadvertently calling chilling attention to the gap between the narrative's aesthetics and its ethics.

My qualified assessments of the ethics of *Lolita*, *'Tis*, and *The Kiss* further clarify the "but" in the "no, but" answer to the question about a one-to-one correspondence between technique and ethics. Nabokov's technical brilliance allows him to create the possibility for us not only to condemn but also to sympathize with Humbert Humbert, and that brilliance indicates an impressive power of sympathy on Nabokov's part. At the same time, however, Nabokov's technical brilliance does not extend to his finding a way to alter his consistent subordination of Dolores and her pain to Humbert and his struggles, and that aspect of his treatment as well as what I have called his perverse relish in creating Humbert's world indicates a serious ethical limitation. This dual awareness of what Nabokov achieves and fails to achieve both technically and ethically makes the narrative simultaneously moving and disturbing, compelling and repellent. In *'Tis* the ethical limits of McCourt's vision of his adult self are directly reflected in the problems with his technique: his withholding the information about his absences from school and his joke at Mrs. Propp's expense in the incident about teaching Shakespeare; his use of cultural stereotypes to stack the deck in his account of the breakup of his marriage. Given McCourt's technical success in *Angela's Ashes* and in much of *'Tis*, it seems reasonable to conclude that the technical deficiency follows from the ethical shortcoming: if McCourt saw himself differently, he could have found different and better techniques for conveying that vision than the ones he has employed.

In *The Kiss* it is much harder to say whether technique follows from ethical vision or vice versa because suppressed narration is a fusion of a technical and an ethical problem. Harrison's depiction of her agency at crucial points conflicts with other, less guarded representations of it, and, consequently, her depiction causes us to question her honesty. These questions, in turn, indicate that she does not fully succeed in accomplishing her very difficult aesthetic and therapeutic purpose. The fusion of technique and ethics in the suppressed narration can also be illuminated by our imagining how Harrison might revise *The Kiss* if she were persuaded either that her narrative contained suppressed narration at key points or that there were some ethical flaws in it. Seeking to eliminate the suppressed narration could very well lead Harrison to a new level of honesty about her agency, and, thus, to a new layer in her ethical exploration of her affair with her father. Alternatively, seeking to work through problems with the ethical dimension of her book could very well lead her to locate those problems in the suppressed narration. In sum, while it would be extremely misleading to say "technique is ethics, ethics technique; that's all you know in narrative studies and all you need to know," it is extremely important to recognize that the two are interdependent and that the kind of interdependence can vary from narrative to narrative.

Having now examined a range of character narrators in narratives that require us to judge their protagonists as they move through the events of the narrative, I turn in the next chapter to two character narrators who are protagonists in lyric narratives, Ernest Hemingway's "Now I Lay Me" and John Edgar Wideman's "Doc's Story." As we shall see, these narratives involve different kinds of progressions and different kinds of audience response, and naturally these differences have significant consequences for our ethical encounters with these character narrators.

# 5 Progression and Audience Engagement in Lyric Narratives

*"Now I Lay Me" and "Doc's Story"*

In this chapter, I turn to character narration in texts more like "Barbie-Q" than like the novels and memoirs examined in chapters 1–4. These texts are recognizable—and typically classified—as narratives because they contain a character narrator who is clearly distinct from the implied author and because the character narrator usually engages in some telling about past events. But these texts also contain one or more of three salient features that we typically associate with lyric poetry, and so I shall refer to them as lyric narratives. (1) The character narrator does not undergo any substantial change within the temporal frame of the main action; instead, the text focuses on revealing the dimensions of the character narrator's current situation. (2) The dominant tense of the narrative is the present; even if, as in "Barbie-Q," most of the sentences of the text focus on past events, the narrative still directs our primary interest to the present situation of the character narrator. In other words, revelations about "what happened" are made not for their own sake but in the service of explaining "what is." (3) The implied author invites the authorial audience to enter sympathetically into the character narrator's perspective but does not ask us to render an ethical judgment of that perspective or of the character narrator.[1] As we shall see, when this feature is present, we still engage

---

1. I believe that the category of "lyric narrative" can be profitably broken down into more specific subcategories that would describe different combinations of static situation, retrospective or present tense narration, and audience engagement, as well as combinations in which lyric dominates but then gives way to narrative and vice versa. Such a taxonomy, however, is beyond the scope of this project; among other reasons, developing an adequate taxonomy would involve considerable study of lyric narratives with noncharacter narrators.

ethically with the text, but focus not on the ethics of the character's actions but on the underlying value structure of the lyric narrative.

Although lyric narratives are not as plentiful as narratives that give a retrospective account of something that happened and ask the audience to judge their characters, these hybrid forms are sufficiently numerous to constitute a significant subgenre. Given their lyric qualities, they are more likely to be among the narratives we group under the umbrella of the short story than that of the novella or the novel, though examples can be found under all three umbrellas.[2] Lyric narratives raise a number of challenging questions for the rhetorical theorist: if the narrative does not trace the developing fortunes (or misfortunes) of a protagonist, what are the mechanisms of its progression? If the character narrator is a present-tense meditator more than a past-tense storyteller, what happens to the relation between disclosure functions and narrator functions? If the implied author does not ask us to judge the protagonist, what provides the initial ethical positioning in these narratives? I shall pursue these questions in relation to two different but very rich and challenging short stories: Ernest Hemingway's "Now I Lay Me" and John Edgar Wideman's "Doc's Story."

"Now I Lay Me," the concluding story in Hemingway's 1927 collection *Men without Women*, is a paradigm case of lyric narrative: Nick Adams's report of his past becomes a way to reveal his present condition, and it is that condition that Hemingway makes the ultimate interest of the story; furthermore, Hemingway asks his audience to enter into the feelings and attitudes associated with that condition rather than to judge Nick. On the other hand, "Doc's Story," the first entry in Wideman's second collection, *Fever* (1989), is a kind of limit case for this study of character narration and a particularly complicated hybrid of lyric and narrative. "Doc's Story" is a frame tale in which the unnamed protagonist of the frame is not the narrator; however, within that frame, Wideman employs a lot of narration from the vision of the protagonist and even some in his voice: a section toward the very end of the story marks some of the narration as his words and the very last sentence is quoted thought: "Would she have believed any of it?" (153). In other words, in these passages of internal focalization where the vision and the voice both belong to the protagonist, the technique borders on character nar-

---

2. Among novel-length narratives, I'd list several of Virginia Woolf's experiments, including *Mrs. Dalloway, To the Lighthouse,* and *The Waves.* Among short stories, in addition to the three I discuss in this book, I'd include several of Woolf's, Cisneros's "Woman Hollering Creek," Hemingway's "A Clean, Well-Lighted Place," Alice Munro's "Prue," Ann Beattie's "Janus," Tillie Olsen's, "I Stand Here Ironing," and J. D. Salinger's "Uncle Wiggly in Connecticut." Needless to say, this list is illustrative rather than comprehensive.

ration. Furthermore, in the embedded tale, the protagonist becomes the narrator but does so by mentally rehearsing another speaker's tale; in other words, by narrating the story to himself, he steps into the role of its observer character narrator—though the distinction between the actual observer and the protagonist is never fully erased.

"Doc's Story" also has a complex kind of lyric narrative hybridity. The frame tale is lyric—it reveals the protagonist's present-tense condition— but the embedded tale is a more conventional narrative that follows what happens the day the Doc of the title, who is blind, played basketball. And the question of judgment is similarly complicated: Wideman asks us not only to enter into the protagonist's condition but also to adopt a critical perspective on it. In short, working through the complexities of "Doc's Story" will require a greater precision in my discussion of lyric narratives as well as a fitting closure to our study of character narration. But before I delve into the specifics of Hemingway's and Wideman's stories, I want, first, to say more about the role of judgment in reading narrative and, second, to provide my own frame for understanding lyric narratives.

The rhetorical approach to narrative, because it seeks to account not just for the cognitive but also for the emotive and ethical dimensions of reading, regards judgment as central to narrative itself. Our emotions and desires about both fictional and nonfictional characters are intimately tied to our judgments of them;[3] and our ethical responses to narrative, as we have seen, are tied both to the ethical quality of characters' actions and to the interaction of our own ethical positions with the ethics of technique and the ethical positions of the implied author. One of the remarkable features of narrative is that it can take an action that we would conventionally regard as ethically sound or ethically deficient, and through the details of its treatment in the narrative, either activate that conventional judgment or reject it in favor of a different and even opposite judgment. Indeed, this power of narrative is one of the reasons that it is, as Martha Nussbaum and others have argued, a site for ethical inquiry that rivals the site provided by the philosophical study of ethics.

This point also suggests that both judgments of a character's actions and the techniques for communicating those judgments can range from the simple and straightforward to the subtle and complex. Thus, for example, narrative judgments are central to the purposes and effects of both *Angela's Ashes* and *Lolita*, though both the techniques and the nature

3. Elder Olson and James L. Battersby have each made a similar point.

of those judgments are markedly different. Even as I regard judgment as central to narrative, I also recognize that individual writers may find it necessary and beneficial for their purposes not to provide the grounds of judgment for a particular set of actions or to render the issue of judgment either indeterminate or ambiguous. In other words, an individual writer may play off the usual centrality of judgment for particular purposes. In lyric narrative hybrids, I believe that such shifts often occur. To clarify that claim, I turn now to more general descriptions of what marks a given text as a narrative, what marks another as lyric, and what marks a third text as a character portrait; these descriptions are all based on the rhetorical definition of narrative I referred to in the introduction: *somebody telling somebody else on some occasion for some purpose that something happened.*

## A Rhetorical View of Narrativity, Lyricality, and Portraiture

From the rhetorical perspective, narrativity is a double-layered phenomenon, involving both a dynamics of character and event and a dynamics of audience response. The phrase "something happened" gets at the first layer, as it indicates that narrative involves a sequence of related events during which the characters and/or their situations undergo some *change.* The phrase also is designed to indicate that the standard tense for narrative is the past. As we have seen, the telling of the change typically proceeds through the introduction, complication, and resolution (in whole or in part) of unstable situations within, between, or among the characters. These dynamics of instability may be accompanied by a dynamics of tension—unstable relations among authors, narrators, and audiences—and the interaction of the two sets of dynamics, as in narratives that employ unreliable narration, may have significant consequences for our understanding of the "something that happened." However, the dynamics of instability are essential to narrative, but those of tension are not. If there is no change in character or situation, we begin to leave the realm of narrative, but if there is such change and no tension among author, narrator, and reader we are in one kind of narrative situation rather than another.

Turning to the second layer, the "somebody else," I highlight two activities of the authorial audience, one that I have taken for granted in the previous chapters and the other that I have made considerable reference to: observing and judging. The authorial audience perceives the characters as other in two ways, as external to themselves and as distinct from their implied authors, and the authorial audience passes intellectual and ethical judgments on them, their situations, and their choices. Furthermore, as noted above, the audience's observer role is what makes the judgment role possible, and the particular judgments are integral to our sympathies and antipathies as well as to our expectations about future events. In short, just as there is a progression of events there is a progression of audience response to those events, a progression rooted in the twin activities of observing and judging. Thus, from the rhetorical perspective, narrativity involves *the interaction of two kinds of change:* that experienced by the characters and that experienced by the audience in its developing responses to the characters' changes.

Turning now to lyricality,[4] I start with a rhetorical definition of lyric that identifies two main modes: (1) somebody telling somebody else (who may or may not be present to the speaker) or even himself or herself on some occasion for some purpose that something is—a situation, an emotion, a perception, an attitude, a belief; (2) somebody telling somebody else (who may or may not be present) or even himself or herself on some occasion about his or her meditations on something. Furthermore, in both kinds of lyric, the authorial audience is less in the position of observer and judge and more in the position of participant. While we recognize that the speaker is different from us, we move from that recognition toward fusion with the speaker—or, to put it in more measured terms, toward adopting the speaker's perspective without any irritable reaching after difference and evaluation. This element of lyricality also depends on the absence of distance between the implied author and the "I" of the poem. Furthermore, the standard tense for lyric is the present. Lyricality, then, in contrast to narrativity is neutral on the issue of change for the speaker—it may or may not be present—and invested not in character and event but in thoughts, attitudes, beliefs, emotions, specific conditions. Furthermore, the dynamics of audience response stem from adopting the speaker's perspective without judging it. Thus, the double movement of lyric is toward fuller revelation of the

4. My ideas about lyric and portraiture have been significantly influenced by Ralph Rader. His essay "The Dramatic Monologue and Related Lyric Forms" offers a highly insightful way to think about the relations among (implied) author, the "I" of the poem, and the (authorial) audience. For a sampling of other good work on lyric and narrative, see Friedman, Gerlach, and Dubrow. Friedman seeks to make connections between the two forms and gender. Gerlach seeks to identify similarities and differences among the short story, the prose poem, and the lyric. Dubrow points to the contested nature of the concept of lyric and notes the value of understanding the mode within specific historical contexts. I am especially grateful for conversations with Dubrow about the intersections of lyric and narrative.

speaker's situation and perspective and, on the audience's part, toward deeper understanding of and participation in what is revealed.

Portraiture, manifest most commonly in one type of dramatic monologue, exists in the space between narrativity and lyricality. In this type of monologue, somebody tells somebody else whatever the speaker judges to be relevant in that rhetorical occasion; furthermore, from the poet's perspective, though not the speaker's, the purpose of the speech is the revelation of the speaker's character. In this sense, the double movement of the form involves a double logic: the speaker's telling progresses according to the logic of the dramatic situation, while the audience's understanding progresses toward a deeper knowledge and understanding of the speaker. Thus, portraiture is neutral on both change and stasis, since its point is neither event nor condition but character. Regardless of what is told, however, the implied author and the speaker are distinct figures, and so are the speaker and the authorial audience. Furthermore, although the audience remains in the observer role, that role involves comprehending and contemplating the character, and judgment may or may not accompany that contemplation. In a sense, the purpose of portraiture is to evoke in the audience a response much like that of Browning's Duke to Fra Pandolf's painting: "There she stands as if alive." Sometimes what we behold is a character whom we judge, as in "My Last Duchess," but sometimes we behold without judging.

Now there is no theoretical or practical reason why, in any specific text, the relationships among events, character, change, and audience activity need to stay within the boundaries of narrativity, lyricality, and portraiture. Indeed, there have been multiple rich experiments with hybrid forms of narrative, lyric, and dramatic monologue over the last hundred years or so. Although Hemingway's and Wideman's stories do not represent the full range of such experiments, they do offer some highly illuminating examples of what has been accomplished both aesthetically and ethically. I begin with "Now I Lay Me," paying special attention to the logic of its progression, its movement from Nick the teller's memories of how he used to stay awake during the war by remembering his past to his memory of a conversation on one specific night to his return to his present situation.

## The Narrative Situation in "Now I Lay Me"

Unlike *The Remains of the Day* or *Lolita*, "Now I Lay Me" contains very little evidence about its occasion of narration. Like Jake Barnes of

*The Sun Also Rises* and Frederic Henry of *A Farewell to Arms*, Nick Adams is telling his tale to an unspecified narratee on an unspecified occasion. We know that some time has passed between the summer of sleepless nights that he is telling about and the time of his telling, but we don't know exactly how much.[5] Because Nick's narratee is uncharacterized and the occasion undefined, the gap between the narratee and the authorial audience is minimal and so the authorial audience will feel that Nick's narration might as well be addressed to us even as we remain aware of the implied Hemingway communicating more to us than Nick realizes. Given this situation, the disclosure functions and the narrator functions work seamlessly together sentence by sentence. Nick's narration is, for the most part, reliable on all three axes, and Hemingway never needs to have the disclosure functions trump the narrator functions. Nevertheless, the implied Hemingway's disclosure to the authorial audience goes significantly beyond Nick's communication to the narratee because Hemingway invites us to see the big picture behind Nick's particular moves in his monologue, invites us to achieve a kind of insight into Nick's situation that Nick himself does not achieve.

The first such guidance from the implied Hemingway concerns the answer to the question of why Nick is telling this story, why his monologue is a memory of the sleepless nights he spent remembering his past, what we might call a metamemory. The title provides an important clue in its use of the present tense and its invocation of the well-known child's bedtime prayer:

> Now I lay me down to sleep
> I pray the Lord my soul to keep.
> If I should die before I wake
> I pray the Lord my soul to take.

Nick the teller is in much the same psychological state as Nick the soldier. Although he may no longer worry that his soul will go out of his

5. The story does let us know that Nick the soldier is in Italy during World War I because "they had taken [John] for a soldier in nineteen fourteen" and John calls Nick "Signor Tenente." The reference to the "October offensive," a bloody affair in which many Italians were killed and which John was fortunate to miss (282) allows us to place Nick the soldier in the summer of 1918. Although the date on which Nick the teller remembers that summer is unspecified, the last sentence of the first paragraph suggests that it is years rather than weeks or months later: "So while *now* I am fairly sure that [my soul] would not really have gone out [of my body], yet *then, that summer,* I was unwilling to make the experiment" (276).

body if he falls asleep, Nick is still living with deep wounds that disturb his nights. Just as his memories during that summer were efforts to cope with his war trauma, his memories of those nights spent remembering are efforts to cope with his current condition.

The unspecified distance in time between that summer and the time of narration and the tense shifts throughout the monologue indicate the continuing power of Nick's memories, their significance for Nick the teller's current sense of self. In this way, the story makes the present of Nick's narration the dominant temporal frame, and invites us to read his memories of that summer near the front for the light it sheds on him now. In other words, Nick's telling is itself the main action in "Now I Lay Me," and Hemingway arranges that telling to provide a lyric revelation of Nick's traumatized condition. Hemingway's disclosure exceeds Nick's narration because Hemingway, unlike Nick, has constructed a logic behind the twists and turns of Nick's monologue.[6] Indeed, this move on Hemingway's part is crucial to our responding to the story as a lyric *narrative* because it underlines the distance between the implied author and his character narrator.

Nick's monologue does function as portraiture to some extent: part of what we infer from the progression is a sense of Nick as character. But since the monologue does not recount any change in Nick the teller's condition or offer any substantial information about the narrative situation, our interest is primarily focused on coming to understand that

6. Although the story has received some fine critical commentary, few critics have analyzed its narrative technique in any detail and no one, to my knowledge, has given it the kind of scrutiny I will attempt here. DeFalco, Hovey, and Brenner have offered illuminating psychoanalytic readings. Flora, in an extended discussion, situates it in relation to the other Nick Adams stories, and reminds us that the monologue is a memory. Steinke develops a nice comparison with "In Another Country"; Josephs relates the story to Hemingway's own out-of-body experience, and Scafella ("'I and the Abyss'" and "Imagistic Landscape") links it to Emersonian philosophy. Fournier cites the evidence of the manuscripts to argue that Hovey's psychoanalytic interpretation overemphasizes the theme of castration; in Fournier's view, it is a marriage story, and she offers an insightful account of the progression of Nick's memories in the first half of the story.

In addition to focusing some attention on matters of form, all these critics, to one extent or another, regard the main interpretive task as thematizing the story in relation either to other Nick Adams stories or to Hemingway's own life. In brief, Nick's memories of the burnings are typically read as based on Hemingway's memories of similar events in his own life, a tendency that has been encouraged by study of the manuscripts at the John F. Kennedy Library. One of the manuscripts shows that at one point Hemingway had Mrs. Adams say "and Ernie's helped me burn the things" (Kennedy Library/Ernest Hemingway 618).

Recently Miriam Clark has offered an insightful discussion of the lyric and ethical dimensions of the story by linking it with other Nick Adams stories and thinking of them as illness narratives.

condition and to participate in the feelings and thoughts associated with it. The ethical force of the monologue depends, in turn, on the way in which this participation implicates us in a set of values that tacitly underlie the whole story.

## Nick's Metamemory and Triple Focalization in the Initial Lyric Phase

Nick's first paragraph is a very peculiar introduction, one that begins in one direction and then quickly veers off in another:

> That night we lay on the floor in the room and I listened to the silk-worms eating. The silk-worms fed in racks of mulberry leaves and all night you could hear them eating and a dropping sound in the leaves. I myself did not want to sleep because I had been living for a long time with the knowledge that if I ever shut my eyes in the dark and let myself go, my soul would go out of my body. I had been that way for a long time, ever since I had been blown up at night and felt it go out of me and go off and then come back. I tried never to think about it, but it had started to go since, in the nights, just at the moment of going off to sleep, and I could only stop it by a very great effort. So while now I am fairly sure that it would not really have gone out, yet then, that summer, I was unwilling to make the experiment. (276)

The first three words ("That night we") indicate that the speaker is about to narrate his memory of an event. Yet in the rest of the first sentence, something curious happens to the narrative movement: "*we* lay on the floor" but only "*I*" listened to the silk-worms. Although Nick apparently has a story to tell about "we," he no sooner begins it than he shifts his focus to "I"—and it turns out that he does not return to "we" until the story is half finished. What can we infer about Nick based on this sudden shift from "we" to "I" and on the long delay before he returns to "that night"? Part of the answer is suggested by what we have already seen about the narrative situation: despite his retrospective stance, Nick has not fully formulated the story he is about to tell; indeed, he is less focused on the narrative than on the feelings that motivate his memories. Furthermore, the sudden veering away suggests that, though he is drawn to recall "that night," there may also be something unpleasant in that memory. The movement of the first sentence suggests that Nick has an approach/avoidance conflict with the specific memory of that night.

Initially, however, Nick's delay appears likely to be momentary as he moves to tell his audience why he "did not want to sleep" (276). Nick did not have insomnia but fear. He could easily fall asleep but believed that if he did, his soul would go out of his body just as he felt it go when he was wounded.[7] Nick gives only a clipped, truncated account of that experience: "I had been blown up at night and felt [my soul] go out of me and go off and then come back" (276). For all of its matter-of-factness, the description is sufficiently disturbing to render Nick's fear perfectly understandable. Nick the soldier has recovered from his physical wounding but not its psychic effects. Yet, the last sentence of the paragraph indicates that Nick the teller has developed sufficient distance from the physical event to overcome his fear of falling asleep in the dark. He can talk about the experience and his fear with considerable equanimity: "So while *now I am* fairly sure that it would not really have gone out, yet *then, that summer I was* unwilling to make the experiment" (276, emphasis mine).

The movement of Nick's telling in the first paragraph, then, suggests that Nick has gotten further in coming to terms with his physical wounding than he has with his detailed memories of "that night." Whatever the contours of his current condition, he is not still afraid that his soul will go out of his body if he sleeps. But the paragraph also sets up strong associations between Nick's physical injury ("I had been blown up at night"), its spiritual and psychological consequences ("I tried never to think about it, but it [my soul] had started to go since, in the nights"), the memories of how Nick spent "that night" and others, and his current situation "now" as he recalls those nights. The presence of this chain suggests that whatever Nick uncovers about any of its links will have consequences for the others. Both this chain and Nick's matter-of-fact telling constitute a strong invitation to empathize with him—both to see the world through his eyes and to share the feelings accompanying such a vision.

Apparently not yet ready to return to what happened "that night,"

7. Allen Josephs argues that Nick is describing what medical experts now call an "out-of-body experience," a specific event in which a person's consciousness detaches completely from the physical body. Whether Nick's experience of wounding (or Hemingway's, for that matter) conforms to the clinical definition of an out-of-body event is arguable, but Josephs's essay nicely emphasizes that Nick is all too able to fall asleep.

Nick offers his recollections of two different kinds of memories: of fishing and of his parents. During the fishing memories, Hemingway often employs dual focalization. The memories begin with an introductory comment using the vision and voice of Nick the teller: "I had different ways of occupying myself while I lay awake." Then with "I would think of a trout stream," Hemingway uses the iterative to mark the shift to dual focalization with Nick the soldier: "I would think of a trout stream" can be glossed as "I am thinking now about what I thought then." As the fishing memories continue, Hemingway adds a third perspective, that of Nick the young boy ("I always ate my lunch very slowly and watched the stream below me while I ate" [276]) so that we have a triple focalization: "I am thinking of myself as a soldier thinking of myself as a young boy." As Nick's monologue of metamemory continues, Hemingway occasionally has Nick the teller skip the perspective of Nick the soldier and go right to that of Nick the young boy. "Sometimes the stream ran through an open meadow, and in the dry grass I would catch grasshoppers . . . and toss them into the stream . . ." (277). This narration actually reinforces the connection between Nick the teller and Nick the soldier because it indicates that Nick the teller is re-enacting the remembering done by Nick the soldier. But Hemingway never leaves Nick the teller's focus on Nick the soldier for very long: "Sometimes I would fish four or five different streams in the night. . . . Some nights too I made up streams, and some of them were very exciting, and it was like being awake and dreaming." Hemingway again emphasizes the connections between Nick the teller and Nick the soldier when he returns to a single focalization and has Nick speak in the present tense of the long-term effect of those nights of remembering: "Some of those streams I still remember and think that I have fished in them, and they are confused with streams I really know" (277).

As a result of the single, dual, and triple focalization, Hemingway emphasizes the similarity between Nick's telling now and his remembering then. Nick the soldier's memories are a way to handle his fear of sleep, a way to keep his soul connected to his body after the trauma of his wounding. Furthermore, his memories of fishing are a way to reconstruct his identity after that trauma through both the care involved in the detailed memory and the rehearsal of the discipline of the sport. And of course, as we see most dramatically in "The Big Two-Hearted River," fishing itself has been a source of healing for Nick. The tight connection between Nick the teller and Nick the soldier implies that Nick the teller needs once again to connect with a disciplined, healing self, one who was able to cope with trauma. The fact that he seeks this connection before he tells of what happened the night "we" lay on the floor listening to the silk-worms eating reinforces the strength of Nick's approach/avoidance conflict. He wants and he doesn't want to revisit what happened that night.

This initial phase of the story is overtly lyric: Nick is not describing a sequence of events that occurred on any one fishing trip but rather evoking the mood and sensibility of his trips and the mood and sensibility of how he kept himself from sleeping. Within that lyric presentation, we see both Nick the young boy and Nick the soldier as not only devoted and disciplined but well-attuned to nature and sensitive to other creatures: salamanders are too "neat and agile and . . . lovely" in color to be used for bait, and he will not use crickets "because of the way they acted about the hook" (277). These descriptions make it relatively easy to adopt Nick's perspective even as he clearly remains a distinct character.

In the next movement of the monologue, Nick remembers the nights when he "could not fish," and so, as he lay "cold-awake," turned to praying for "all the people [he] had ever known" (277). As a soldier Nick turned from (remembering) fishing to (remembering) people, presumably when his fear became too great for the fishing memories to occupy his mind sufficiently. So, the turn to people for both Nick the teller and Nick the soldier is a turn to more compelling—and potentially more disturbing—subjects. Nick the teller betrays his awareness of the potential disturbance by initially keeping himself at a greater distance from Nick the soldier than he did during the fishing memories. That distance is established by his switching from first person to second, and from assertions ("I could not fish") to conditionals ("If you try to remember all the people you have ever known . . .") (277). Nevertheless, in the middle of this distanced perspective, in the space between the dashes of the longest sentence in the story, Hemingway again uses dual focalization to have Nick the teller's memories of the distant past merge with those of Nick the soldier:

> That took up a great amount of time, for if you try to remember all the people you have ever known, going back to the earliest thing you remember—which was, with me, the attic of the house where I was born and my mother and father's wedding cake in a tin box hanging from one of the rafters, and, in the attic, jars of snakes and other specimens that my father had collected as a boy and preserved in alcohol, the alcohol sunken in the jars so the backs of some of the snakes and specimens were

exposed and turned white—if you thought back that far, you remem-
bered a great many people. (277)

Richard Hovey and other psychoanalytic critics make much of the images of cake and snakes, and their links to male and female genitalia,
which in turn link the whitened snakes in alcohol to fears of castration.
I, too, acknowledge this psychoanalytic dimension of the passage, but I
want to call attention to other, less often noticed elements of it. First,
there is the switch from "*people* you have ever known" to "the earliest
*thing* you remember." The things, then, are standing in for the people:
the cake for Nick's mother and father together—ominously hanging
from the rafters as if the marriage it symbolizes has become suicidal—
and the snakes for Nick's father alone. The switch introduces a tension
in the story: why does Nick substitute these things for his parents, and
why does he isolate his father in memory here?

The second striking feature of the sentence, especially in comparison
to the fishing memories, is that Hemingway quickly shifts away from
dual focalization and returns to Nick the teller's more distanced perspective: after the dash, Nick's narration returns to the second-person
pronoun and conditional verb forms and maintains this way of telling for
the rest of the paragraph. Nick also shifts away from the memory of people and things to the memory of his praying for them, and to the effectiveness of the prayers in passing the time. At the same time, the specific
prayers, "Hail Mary" and "Our Father," are easily associated with images of Nick's parents.[8] The psychological dynamics of these shifts are
similar to those operating in the story's opening sentence: Nick the teller
approaches the act of remembering his parents, especially his father, and
then swerves away from the memory. Again, the situation seems to be
one of approach/avoidance.

After the successive focus on people, things, and prayer, Nick turns to
events; he also drops the second-person and the conditional: "I tried to
remember everything that had ever happened to me. . . . I found I could
only remember back to that attic in my grandfather's house. Then I
would start there and remember this way again, until I reached the war"
(277). It is as if Nick, having turned away from a painful memory, is now
readying himself for another attempt at facing it.

----

8. For more on this point, see Fournier's impressive close reading. For those interested
in the biographical connections, it is perhaps worth pointing out that Hemingway's
mother's name was Grace, so just as Nick's "Hail, Mary, full of grace" recalls Mrs. Adams
for him, it also recalls Grace Hall Hemingway for his creator.

## Mini-Narratives within the Monologue

The next section of the monologue contains two mini-narratives involving memories about burning, one with "no people" and one with "two people" (278). The first mini-narrative involves the burning of his father's childhood specimens that had been in the attic of his paternal grandfather's house, a burning associated with the family's moving from that house "to a new house designed and built by my mother" (277). The narrative with people involves his mother's burning his father's adult collection of knives, tools, and arrowheads. Both mini-narratives begin with the present-tense assertion "I remember," Hemingway's way of signaling that these memories are crucial for Nick the teller. But Hemingway still keeps the link between Nick the teller and Nick the soldier by ending each mini-narrative with a return to Nick the soldier's perspective. At the end of the first, Nick shifts back to past tense and to his memory of spending the nights praying: "I *could not remember* who burned the things even, and I would go on until I came to people and then stop and pray for them" (278, emphasis mine). Nick closes the second account with a similar return to the past, "I would pray for them both" (278).

The use of the narrative mode reinforces the sense that Nick is now articulating his most troubling memories. The detailed recounting in the second mini-narrative also marks it as the key moment in this first half of the story. As many readers have remarked, Nick finds the memory a very painful one because it shows his mother's smooth and effective power play over his father. She burns his father's possessions under the guise of "cleaning out the basement, dear" (278), and his father is incapable of doing anything about it. Nick's telling involves a dual focalization of his adult perspective and his child perspective: "I stayed outside on the grass with the two game-bags. After a while I took them in." As this matter of fact recounting indicates, despite the pain of the memory, Nick's voice retains its tone of calm acceptance. But in the summary sentence, Nick inadvertently reveals how the memory still wounds him, as Hemingway reconnects the memory of Nick the teller with that of Nick the soldier: "In remembering that, there were only two people, so I would pray for them both" (278). The emotive force here is very powerful: we sense Nick's pain, both as witnessing child and as remembering adult, precisely because he is uncharacteristically unreliable here as he tries to erase himself from the scene by underreporting it: despite what he says, we know that there were *three* people involved. Nevertheless, we find the effort to focus on his parents and to keep his voice gentle deeply poignant.

Given what Nick has witnessed, we can now understand why he first substituted things for his parents and why he isolated his father's things. We can also understand why in saying his prayers on "some nights . . . I could only get as far as 'On earth as it is in heaven' and then have to start all over and be absolutely unable to get past that" (278). The line of the Our Father just before "On earth as it is in heaven" is "Thy will be done." Nick's father has been too weak to assert his will, and in his home it is "our mother" whose will is done. Nick cannot get to the next line, "Give us this day our daily bread," because he cannot envision his father as the powerful provider. And given what he has seen happen to his father, we can infer that Nick the teller is still plagued by anxiety about being a husband, a father, a provider.

Hemingway's handling of Nick's remarks about the "Our Father" is an instructive example of his art of omission, one that has implications for our interpretive decision about Nick's role in the burnings. Hemingway leaves out everything about the prayer except the one phrase "On earth as it is in heaven," and he even has Nick say that "I could not remember my prayers" (278). Once we supply the lines before and after "on earth as it is in heaven," we can readily infer the rest of Nick's psychological situation and thus the reason he cannot get to the next line. Because Hemingway's technique requires our active involvement in coming to understand Nick's situation, we become more deeply involved with Nick on the emotive level as well.

With regard to the narrative of the second burning, Nina Fournier cites biographical and manuscript evidence to suggest that Hemingway is also employing his art of omission here. She sees Nick's reference to "only two people" as an act of denial and appeals to the evidence of the manuscripts that shows Hemingway having Mrs. Adams say that "Ernie" and then upon correction "Nick" helped her with the burning. Consequently, on this account, we need to infer from the "thing left out" that much of the pain in Nick's memory—and the reason why it is so difficult for him to return to it—is that he was complicit in his mother's emasculation of his father.

This reading has the advantage of adding yet another layer to Nick's already complicated psychological dynamics, but I'd suggest that here the thing left out actually falls away from the story. In my view, Hemingway deleted Mrs. Adams's line about Nick's helping not because he wanted us to infer Nick's complicity but because he wanted to keep Nick in the observer role, to make him not an actor but a bystander. Although it is impossible to prove a negative (in this case that Hemingway doesn't want readers to see Nick as having helped), I find it telling that Hemingway does not leave us a cue analogous to the one offered in "I could only get as far as 'On earth as it is in heaven.'" One likely place for Hemingway to have provided the cue is Nick's general description of his mother's penchant for cleaning. By employing a somewhat ambiguous description such as "my mother was always having us clean things out . . . . At the end of one of these cleanings my father returned," Hemingway could have subtly signaled Nick's involvement. But Hemingway has Nick assign explicit and exclusive agency to his mother here: "My mother was always cleaning things out. . . . One time . . . she made a good thorough cleaning out in the basement and burned everything that should not have been there" (278).

I also favor the view that Nick is a witness rather than a participant in the scene between his parents because that role fits with the logic of analogy on which the story is built. Just as the mortar shell hits Nick unawares, so too does his mother's emasculation of his father. With this point, we can move beyond the particulars of the scene to the larger patterns of the story.

In traditional narrative, the logic of story is the logic of connected events: one thing happens which leads to another thing and so on until the author finds some way to resolve the sequence. In lyric narrative, as I noted above, the logic of event gives way to the logic of revelation and exploration of a character's emotions and attitudes in a particular situation. The movement from beginning to end typically follows the movement of the speaker's thoughts, but these thoughts are not typically a review of his or her identity and situation. Instead, as the speaker's thoughts follow their apparently autonomous direction, the author finds a way to convey to the reader a rounded awareness of the speaker's character and situation. In "Now I Lay Me," Hemingway's strategy of revelation depends upon a set of analogies. Nick the teller is analogous to Nick the solider. Nick's physical wound is analogous to his psychic wound. Nick's parents, but especially his mother, who is the main actor in that psychic wounding, are analogous to the mortar shell that blew him up at night.

Given this analogical design, Hemingway's use of Nick's present-tense memory of the burnings provides the answer to the lingering question stemming from the first analogy: why is Nick the teller in much the same condition as Nick the soldier? As we see from the end of the first paragraph, Nick is no longer afraid of falling asleep in the dark. What is troubling him, instead, is the continuing effects of his psychic wounds, effects that make marriage and the intimacy with another human being it requires impossible. If Nick the soldier needs some way of coping with the fear engendered by his having been blown up at night, Nick the teller needs some way of coping with the aftermath of that experience as it reminds him of an earlier analogous experience, one that he finds himself repeatedly recalling when he has difficulty going to sleep. In other words, the war wound is so psychically damaging because it is the second traumatic experience Nick has been the victim of, and the lyric mode of "Now I Lay Me" captures the particular and enduring consequences of those traumatic experiences for Nick.[9] Even as this logic of analogy and trauma increases our sympathy for Nick, it also complicates the ethical component of our reading. I shall return to this point after tracing the movement of the second half of Nick's monologue.

## The Narrative of "That Night"

Having faced the most painful memory, Nick can then return to the "we" of the story's first sentence—himself and his orderly John—and to the events of "that night" when they lay on the floor and listened to the silk-worms eating. Though Nick's physical wound is analogous to his psychic wound, there is also a significant difference. Nick is not drawn to replay the scene of the bombing (note again how brief his description of the bombing is and that he stops his memories once he "reached the war" [277]). He is, however, drawn to think again and again about marriage. And now the approach/avoidance conflict becomes understandable. Nick's memories are painful enough to be capable of wounding him again, so naturally he wants to avoid them. Yet his desire for the intimacy that he seems unable to have motivates him to keep returning both to the scene between his parents and to the night he spent talking and thinking about marriage with John, a night that is clearly linked for him with both his physical and his psychic wounding. Furthermore, at this point, Hemingway's repeated references to the silk-worms also become intelligible. He is establishing another analogy, one between the instinctive and persistent eating of the silk-worms and the instinctive and

9. The introduction to Cathy Caruth's *Unclaimed Experience*, "The Wound and the Voice," offers an excellent discussion of the relation between trauma and telling.

persistent replay of memory in Nick the soldier and Nick the teller. That the outcome of the silk-worms' persistent activity is positive gives us some hope for the outcome of Nick's instinctive remembering.

After some expository information from Nick the teller's perspective about John, an Italian whom "they had taken for a soldier in nineteen fourteen when he came back [from Chicago] to visit his family," Nick narrates his interactions with John through his perspective at the time of the action. The opening sequence of their conversation shows a surprising side of Nick's attitudes. He is the one who asks John, "[Do] you want to talk a while?" (279), but then only a few lines later he is the one who implies that they should stop talking: "Don't you think we'll wake them up, talking?" (279). The sequence between these lines is worth a closer look.

> "Tell me about how you got married."
> "I told you that."
> "Was the letter you got Monday—from her?"
> "Sure. She writes me all the time. She's making good money with the place."
> "You'll have a nice place when you go back."
> "Sure. She runs it fine. She's making a lot of money."
> "Don't you think we'll wake them up, talking?" I asked. (279)

Nick's ambivalence about marriage comes through in the double messages he sends here: he asks—indeed, commands—John to talk about marriage, but when John's talk is so positive ("she writes me all the time"; "she's making a lot of money") he suggests that they stop talking. Nick the soldier's ambivalent feelings are still shared by Nick the teller. He is returning to his memory of this night as a way to revisit those feelings, but, as we shall see, the revisiting doesn't lead him to work through them to any new attitudes.

After failing to hear Nick's gentle suggestion that they stop talking, John takes the lead in the conversation, commenting on the other men and his difference from them (they "sleep like pigs" but he is "nervous"), making small talk about smoking and the silk-worms, and then asking Nick, "Is there something really the matter that you can't sleep?" Again the ensuing sequence is worth a close look:

> "I don't know, John. I got in pretty bad shape along early last spring and at night it bothers me."

"Just like I am," he said. "I shouldn't have gotten in this war. I'm too nervous."

"Maybe it will get better." (280)

John's question offers Nick the opportunity to open up, to risk an intimate communication. Nick certainly does not embrace John's invitation ("I don't know"), but he does not absolutely refuse it, since his rather general report ("I got in pretty bad shape along early last spring") leaves the door open for further questions about what exactly happened last spring. But John is too self-absorbed to go through that door, opting instead to claim his similarity to Nick ("Just like I am"). Nick lets the door close by trying to reassure John rather than trying to explain that it's not nervousness that keeps him awake at night.[10]

A little later, the pattern repeats and then the conversation returns to marriage. Nick asks John, "How are your kids?" John replies that "they're fine," that they're the reason he can be an orderly rather than on the front line and that "they're fine kids but I want a boy. Three girls and no boy. That's a hell of a note." Nick, who will probably never have a family, can't take any more, so once again he tries to end the conversation: "Why don't you try and go to sleep?" (280–81). John, ever so slow on the uptake, again misses the hint and instead turns the conversation back to Nick's inability to sleep:

> "No, I can't sleep now. I'm wide awake now, Signor Tenente. Say, I'm worried about you not sleeping though."
>
> "It'll be all right, John. . . ."

10. In light of the recent critical interest in Hemingway's complex attitudes toward and representations of sexuality (see especially the work by Moddelmog and Scholes and Comley), I think it is important to note that the situation here—two men lying near each other at night unable to sleep—invites us to look for homoerotic overtones in the interaction between Nick and John but that the interaction itself indicates a surprising lack of such overtones. Again, one cannot prove a negative, but Hemingway shows that the conversation moves not toward but away from intimacy and that Nick and John are both more preoccupied with their private worlds than they are concerned with connecting. Given this apparent lack of interest in connecting during that night, I am not inclined to see Nick's memory of it as a replay of his homoerotic desire for John.

In "A Simple Enquiry," by contrast, Hemingway uses the dialogue between the major and his orderly to explore the complications of same-sex desire in a situation where it is combined with power differentials and a strong prohibition. Part of the effectiveness of "A Simple Enquiry" depends on its leaving open the question of the orderly's desire (he claims he is not "corrupt," but the story closes with the major wondering "if he lied to me" [251, 252]). Similar questions about Nick's and John's desire seem closed off in "Now I Lay Me."

"You got to get all right. A man can't get along that don't sleep. Do
you worry about anything? You got anything on your mind?"

"No, John, I don't think so."

"You ought to get married, Signor Tenente. Then you wouldn't
worry."

"I don't know."

"You ought to get married. Why don't you pick out some nice Italian
girl with plenty of money? You could get any one you want. You're young
and you got good decorations and you look nice. You been wounded a
couple of times."

"I can't talk the language well enough."

"You talk it fine. To hell with talking the language. You don't have to
talk to them. Marry them." (281)

There are two important differences in this repetition of the earlier
pattern: Nick does not give John any opportunity to find out more about
what is really wrong with him, and John's self-absorption shows not in
his direct identification with Nick but in his confident recommendation
of marriage as the cure for Nick's ailments. John's idea of marriage clearly
does not include either equality or emotional intimacy; instead, it emphasizes material comfort ("marry the one with the most money," he
says a few lines later) and sexual release—I don't suppose I'm the only
reader who hears other verbs underneath "marry" in John's recommendation, "Marry them." After John articulates this view of marriage, Nick
more forcefully moves to end the conversation, twice saying ""let's sleep
a while," and finally succeeds.

In his current psychically wounded state, Nick is drawn back to this
conversation because it is both reassuring and alluring. Nick envies
John's satisfaction with his own family life, even as he can feel superior
to the view of marriage that John advocates. In short, the act of remembering functions for Nick as a (false) reassurance that he is right not to
get married (if marriage is to be as John describes it), even as it shows us
how much he desires a better marriage than the one his parents had or
one following John's model.

Having replayed the conversation, Nick is now ready to conclude his
metamemory. He initially stays with the perspective of Nick the soldier,
recalling that though John did go right back to sleep (no surprise there),
he "had a new thing to think about": "all the girls I had ever known and
what kind of wives they would make" (281). In effect, Nick the soldier
tried to imagine taking John's advice. In a short time, however, Nick lost

interest and went back to thinking about trout fishing because "the girls, after I had thought about them a few times, blurred and I could not call them into my mind and finally they all blurred and all became rather the same and I gave up thinking about them almost altogether" (282). In a sense, he too successfully adopted John's view: he could not retain his memories of individual women. Strikingly, with this recollection, un-like with his earlier ones, Nick the teller does not merge with Nick the soldier, does not ever comment in the present tense on this part of the memory or on any of the women he might have married. The implica-tion is that the possibility is not real enough for him to consider it. Con-sequently, the narration suddenly leaves the events of that particular night, and the perspective for the conclusion of the story returns to Nick the teller.

> But I kept on with my prayers and I prayed very often for John in the nights and his class was removed from active service before the October offensive. I was glad he was not there, because he would have been a great worry to me. He came to the hospital in Milan to see me several months after and was very disappointed that I had not yet married, and *I know he would feel very badly if he knew that, so far, I have never married.* He was going back to America and he was very certain about marriage and knew it would fix up everything. (282, emphasis mine)

The passage completes the monologue not only because it recounts the aftermath of "that night" but also because the penultimate sentence brings Nick and his audience into the present of the telling and states the main fact of Nick's existence. In addition, the passage calls attention one last time to the differences between John's and Nick's views of mar-riage. John is confident that the kind of marriage he recommends would fix everything for Nick, but Nick obviously lacks that confidence. Nick, of course, is right: John's view of marriage is too narrow, and, indeed, too sexist to provide the kind of intimacy Nick wants—and could most ben-efit from. Ironically, Nick's psychic wounds are such that they also keep him from what he most needs to heal. The analogical structure of the story indicates that, for Nick the teller, getting married would be much like falling asleep in the dark for Nick the soldier. Both events would leave him vulnerable to the sensation of getting "blown up at night," of having his soul leave his body. For someone who has experienced that twice already, putting himself in a situation where it could happen a third time is just too hard—even if he is also deeply desirous of that situation. How much easier to think about fishing.

Just as Nick the soldier's memories got him through the night but did not overcome his fear, so too Nick the teller's memories pass the time without enabling him to resolve anything. In this respect, the persistent activities of the silk-worms are clearly more productive than Nick's persistent memories. As it reaches its conclusion, "Now I Lay Me" completes its revelation of what it's like to be in Nick's situation, living with the consequences of his traumatic experiences, and it positions us to participate in the feelings associated with that situation. Nick's voice of gentle resignation actually enhances our sense of how deeply he is wounded, precisely because it cannot mask all his pain. Unlike John, we have access to what ails Nick—both in the past and in the present—and unlike John, we can see no easy cures.

## The Ethical Dimension

Although in the authorial audience we are not making judgments about Nick that influence our expectations, hopes, and desires for what is going to happen, we do engage with the implicit value structure underlying "Now I Lay Me." As character, Nick displays discipline, kindness, and sensitivity: the kindness and sensitivity are clear in Nick's attitudes as fisherman, in his prayers for others, especially his mother and father, and in his solicitousness toward John; the discipline is evident in his approach to fishing and in his careful orchestration of his memories during his summer. Indeed, through the discipline exerted upon his memories, Nick the soldier is able to get through that summer of sleepless nights, even as the discipline does not extend to the point that he represses his most painful memory. Furthermore, although the repeated returns to that memory do not lead to any resolution, or any healing of the scars it left, the story does not suggest that Nick's discipline should lead him to close off the memory and just move on. Instead, it asks us to enter into a sympathetic involvement with Nick's condition of needing to return to that memory. And of course, Nick's return to the memory is connected with his kindness and sensitivity: having exposed himself to the wound, Nick is nevertheless able to pray for the "two people" in the scene.

The value of discipline is also linked to the most famous of Hemingway's values, courage—also frequently called grace under pressure. What's important about the value in "Now I Lay Me" is not that Nick displays any great courage in any of the events he tells about: he is after all a victim in the two scenes of wounding he reports. The courage, instead, is to be found in the ethical position of the narrator in relation to his audience, in Nick's act of telling itself. It is found in the gentle resignation of his voice, his ability to report his painful memories in such a straightforward manner. Nick's telling reveals him to be a man well aware of his feelings, even if he does not understand them all; the telling also reveals him to be a narrator who respects both the intelligence and the sensitivity of his audience.

This last point takes us to the story's valuing of intimacy. We find that value not just in what's implied by Nick's rejection of John's view of marriage, and not just in our larger sense that Nick both needs and is afraid of intimacy. We find it above all in the lyric revelation of the monologue itself: Nick's telling offers an intimate sharing that he never achieves with John and that he seems afraid of trying to achieve with a woman. Again the narrative situation makes a difference in our ethical experience. Because Nick's audience is never characterized, we are more likely to feel ourselves the direct recipients of his intimate sharing. In this respect, the value of intimacy is at the bedrock of the story's ethics.

The implied Hemingway of course positions us to participate in these values of his character narrator, but his own connection to intimacy is slightly more nuanced. The biographical evidence and the manuscript evidence that shows him having written "Ernie" for "Nick" in one typescript of the story indicate that Hemingway is fictionalizing his own childhood. Such fictionalizing involves both a willingness to reveal his own painful memory and an effort to disguise that revelation and keep some distance from it. Such fictionalizing is also a means to invest the private and the personal with a more general significance.

Finally, the implied Hemingway, not Nick, is responsible for one element of the story's value structure, the analogy between the mortar shell and Nick's mother, that pulls in the opposite direction from the rest of that structure. Since the analogy is a crucial building block of the story's lyric structure, the pull is very strong indeed. To feel with Nick is also to assent to Hemingway's implicit assumptions that (some) women are castrating bitches and that their malevolent force is very much like that of a mortar shell exploding in a trench. Without the analogy, the logic of the story doesn't work. With the analogy, the ethical component of the story is compromised.

Since the analogy is so fundamental to the structure of the story, both cognitively and ethically, I see no way of mitigating its effect other than claiming that we ought not view Nick's mother as having any larger representative or thematic function—or indeed, any role in conveying Hemingway's attitudes toward women while he is writing "Now I Lay Me." This claim, however, is not very persuasive, precisely because of the nature of character in narrative, which, as I have noted in the introduction to this book and in earlier work, involves not just mimetic and synthetic but also thematic components. To argue that Hemingway's representation of Nick's mother does not convey Hemingway's negative attitude toward women is to argue that her character does not have a thematic function. But the logical extension of that argument is that Nick does not have any thematic function either. That conclusion seems to me to undermine much of the power of the story, since that power depends on our viewing Nick as one kind of traumatized young man. More generally, while it is certainly possible for a writer to create a character without a significant thematic function, the default position is for such creations to have thematic functions; consequently, the writer must do something to indicate the deviation from the default position. Although it is of course impossible to prove a negative, I find no evidence that Hemingway wants to block our normal move to thematize his characters.

Since this conclusion about the ethical deficiency of Hemingway's representation of Nick's mother will seem unsurprising and predictable to many, given Hemingway's still current reputation as a writer who, to put it kindly, consistently values his male over his female characters, I would like to place this conclusion within the larger context of Hemingway's representations of women. That context shows a considerable range of representations and ethical positions. For example, I have argued in *Reading People, Reading Plots,* that Hemingway's representation of Catherine Barkley in *A Farewell to Arms,* while not without its ethically problematic dimension, includes her possessing a knowledge of the world equal to the implied author's and far superior to Frederic Henry's. Furthermore, Hemingway constructs the progression so that Catherine is the primary positive influence in Frederic's slow maturation. In "Hills Like White Elephants," Hemingway's representation of the conflict between the pregnant Jig and her lover indicates that Jig is both emotionally and ethically more discerning than he, a difference that makes her situation all the more poignant. Finally, to take another example from the collection *Men without Women,* Hemingway builds "In Another

Country" on a comparison between two kinds of wounds, the unnamed protagonist's physical wound, and the major's emotional wound from having lost his wife. In showing the extremely powerful effect of the major's wound, Hemingway pays tribute to the wife, and, by the same logic of thematizing that operates in "Now I Lay Me" (which, by the way, Hemingway initially titled "In Another Country—Two"), pays tribute to the force of women's love. This brief survey also returns us to the utility of the concept of the implied author. The implied authors of the four narratives—"Now I Lay Me," *A Farewell to Arms*, "Hills Like White Elephants," and "In Another Country"—have different attitudes (sometimes overlapping, sometimes conflicting) toward women, though each implied author has a clearly recognizable attitude within each narrative.

To reiterate, the problem I find in "Now I Lay Me" is that the logic of the story is built on the analogy it makes between Nick's mother and the mortar shell. Given the importance of that analogy, my overall emotional engagement with Nick—and my relation to the implied Hemingway in this story—become much more ambivalent. Precisely because the lyric structure invites my participation in Nick's feelings and the implied author's values, I am now uncomfortable about sharing the intimacy the story offers. I find that I can neither repudiate nor fully celebrate the experience it offers. Instead, I retain my admiration for Hemingway's brilliant handling of the story's technique and become caught between my respect for much of its ethical basis and my instinctive rejection of this fundamental analogy. "Now I Lay Me" remains for me one of the most powerful and most disconcerting of Hemingway's brilliant corpus of short stories. On a sleepless night, I can imagine slowly rereading—or just recalling—it from beginning to end. As with Nick's memories of his parents, the fascination of the story remains no matter how many times I go over it. Indeed, as I do my version of Nick's repetitive memories, I find myself adapting Hemingway's title: "Now I Lay Me Down to Read."

## Rhetorical Theory and Reading across Identity Borders: "Doc's Story"

In an interview with James W. Coleman (1988) John Edgar Wideman makes two observations of special significance for a rhetorical theorist:

1. I try to invite the reader into the process of writing, into the mysteries, into the intricacies of how things are made and so, therefore, I

foreground the self-consciousness of the act of writing. And try to get
the reader to experience that, so that the reader is participating in the
creation of the fiction. . . .

    2. There's often a confusion between the person I am and what I do in
my work. If the work is serious it should stand on its own. It shouldn't
need the prop of personality behind it. Another side of this cult of personality is that it perpetuates our confusion about race. The author's
race or sex determines the kind of critical commentary that appears
about his or her work. This stupidity is institutionalized in traditional
literary studies. (TuSmith, 77, 79)

As I turn to "Doc's Story," I also want to address more fully than I yet
have the relation between my rhetorical approach and the issue of difference that has loomed so large in much recent theorizing in cultural
studies. Indeed, one commonplace of our poststructuralist, postmodern
critical age is that all knowledge is relative to analytical frameworks,
epistemological perspectives, subject positions. My partial agreement
with that commonplace can be found in the principle that our ethical
encounters with narrative will inevitably be affected by our individual,
flesh-and-blood ethical commitments and so it is not possible to claim
universality, or anything approaching it, for the ethical engagements I
offer here. But my agreement with the commonplace is only partial because I also believe that knowledge and understanding can be shared
across frameworks, perspectives, and positions, and, indeed, that the activities of writing literature and literary criticism actually depend on
such a belief. If we do not believe that we can connect across difference,
why bother writing or reading literature and why bother teaching or
writing about it? Of course one of the key elements of rhetorical theory,
the concept of an authorial audience that flesh-and-blood readers may
succeed in entering, rests on the possibility of connecting across difference, on being able to move from our individual subject positions to the
one constructed by the author for his or her ideal reader. In turning to
"Doc's Story," I want to foreground these issues of reading across difference not only because of the racial difference between me and Wideman
(I'm white; he's African American) but also because the story itself
touches upon these issues as it offers a lyric exploration of the longing
of an African American male protagonist for his departed white female
lover.[11]

    11. One important stream of work within reader-response criticism, to take just that
branch of theory most directly concerned with the activity of reading, has been on the importance of difference, with Flynn and Schweikart's 1986 collection *Gender and Reading*

In "Doc's Story," the narrative present is some unspecified winter in the post–Civil Rights era of American history; the protagonist, an unnamed adult African American male living in Philadelphia, has broken up with his white lover (also unnamed) the previous spring and finds himself in need of the right story "to get him through [the] long winter because she's gone and won't leave him alone" (146). That story, which he first heard on the basketball court in Regent Park the previous summer, is about Doc, one of the Regent Park regulars who was successful in the white world and who, after going blind, played a legendary game of basketball in which he "held his own" (152). Wideman presents the protagonist's remembering of the story as one in which the protagonist moves, for all intents and purposes, into the positions of narrating-I and narratee. After the protagonist rehearses Doc's story, the larger narrative continues in the present tense with the protagonist thinking of his departed lover, including the final moments she spent with him in Regent Park. During that meeting, something got in his eyes, temporarily blurring his vision, and "before he could blink her back into focus, before he could speak, she was gone" (153). The story concludes with the protagonist wondering whether his telling her Doc's story would have persuaded her that the two of them could make it as a couple: "*If a blind man could play basketball, surely we . . .* If he had known Doc's story, would it have saved them? He hears himself saying the words. The ball arches from Doc's fingertips, the miracle of it sinking. Would she have believed any of it?" (153).

The embedded story of Doc playing basketball has a high degree of narrativity at least until its end (and I will return to its ending), while the frame story has minimal narrativity: although it does allow us to infer something of the history of the protagonist and his lover, the focus is on the protagonist's current condition, his sense of loss and longing, emotions that the audience is asked to participate in rather than judge. Nevertheless, Wideman asks us to question the protagonist's understanding

---

being one exemplar of work in that mode. For that reason, I find it all the more significant that Schweikart's "Reading as Communicative Action" (2000) calls for more attention to the question of reading across differences.

One useful model that arises from work on difference itself would be to adapt Gloria Anzaldúa's notion of "mestiza consciousness" to the act of reading: all readers have multiple parts of their identities, some of them in paradoxical relation to each other, but in order to read well, each of us must be able to draw on those different parts of our identities at different times. I find such an adaptation useful for talking about flesh-and-blood readers, but in this book my focus is on how flesh-and-blood readers may find common ground in the authorial audience.

in a way that Hemingway never asks us to do in relation to Nick. Wideman gives us considerable evidence that the protagonist's vision of both himself and his lover is still occluded by his desire for reunion. Nevertheless, this inference increases the emotional power of the story, because it emphasizes the gap between desire and its effects, on the one hand, and the actual state of affairs between the lovers, on the other. This relationship between cognitive understanding (the protagonist does not understand his situation) and emotional response (his situation becomes even more poignant) raises questions about the role of readerly judgment in this lyric narrative. Is there a connection between the protagonist's failure to see and his ethical relation to the lover—or even to himself? Furthermore, even as I make this claim about the protagonist's ongoing occluded vision, I can't help but wonder, especially given the identity borders between me and Wideman, about my vision of his story: "What am I not seeing?" is a question that inevitably hangs over my responses and inferences. Consequently, after working through the rhetorical analysis, I will revisit my conclusions in light of this question.

Where "Now I Lay Me" is built on the analogies between Nick the teller and Nick the soldier and between Nick's psychic and his physical wounding, "Doc's Story" is built on the interrelations between the embedded narrative about Doc and the lyric frame story of the protagonist. A flesh-and-blood reader can enter the authorial audience—and, in Wideman's words, participate in the making of the fiction—by inferring the comparisons and contrasts Wideman builds into his construction of the two stories. In order to track the comparisons, contrasts, and corresponding inferences, it will be helpful to distinguish among three nested narratives: the innermost story about Doc, which I will call "Doc Plays Ball"; the middle-level story about the unnamed protagonist, which I will call "The Protagonist Longs"; and the synthesis of these two stories, "Doc's Story" itself.

The most salient feature of "Doc's Story" is "Doc Plays Ball." Not only is the embedded story given the most space in the text, it is also the main textual source for the inference that the racial identity of the author is shared by the implied author. For in "Doc Plays Ball," the implied Wideman draws on the rich tradition of African American oral narrative. The tale, whose exact "orbit was unpredictable" (147), clearly circulates among the basketball players and is clearly marked as community property. The narrator reports that the protagonist has heard the story three times and identifies the occasion when he first heard it: after the telling of a story by a character named Pooner about gang warfare in North

Philadelphia. Wideman manages the shift to the story itself in a way that points to the protagonist's retelling it to himself. At the end of Pooner's narration, Wideman writes, "One of the fellows says, I wonder what happened to old Doc. I always be thinking about Doc, wondering where the cat is, what he be doing now . . . " (148). Then, after this ellipsis, Wideman moves to the narration of "Doc Plays Ball": "Don't nobody know why Doc's eyes start to going bad" (148). The ellipsis has two functions: (1) it further separates the story from any individual character narrator; the "fellow" who wonders about Doc may or may not be the one who tells the tale; (2) it implies a time shift from the moment when the protagonist first heard the tale to the present of "The Protagonist Longs" when he tells it to himself. This implication is then reinforced by the free indirect discourse questions that come immediately with the return to the narrative present of "The Protagonist Longs": "If he had tried to tell her about Doc, would it have made a difference?" (152).

The version of "Doc Plays Ball" that the protagonist retells himself is a tour de force of oral narrative in Black English Vernacular, full of metaphor, hyperbole, and innovative syntax. The style contrasts with the more standard diction and syntax of "The Protagonist Longs," though here, too, Wideman proves to be a master stylist and the narrator has a distinctive voice; indeed, Wideman's stylistic virtuosity is itself worthy of a full analysis. There is no doubt that "Doc Plays Ball" resonates differently for someone who uses Black English Vernacular and is familiar with African American oral narrative traditions than it does for me. There is also no doubt that "Doc Plays Ball" resonates differently for someone like me who has played serious playground basketball than for readers who have not. Nevertheless, the functions of "Doc Plays Ball" within "Doc's Story" are equally available to these different kinds of readers: all of us can still enter the authorial audience, even if we do not all sit in the same row. Before I can analyze those functions, I need to turn to some salient features of "The Protagonist Longs."

Although lacking the surface brilliance of "Doc Plays Ball," "The Protagonist Longs" is a rich and innovative story in its own right. As a tale with greater lyricality than narrativity, its progression is governed not by a sequence of instability, complication, and resolution but rather by Wideman's decisions about the best way to reveal, piece by piece, the protagonist's situation of loss and longing. "The Protagonist Longs," however, is not in and of itself sufficient for a full revelation of the contours of that situation, and so Wideman sets up "Doc Plays Ball" as the most important element in that revelation. By itself, "The Protagonist

Longs" is a slight narrative and a minimal portrait: it does not give us a detailed picture of the main character, and it offers a sketchy narrative about the lovers' relationship, though they had been together for years.

One consequence of this relative slightness is that the few specifics offered take on considerable importance. We learn that the lovers were "opposites attracting" (152), that they'd picketed a Woolworth's "for two years" (145), that she was hardheaded and practical, and so regarded as "superstition" the supernatural stories about slavery he would sometimes tell (152). We also learn that at the end "it was clear to both of them that things weren't going to work out," but also that "more and more as the years went by, he'd wanted her with him, wanted them to be together" (152). These details and the scene in which she leaves while he is not looking lead to the inference that she acted on her hardheaded practicality. If it were up to him, they'd still be trying to work things out, however clear it was that they wouldn't succeed.

## Disclosure Functions and Narrator Functions

It is not until we examine the interaction between "Doc Plays Ball" and "The Protagonist Longs" and particularly until we try to understand why the protagonist turns to "Doc Plays Ball" for solace that we can get at the emotional core of the story. As in "Now I Lay Me," the disclosure functions and the narrator functions work well together sentence by sentence but the implied author offers significant disclosure beyond anything the narrators communicate. In "Now I Lay Me," that disclosure comes through the authorial audience recognizing the underlying logic of Nick's monologue by association; in "Doc's Story," that disclosure comes through the authorial audience recognizing the logic of the relation between the frame and the embedded tales. Furthermore, unlike the situation in "Now I Lay Me," where the authorial audience participates in Nick's emotional situation as character narrator, in "Doc's Story" the authorial audience does not enter into the character narrator's emotional situation during "Doc Plays Ball," but rather uses that narration as a means to discover that situation. While the protagonist provides the obvious connection between his situation and "Doc Plays Ball" in his imagined appeal to his lover, "*If a blind man could play basketball, surely we . . . ,*" Wideman invites the authorial audience to recognize other comparisons and contrasts that the protagonist himself recognizes either dimly or not at all. To put this point another way, the character narration is generally reliable on all three axes (I will note one exception below), and it does not involve any violation of what would be plausible telling along the narrator-narratee track. For example, the protagonist's narration of "Doc Plays Ball" to himself is not an instance of redundant telling, since that narration is well motivated by the tale's status as a source of both solace and worry for the protagonist.

The major inference we need to make is that Doc himself is a role model for the protagonist, someone able to achieve what the protagonist desires. First, Doc has succeeded in the white world, not just as an athlete but also as a man: he taught at the university, integrated a white neighborhood, and was neither deterred by the racism that accompanied these efforts nor forgetful of his roots. When he was teaching, "Doc used to laugh when white people asked him if he was in the Athletic Department"—"till the joke got old" (147). Doc's white neighbors didn't like his bringing his friends from the playground to his house to cool off with water from his hose, "didn't like a whole bunch of loud, sweaty, half-naked niggers backed up in their nice street" but "Doc didn't care. He was just out there like everybody else having a good time" (147).

For the protagonist, succeeding in the white world would mean being able to maintain his relationship with his lover without forgetting his own roots. The limited details of their relationship indicate that they are ultimately driven apart by disagreements and other differences stemming from their racial difference. Though the picketing of Woolworth's indicates their shared concern with civil rights, her regarding the stories of slavery days, "when Africans could fly, change themselves to cats and hummingbirds, when black hoodoo priests and conjure queens were feared by powerful whites" (152), as superstition indicates the cultural divide between them. For her the stories were interesting because of what they suggested about "the psychology, the pathology of the oppressed" (152). Since her hardheaded practicality is one sign that they were "opposites attracting," his recollection that she never listened expecting to "hear truth" indicates that he did find such truth in the stories (152). The protagonist recognizes their differences but desperately wants to believe that those differences could have been overcome. In Doc himself and in "Doc Plays Ball," he recognizes, at some level of his consciousness, not just a story about overcoming seemingly insurmountable obstacles but also a possibility of successfully negotiating the cultural divide between white and black.

Moreover, the protagonist is attracted to "Doc Plays Ball" because the story shows that Doc is able to take command of any situation, as exemplified in the sequence of actions that leads him to play despite his blindness. This sequence forms a very traditional narrative, one with initial instabilities, complications of those instabilities, and a resolution of them. The main instability is introduced when Doc, usually an unerring free throw shooter, misses badly on one summer Sunday, and a younger player, aptly nicknamed Sky, snatches the ball out of the air and dunks it for him. The instabilities are complicated by what happens next: the assembled players loudly applaud Sky's dunk, but Doc quiets everybody by saying, "Didn't ask for no help, Sky. Why'd you fuck with my shot, Sky? . . . You must think I'm some kind of chump . . . " (150–51). After keeping Sky standing uncomfortably before him long enough to make his point that Sky's action was an insult, however unintentional, Doc tells Sky to forget it and asks to play in the next game. Doc's position in the group is such that no one, especially not Leroy, the player picking the next team, will deny Doc's request. Once Leroy picks Doc for his team, resolution quickly follows: the game was a "helluva run. . . . Overtime and shit. . . . And Doc? Doc ain't been out on the court for a while but Doc is Doc, you know. Held his own" (152). In short, "Doc Plays Ball" is a narrative whose initial instability puts Doc on the verge of losing status in his community but whose resolution shows him substantially enhancing that status.

Indeed, the one instance of unreliability in the tale is very significant in underlining that Doc is even more powerful than the protagonist realizes. The unreliability is an instance of underreading, and it involves the narration of Doc's missed foul shot: "That Sunday something went wrong. Couldna been wind cause wasn't no wind. I was there. I know. Maybe Doc had playing on his mind. Couldn't help have playing on his mind cause it was one those days wasn't nothing better to do in the world than play. Whatever it was, soon as the ball left his hands, you could see Doc was missing, missing real bad" (150). Since the protagonist has moved into the role of the "I," we know that he wasn't literally there, but the very fact that he simply rehearses this part of the narration indicates that he doesn't perceive what Wideman wants his audience to: Doc missed on purpose in order to command the attention of all the players and to put Leroy in the situation of having to choose him for the next game. In short, Doc manipulated the whole situation so that he could play on this Sunday that was "one them good days when it's hot and everybody's juices is high and you feel you could play till next week" (149).[12]

12. This account of Doc's motives differs from that offered by Keith Byerman, who sees Doc's response to Sky as indicating "a psychological struggle with his new identity as a blind man" (41).

The protagonist is drawn to Doc because he desires a similar kind of command in his life, a command that he clearly lacked in the final meeting with his lover. "They were walking in Regent Park and dusk had turned the tree trunks black. . . . Perhaps he had listened too intently for his own voice to fill the emptiness. When he turned back to her, his eyes were glazed, stinging. Grit, chemicals, whatever it was coloring, poisoning the sky, blurred his vision. Before he could blink her into focus, before he could speak, she was gone" (152). This implicit contrast with Doc is hard to miss. Doc's blindness is something that he overcomes or even uses to his advantage. The protagonist's blindness, though momentary, puts him at such a disadvantage that his lover leaves even before he realizes it.

Thus, the protagonist turns to "Doc Plays Ball" because it gives him hope not only for the relationship but also for himself—not to be Doc exactly but to have Doc's abilities. But Doc's story also "bothered him most" (147) because he worries that he lacks those abilities. In testing my initial inference that the protagonist's worries are well founded and his hopes unrealistic, I find considerable confirming evidence. It is significant, first, that the protagonist reacts to losing his lover not by seeking ways to bridge the cultural divide between them but by moving further into a subculture distinct from hers: the Regent Park playground is not just an African American space, it is an African American male space. The basketball and the stories—and the protagonist's becoming the teller of "Doc Plays Ball"—emphasize the point. The protagonist remembers that, on the occasion when he first heard "Doc Plays Ball," it was immediately preceded by "the one about gang warring in North Philly" in which one gang "lynched this dude they caught on their turf. Hung him up on the goddamn poles behind the backboard" where the next morning "little kids" found him "with his tongue all black and shit down his legs" (148). Furthermore, "Doc Plays Ball" is very much a story of the African American male urban subculture: it is about a male hero, whose heroism consists of individual achievements, especially, though not exclusively, athletic ones.

Second, the protagonist seems unable to understand something that Wideman invites his audience to see: the difference between his own response to "Doc Plays Ball" and the likely response of his lover. For him, it is literal truth, verified by an eyewitness and, thus, something he sees in his mind's eye as he retells it: "I was there. I know" (150). For her, we infer, especially given the unreliability surrounding those phrases, it would be an urban legend, no more truthful than the stories about

Africans who could fly. Furthermore, the protagonist's denial, the occluded vision that prevents him from seeing how the woman would respond to the story, also suggests ways in which he is not like Doc. "Doc
Plays Ball," indeed, Doc's whole life, is about a man overcoming obstacles, not about a man denying them.

At this point, we are ready to return to the question of how readerly
judgment works in "Doc's Story," especially in relation to Doc and to
the protagonist. Like the protagonist—and the teller of "Doc Plays
Ball"—we judge Doc very positively, admire his abilities, want him to
succeed, and take some satisfaction in his success. But we also always
see him from the outside, filtered through the perspective of the protagonist. Indeed, because we see his story through this filter, we subordinate our responses to Doc to our responses to the protagonist. And those
responses are more complicated, since the protagonist is less fully characterized than Doc, since the protagonist does not act in any ways that
alter his initial situation, and since we nevertheless see his vision of his
situation as inadequate. Perhaps the most significant element of our
complicated reaction is that we do not see any ethical consequence to
his limited vision: that is, the protagonist's failure to see his situation
clearly is not a sign of an ethical deficiency but instead a sign of the depth
of his heartache and his desire. Furthermore, Wideman's limited characterization of the protagonist in combination with the lyric structure of
the narrative and the technique of focalizing most of "The Protagonist
Longs" through the protagonist's consciousness allows us ultimately to
see him not from the outside but from the inside. Rather than judging
him, we participate in his feelings of loss and longing. The power of the
ending, then, arises through the synthesis of our clearer vision of the protagonist's situation and our capacity to feel with him. In sum, Wideman
has invited us to participate in completing the fiction by recognizing his
innovative narrative structure, one that harnesses the powerful vernacular narrative of "Doc Plays Ball" to the lyric revelation of "The Protagonist Longs" and that also uses our understanding of the protagonist's
limited vision to deepen the poignancy of his heartache and his longing.

## Reexamining the Design, Reading Wideman's Ethics
of Reading

What, then, about the possible limits of my vision as I try to move
from my responses as flesh-and-blood reader to an understanding of

Wideman's invitations to his audience? Although of course one cannot finally see what one is unable to see, I find that some elements of the story lead me to reconsider some of my claims. "Doc's Story" is, in part, a narrative about ways of reading: the lover has one way of reading the protagonist's stories of the supernatural and he has another; the protagonist has one way of reading "Doc Plays Ball," and Wideman guides his audience to have another. It makes sense to compare Wideman's representations of different ways of reading with the kind of reading I have offered to this point and to consider the implicit ethics of each by considering the ethical position the implied Wideman takes toward each. So far, that reading is very close to the lover's mode: with hardheaded practicality, I have concluded that the answers to the protagonist's final questions are negative. This realization gives me pause, because I infer that Wideman wants us to question the lover's mode of reading. She is an exemplar of the nonrhetorical reader, one who does not bother to enter the authorial audience, preferring instead (however unreflectively) to impose her own cultural assumptions on another culture's narratives. By reading Wideman's story with hardheaded practicality—and attributing that reading to the authorial audience—am I doing the same ethically questionable thing? One way to answer is to start with another question: does Wideman want his audience to regard "Doc Plays Ball" as a true story or an urban legend? In other words, does Wideman invite us to adopt the protagonist's view of the story, or does he invite us to adopt his lover's likely view, or some third view—and if a third view, what is it?

The flesh-and-blood Wideman, who himself was an all–Ivy League basketball player at the University of Pennsylvania and has recently published a book about his life-long association with the game called *Hoop Roots*, knows that playing basketball with any skill without being able to see is impossible, very much the stuff of urban legend. Passing, catching, shooting, cutting, rebounding: a blind man, no matter how gifted and how capable of compensating for loss of sight with his other senses, simply couldn't do these things well enough to "hold his own" in a serious playground game. Yet the implied Wideman constructs many elements of the text to make "Doc Plays Ball" a plausible story up until the resolution, including having the protagonist remember what he knows about Doc beyond "Doc Plays Ball." The information about Doc's success in the white world is authoritative. "Doc Plays Ball" itself has a plausible starting point because a formerly skilled player who loses his vision could become an accurate free throw shooter. And the story is itself so loaded with specific, concrete details—not just the names of players such as Sky and Leroy but also the ways in which Doc uses his knowledge of the players to take command of the situation—that it sounds at least as much like history as like legend. Yet there are also some important elements that suggest it is legend. As noted above, it is not a story that is owned by—or closely associated with—an individual teller but rather one that belongs to and circulates in the whole community. In addition, the resolution quickly becomes anticlimactic as the story loses its specificity, offering only very sketchy details of the game itself: Leroy is the only other player identified, there is no testimony about any particular moves Doc makes, and no definitive report on which team won. It's as if Wideman wants us to focus on everything up until the resolution as the literal truth and recognize the resolution as entering the realm of legend.

More generally, we can infer that Wideman wants his audience to understand the story not as literally true but as capturing some truth about both Doc and the community that is so invested in his story. Doc is an extraordinary individual whose achievements in his subculture and in the white world are not just tellable but significant because they offer those who share his story hope and even inspiration. Furthermore, the community is invested in the story because they need it to counter the truths in stories such as the one Pooner tells about gang wars.

Significantly, this answer moves the authorial audience away from simple hardheaded practicality and its questionable ethics without fully deviating from the reading strategy of the white woman: it interprets "Doc Plays Ball" as revealing something about the psychology—though not the "pathology" (and there is the ethical difference)—of the community in which the story circulates. This movement, along with the inference that the story is a legend with some basis in literal truth, puts new emphasis on the protagonist's imagined address to his lover at their final meeting in Regent Park, the one during which his vision had blurred temporarily:

> If he'd known Doc's story he would have said: *There's still a chance. There's always a chance. I mean this guy, Doc. Christ. He was stone blind. But he got out on the court and played. Over there. Right over there. On that very court across the hollow from us. It happened. I've talked to people about it many times. If Doc could do that, then anything's possible. We're possible . . .*
> *If a blind man could play basketball, surely we . . .* (153)

This passage opens up another set of answers to the protagonist's final question, "Would she have believed any of it?" The difference between "Doc Plays Ball" and the supernatural tales may be sufficient for the woman to believe *some* of it—and also to hear behind the story and the protagonist's eagerness to have her believe it the truth of the protagonist's love and of his desire for them to be together. Given that she stayed in the relationship for so many years, we can readily infer that she, too, has a certain desire for it to work, and that she might find some hope in the protagonist's telling of this story. In other words, these inferences shake the confidence with which I have answered "no" to the protagonist's questions without moving me toward a confident "yes." Instead, these inferences render the story's final questions open not just for the protagonist but also for the authorial audience.

Understanding the final questions as genuinely open has several significant consequences. First and most evidently, this understanding injects an element of hope into the ending, even as the depth of the protagonist's longing—and our empathy with it—remains unchanged. Second, this understanding alters our sense of the protagonist's flawed vision: although he is too invested in the possibility that "Doc Plays Ball" would have made a difference to recognize why it might not, that investment itself now seems less rooted in denial. Third, this understanding alters our inferences about Wideman's treatment of reading across differences. My initial conclusions make the content of the story run somewhat counter to Wideman's own invitation to his readers: in that account, Wideman represents an unbridgeable gap across the racial and gender differences of the protagonist and his lover, even as Wideman asks those readers who are not male and African American to bridge whatever gaps there may be between him and them. I do not mean to suggest that this initial reading uncovers a flawed logic in Wideman's construction or that it shows that the story is at cross-purposes with itself: certainly one could imagine a successful story written along these lines. But the revised view invites us to thematize questions of reading across difference both on the level of the protagonist's relation with his lover and on that of Wideman's relation to his audience. In each case, the story suggests, we need to remain conscious of the gaps, but in each case, there is hope, though not certainty, that the gaps can be bridged. In that way the story both locates and exemplifies this ethical stance toward the question of reading across differences.

In this connection, it is worth emphasizing that even if the lover were to have her faith in their future restored by "Doc Plays Ball," her reading of that story would still be different from the protagonist's. He would believe "It happened" (153), and she would believe that it ultimately conveys a figurative rather than literal truth. The differences between the lovers would remain, and those differences would continue to be a source of both attraction and contention. Similarly, this revised understanding of Wideman's communication does not erase all difference between him and his audience, and it does not stop me from continuing to wonder, "What am I not seeing?" At the same time, however, it does make me more optimistic that both Wideman and I are right to believe that communication across differences is possible.

Finally, this new understanding sheds further light on the relation between the narrative form of "Doc Plays Ball" and the lyric mode of "The Protagonist Longs" and, indeed, of "Doc's Story" itself as a lyric narrative. As noted above, one of the innovative features of "Doc's Story" is the way it subordinates the embedded narrative to the larger lyric structure. Understanding that subordination as one which leads to the conclusion that the protagonist's final questions are genuinely open helps us recognize the effectiveness of Wideman's technique. The clear narrative resolution of "Doc Plays Ball" sets up the openness of "Doc's Story"'s lyric narrative structure. And that openness makes the lyric component itself more effective than if there were a clear answer, positive or negative, to the protagonist's questions. Because the authorial audience sees both possibilities, we move closer to the protagonist as we appreciate and participate in his sense of loss and longing. Once again, then, we see intersection of ethics and technique: moving toward the more ethically sound position on how to read deepens the emotional power of the story.

## Other Dimension of Ethical Response

As with any narrative, our ethical engagements with "Doc's Story" also depend on the story's underlying value structure. And there are two primary sets of values that Wideman's communication both relies upon and endorses, the first having to do with the story's characters and events and Wideman's treatment of them, and the second having to do with the story's self-reflexiveness—its thematizing of its own form. The first set includes the following: a community provides comfort in times of trouble; difficult obstacles can be overcome; those who are able to overcome such obstacles not only deserve respect but rightfully inspire others;

communication, even love, across racial barriers is one such obstacle. The second set includes a belief in the power of narrative, a similar faith in the power of lyric empathy, and an overriding commitment to communication across racial borders. At the same time, Wideman's endorsement of the values concerned with communication across borders is tempered by a realization of its difficulty. Although I can imagine some flesh-and-blood readers objecting to elements of this value structure—some, for example, might find it self-indulgent for a fiction writer to proclaim the power of narrative—for my own part, I find participating in the story's creation to be both ethically challenging and ethically rewarding. I am not only willingly persuaded but also greatly encouraged by Wideman's vision of possibility even as I'm deeply moved by the protagonist's plight.

"The ball arches from Doc's fingertips, the miracle of it sinking." The meanings flow from author to audience, writer to reader and then back again, the miracle of literary communication. Can you share our belief in it?

# Epilogue

*Serial Narration, Observer Narration, and Mask Narration*

Since the number of narratives with character narrators is almost beyond counting, I cannot claim to have offered a comprehensive account of variations in the technique and of its ethical consequences. Indeed, one of the lessons of this book is that, although technique and ethics are interdependent, the nature of that interdependence will vary from one narrative to the next, because the ethics of reading involves so many interacting positions. Before I conclude, however, I would like to comment briefly on how the principles developed in the previous chapters can help us understand the rhetorical dynamics of three prominent varieties of character narration that I have not given much, or any, attention to here. The three are what I call *serial narration,* the implied author's use of more than one character narrator to tell the tale; *observer narration,* the implied author's use of a character narrator other than the protagonist to tell the tale; and *mask narration,* the implied author's use of the character narrator to express his or her own thoughts and beliefs.

With the exception of *Lolita,* which includes John Ray Jr. as well as Humbert Humbert, and "Doc's Story," which includes both the noncharacter narrator and the protagonist narrator, the narratives I've examined have had a single character narrator. But of course from the inception of the epistolary novel, authors have made effective use of a series of character narrators within a single narrative. The most important consequence of serial narration is one we have seen in "Doc's Story": the disclosure functions work not only in relation to the narrator functions of each narrator but also across the serial narration; disclosure, in other words, arises both within individual narrations and as a result of their interaction. The second significant consequence of serial narration is that it allows the author to work with clearly demarcated perspectives, and, thus, potentially with the whole range of techniques we have seen in this book. In *As I Lay Dying*, for example, William Faulkner employs a serial narration that multiplies perspectives, as he gives us monologues from every member of the Bundren family, from some of their neighbors, and from characters the family meets on their journey to Jefferson with Addie's coffin. Faulkner also gives a very telling illustration of how disclosure functions trump narrator functions: Addie's narration from beyond the grave is not motivated by any unfinished business she has with the (uncharacterized) narratee but rather by Faulkner's need to include her perspective on Anse, their children, and the current quest to bury her. The individual monologues are often memorable in themselves, especially Darl's clairvoyant reporting of the moment of Addie's death, Cash's restricted narration in his listing of specifications for Addie's coffin, and Vardaman's provocative misreading, "My mother is a fish." But perhaps even more impressive than any of Faulkner's brilliant individual uses of reliable, unreliable, and restricted narration is his ability to use the serial narration to communicate both how radically different each Bundren's experience of the journey is and how those differences define the larger family experience of the journey through flood and fire to bury Addie's body in Jefferson.

With the exception of "Doc's Story," the narratives I have examined here all employ a character narrator who is also a protagonist, and so I want to turn now to consider what I call observer narration, that is, narration by a character narrator who is not a protagonist. These observers can play a wide variety of roles in the narrative action, ranging from that of protagonist's sidekick (e.g., Arthur Conan Doyle's Watson) to peripheral agent (e.g., Ring Lardner's Whitey in "Haircut"), from that of a participant who affects and is affected by the action (e.g., Herman Melville's Ishmael, F. Scott Fitzgerald's Nick Carraway) to that of a reporter who is affected by but does not affect the actions of the main characters (the unnamed character narrator of Alice McDermott's *Charming Billy*; or, in a particularly interesting recent variation, Alice Sebold's Susie Salmon in *The Lovely Bones*, who narrates beyond the grave: for the most part, she tells the story of the effect of her death on her family and friends, though Sebold allows her to influence the action at a few key points and generates a few minor instabilities about Susie's progress in the afterlife). It is even possible for the observer to be someone who neither affects nor is affected by the main action beyond being moved to pass on the tale (some character narrators who give way to other narrators such as John Ray Jr. fit this pattern; a character narrator who discovers a story about the past and wants to pass it on would be another example). The implied author of observer narration can of course employ any and all of the techniques I have examined in this book, but there are two potentialities of observer narration that deserve special attention.

1. An observer narrator's quest for the story that he or she tells can itself become part of the represented action, something that significantly affects the authorial audience's response to the narrative. In Joseph Conrad's *Lord Jim*, for example, Marlow's quest to comprehend Jim and his actions on the *Patna* and in Patsun is part and parcel of Marlow's recounting Jim's story. That Marlow's quest is ultimately unsuccessful ("he passes away under a cloud, inscrutable at heart" [253], Marlow says at the end) nevertheless increases the tragic effects of the novel, and, indeed, without that quest, Jim would be only a character who had failed on the *Patna* and failed again in Patusan.

2. Implied authors are more likely to have disclosure functions egregiously override narrator functions when employing observer narration. I have written elsewhere (*Narrative as Rhetoric*) about Fitzgerald's granting Nick the powers of an authoritative noncharacter narrator to narrate the scene in Michaelis's garage the night after Myrtle Wilson was killed. Melville's expansive use of Ishmael is notorious, and, indeed, worthy of a book-length study in itself. McDermott's character narrator at times functions only as an authoritative narrator, but then at others her perspective as the daughter of the eponymous Billy's best friend becomes crucial to the rhetorical dynamics of the novel. The list of examples could go on, but the more pressing issue is why observer narration lends itself to this wide divergence between disclosure functions and narrator functions more readily than character narration by a protagonist.

The explanation, I believe, resides in the principle underlying the examples of disclosure functions overriding narrator functions we have already seen: the overriding increases the rhetorical power of the narrative. With observer narration our interest ultimately is in the characters other than the character narrator—it's Ahab, Gatsby, and charming Billy rather than Ishmael, Nick, or McDermott's narrator that are at the center of their respective narratives—and we will license the implied author to take liberties with the disclosure functions, provided that those liberties result in a more satisfying reading experience for us, one that is more aesthetically and ethically challenging and rewarding. In these cases, the implied authors want—or, better, need—to take advantage both of the effects that accrue to the use of a character narrator and of those that accrue to the use of an unrestricted, reliable noncharacter narrator, especially the delivery of a broad range of information with authority, efficiency, and the privilege of offering inside views of other characters. Without such flexibility in the narration, their larger purposes cannot be achieved. Readers grant that flexibility because they benefit from engaging with the narratives. Beyond this general principle, I do not believe we can develop rules that govern when disclosure functions can and cannot override narrator functions. But it is fair to say that the technique involves high risks as well as high rewards, because it violates other conventions of narration, particularly the dictum that once an author chooses to use character narration, she should respect the limitations of that character's knowledge and perceptions. Consequently, if the overriding does not produce a substantial addition to the narrative, it will come across as an awkward contrivance at best and a sign of the author's utter ineptitude at worst.

Because character narration is an art of indirection, I have to this point emphasized the indirect communications it makes possible. But what happens when an author wants to use character narration for more direct communication with the audience? What happens, in other words, when the author wants to have the character narrator be an efficient and effective medium for conveying his or her own thoughts and beliefs without having the disclosure functions egregiously trump the narrator functions? Obviously reliable unrestricted narration is the technique that requires the least indirection, since it entails the implied author's endorsement of the character narrator's reports, interpretations, and evaluations. Furthermore, in nonfiction reliable unrestricted narration is eminently well suited to direct communication because the technique means that disclosure functions and narrator functions completely coincide; or to put it another way, in nonfiction the technique means that the implied author and the narrator speak with one voice and the authorial audience and the narratee listen with the same ear. I would venture to say that it is the fit between this technique and the purposes of much nonfiction that lies behind advice to memoirists about the importance of reliability and present-tense reflection.

We can return to the conclusion of section 16 of *The Kiss* for a helpful illustration of such direct disclosure: "I left the space [on my mother's headstone] below the dates empty, because on that afternoon the only word that I could imagine carved in that blank struck me as one I didn't deserve to use, rather than the truth that it was. Is." And then the last paragraph of the section is the single word "Beloved" (204). The phrase "on that afternoon" signals that Harrison is employing her current perspective on Kathryn as she interprets both that past and this present. With that perspective, Harrison claims that the truth of both past and present is reflected in the word she left off the headstone and inserted in the dedication to her book. The direct communication works smoothly, efficiently, and effectively.

With fictional narration, the situation is more rhetorically challenging, because the "I" of the character narration is neither the author's current nor former self, but someone distinct from the author. Consequently, even in reliable unrestricted narration, the implied author is not speaking in his or her own voice, and, if the narration abruptly departs from the previously established vision and voice of the character narrator, we are likely to find it rhetorically ineffective and ethically suspect. For these reasons, the implied author who wants to use the art of indirection for a more direct communication needs to find a way to have the character narrator tell not just reliably but also plausibly. Such telling, which I call *mask narration*, depends upon the implied author being able to draw upon the character narrator's experiences as the ground for the utterance, and in that way not only make the direct communication plausible but also make it even more forceful.[1] Consider the following two passages, the first from Frederic Henry's narration in the middle of Ernest Hemingway's *Farewell to Arms* and the second from Philip Marlowe's narration at the very end of Raymond Chandler's *Big Sleep*.

> I was always embarrassed by the words sacred, glorious, and sacrifice and the expression in vain. We had heard them, sometimes standing in the rain almost out of earshot, so that only the shouted words came through, and had read them, on proclamations that were slapped up by billposters over other proclamations, now for a long time, and I had seen nothing sacred, and the things that were glorious had no glory and the sacrifices were like the stockyards at Chicago if nothing was done with the meat except to bury it. There were many words that you could not

---

1. My development of these ideas about mask narration is indebted to Ralph Rader's discussion of the "mask lyric" in "The Dramatic Monologue and Related Forms." I have previously introduced the concept in chapter 5 of *Narrative as Rhetoric*; my main example there is the conclusion of *The Great Gatsby*, where Fitzgerald uses Nick Carraway to present his own reflections about the new world, the green light on Daisy's dock, Gatsby's capacity for wonder, and all of us beating on against the current.

stand to hear and finally only the names of places had dignity. Certain numbers were the same way and certain dates and these with the names of the places were all you could say and have them mean anything. Abstract words such as glory, honor, courage, or hallow were obscene beside the concrete names of villages, the numbers of roads, the names of rivers, the numbers of regiments and the dates. (184–85)

What did it matter where you lay once you were dead? In a dirty sump or in a marble tower on top of a high hill? You were dead, you were sleeping the big sleep, you were not bothered by things like that. Oil and water were the same as wind and air to you. You just slept the big sleep, not caring about the nastiness of how you died or where you fell. Me, I was part of the nastiness now. (139)

In these passages, Hemingway and Chandler use their respective character narrators to voice their own beliefs. Both authors, I daresay, would be comfortable with the idea of having these passages lifted from their novelistic contexts and put on posters attributing the thoughts to them rather than to their character narrators.[2] But the mask narration works somewhat differently in each case, and those differences help explain why the passage from *A Farewell to Arms* is more likely to be lifted from its context and why the passage from *The Big Sleep* is more rhetorically effective in context. First, Frederic Henry's commentary is far less tied to the specific events that he has been telling us about than Marlowe's. Hemingway places the passage shortly after Frederic returns to the front from his long convalescence in Milan where he has fallen in love with Catherine Barkley. Although Frederic has learned something from Catherine's gentleness and from her knowledge of the world and is beginning to grow beyond the callowness he exhibits early in the narrative, he has not previously expressed sentiments resembling the ones here. If Hemingway wants to use the passage not only as mask narration but also as a sign of Frederic's increasing maturity, he is still asking his audience to make a considerable leap. That Frederic uses the present tense and says "always" contributes to the problem: the Frederic who without irony says the "war was no more dangerous to me myself than war in the movies" (37) is markedly different from this Frederic who says "the

2. These passages are what Susan S. Lanser ("Beholder") calls "attached discourse," that is, discourse in which the primary "I" of the text is identified with the author. In "detached discourse," by contrast, the primary "I" of the text is clearly different from the author. Lanser's distinction perceptively cuts across the fiction/nonfiction divide.

things that were glorious had no glory and the sacrifices were like the stockyards at Chicago if nothing was done with the meat except to bury it." Furthermore, although Hemingway does motivate the narration through Frederic's conversation with the Italian patriot Gino, who says, "We won't talk about losing. . . . What has been done this summer cannot have been done in vain" (184), the experiences that Frederic refers to—listening to the words shouted in the rain; reading them on proclamations—have not been dramatized in his narrative. For all these reasons, Hemingway barely keeps Frederic's mask on throughout the passage, and it's hard to avoid concluding that the passage is a set piece that Hemingway would use the first chance he got. Be that as it may, because the mask is on so loosely, there's no problem with extracting the passage from the novel and presenting it as Hemingway's rather than Frederic's.

Chandler clues his audience to the mask narration by having Marlowe employ the title phrase twice (by convention, we understand the title as conferred by the implied author, not the narrator), and by having Marlowe use the impersonal "you" in the beginning of the passage. But the movement of the passage from the initial generalizations about the indifference of those who are sleeping the big sleep to Marlowe's admission that he is part of the nastiness keeps the mask firmly in place. Although Chandler is using Marlowe to express his own thoughts about the difference between the living and the dead, Chandler connects those thoughts so tightly to Marlowe's situation that they actually set up Marlowe's remarkably self-knowing comment: "Me, I was part of the nastiness now." As a result, the mask narration not only grows organically out of Marlowe's situation but its sentiments gain force because they have Marlowe's experience with the Sternwoods, with Eddie Mars, indeed, with the entire previous narrative, behind them. Chandler also adds to the effectiveness of the mask narration by, in effect, turning the volume down on it. Rather than end the novel with this sententious passage (and its extension into Marlowe's hope that the nastiness would not reach General Sternwood), he moves to a final three sentences of reliable narration. In these sentences, Marlowe the character, who is clearly distinct from Chandler, is prominent: "On the way downtown I stopped at a bar and had a couple of double scotches. They didn't do me any good. All they did was make me think of Silver-wig and I never saw her again" (139).

This comparison of Hemingway and Chandler takes us back, finally and appropriately, to the issue of the relation between disclosure functions and narrator functions, and particularly the question of why Hemingway's less elegant use of the character narrator's mask is more of a rhetorical problem than the liberties taken with observer narration by authors such as Melville, Fitzgerald, and McDermott. The answer involves the difference in the authorial audience's relation to vision and to voice. Audiences are more likely to overlook or make allowances for liberties taken with vision because we are so dependent on narrators for their visions of narrative worlds. It is not just that without those visions we have no access to those worlds, but also that we typically desire the greater access accompanying visions that bring greater disclosure. On the other hand, we are less likely to grant liberties with voice in mask narration because the technique depends on the thoughts and beliefs coming from the narrator's experience as character, and thus it depends on the connection between voice and character. If the implied author seems to be speaking without the mask, the narration will seem a clumsy contrivance.

In the preface to this book I commented upon the interconnections between telling and living: our living prompts us to tell, and our telling affects how we go on living. Since one of the activities of living is reading the tellings of others, we might fancifully describe *Living to Tell about It* as an indirect telling, through that odd form of observer narration we call rhetorical criticism, of my activity as a reader of "Barbie-Q," *The Remains of the Day, Angela's Ashes, 'Tis, Lolita, The Kiss,* "Now I Lay Me," and "Doc's Story." Its purpose has been to enhance the living of other readers by giving them greater access to the pleasures and the problems, the challenges and rewards, of stories told by those who are participants in their actions. In the living that preceded and accompanied my telling, I have spent many complicated hours—some frustrating and disappointing but more of them rich and rewarding—with Cisneros's young girl, Stevens, Frankie McCourt, Humbert Humbert, Kathryn Harrison, Nick Adams, and Wideman's unnamed protagonist, and I hope that, whatever the faults of my telling, it will encourage you to spend your own complicated hours with these and other character narrators. Our rhetorical exchanges with such tellers have the capacity to enrich our own living.

# Appendix

*Character Narrators Talking among Themselves; Or, Charlie Marlow, Rhetorical Theorist*

If I may echo another frame narrator, this could have occurred nowhere but in Characternarratorland, where the living of our lives affects the way we tell our stories, where the telling of our stories affects the way we go on living, and where part of our living is given over to talking about our telling.

We were sitting round a metal table drinking and talking, doing our best to ignore the stares and whispers from another group of five seated at the next table, a group that seemed to be streamlined versions of people we'd seen in other places. Our company consisted of two former governesses, a butler, a sailor, and me. The governesses made quite a contrast: Jane Rochester, the epitome of self-confidence, had inherited a fortune and married her former employer; the other, who always said her name didn't matter, had a troubled, haunted look, not surprising for some one who's had one of her charges die in her arms and at least half of her readers believing that she's insane. The butler, Stevens, was a likable fellow, though given to awkward attempts at bantering with the rest of us. He'd never experienced anything like my year in New York in the 1920s, but he, too, knew about corruption and complicity. The sailor, Marlow, was the most philosophic and most garrulous member of our group. Despite our differences in experience, temperament, and personality, the five of us shared the fellowship of the storytelling craft—and the ordeal of having our tales subject to doubt, disbelief, outrage, and other forms of the higher criticism. Whenever we got together, it wasn't long before either Marlow or Jane would start holding forth; this day Marlow began.

"We're always suspicious characters because we're always suspicious narrators—and vice versa. I can't believe how long it took me to learn that simple, ineluctable fact of our existence. You can work, fight, sweat, nearly kill yourself, to tell the truth—or to keep from telling the truth—and it makes no difference. We use the most vertical of pronouns, the single black bar that looks as if it were striking a blow for ourselves and our tales, an effort to press our actions, our thoughts, our visions into the very foundations of our telling so that the listener can rest upon them, build upon them, above all rely upon them. But it's no use. As soon as we speak or write, we are suspected of, well, you name it—being too self-interested, too romantic, too naïve, too corrupt, too *too*. If one of us were perfectly selfless, realistic, mature, morally sound, no one, I fear, would ever notice. Our tales, alas, are always appropriated by the likes of those five at the next table, those who always intervene—sometimes subtly, sometimes heavy-handedly—between our telling and our audiences. Those audiences too contribute to our problems—their own interests, their own habits of listening interfere, like an iceberg in a ship's path, with the meanings we attach to our words. I daresay that if these words I am now uttering were recorded, some listeners would regard them not as a description of our plight but evidence of my penchant for special pleading, my overweening self-interest. . . . Pass the whiskey."

Mrs. Rochester seemed about to speak, but as everyone else murmured approval, she held her tongue.

"Take 'Youth,' my first extended effort, a straightforward tale about the sense of accomplishment, power, and future promise that accompanies youthful success at sea. This story, you probably won't be surprised to know, has come in for a certain amount of critical bruising—though the kinds of bruises may surprise you: I'm too romantic in the telling; my youthful self really learns nothing; I have no psychological depth to me; I'm too impressed with my own importance. Now I accept the bruising as part of our lot in life—if you spin yarns, you're asking for some backspin. It's the causes that get to me—the habits of suspicion and readerly self-interest underlying the bruising."

Here Jane broke in: "My dear Charlie, I believe you mind the bruising very much—indeed, perhaps more than any of us, with the possible exception of Nick. Surely you ought not lay blame upon your readers until you've examined your story more thoroughly. I hope you won't think me too bold when I suggest that 'Youth' *is* an unsatisfying story, especially when compared with the riches you offer in *Heart of Darkness*. I take exception, it won't surprise you to learn, to 'Youth''s emphatic statement that women don't belong at sea. But that's not my only concern. There is so little conflict among the human characters. It's you, Charlie, and your Captain and crew against the elements—the weather, the sea, the boat, the cargo. These ingredients allow you to provide an entertaining story but not much more. And"—with a look at the rest of us—"I believe that I am not alone in this opinion. Please pass the spring water."

Marlow looked expectantly as the butler, the governess, and I began calculating whether offering an opinion here would result in our getting caught in the middle between Marlow and Jane. Soon Stevens's instinctive good manners led him to break the silence.

"Mrs. Rochester, I acknowledge the accuracy of your description. I would concur that you've located a significant difference between 'Youth' and *Heart of Darkness*, where Captain Marlow's conflicts are both internal and external and where the external conflicts include other characters. Yet I have learned to question the assumption that there is just one ideal for each of our endeavors. Must we always privilege narratives with conflict between humans over those with conflict between humans and nonhuman forces? Might not 'Youth' be serving different interests from *Heart of Darkness* and so be eminently deserving of commendation for that service?"

Emboldened by Stevens, I broke in. "I used to say that I was one of the few honest men I'd ever known, but I honestly can't claim to be any more honest than Mrs. Rochester. Yet to be honest in turn, I find that Mrs. Rochester and Stevens are both leaving out something very important about the human side of the story—the relationship between the twenty-year-old youth and the forty-two-year-old narrator, the hardworking second mate and the experienced veteran of the sea. That relationship, I'd say, is a boat making its way against the current, carrying the thematic cargo about the power and transience of youth."

The unnamed governess now broke her silence: "My perceptions, I've come to believe, are not entirely trustworthy, but there is, to my eye, a human tension between Captain Marlow and the frame narrator that offers considerable interest. The Captain's thematic cargo weighs, in my scale, rather more than his companion's. Our friend testifies not just about the wonder of youth but also about its enduring effects—at forty-two he still sees the East as he saw it at twenty. Youth, for our friend's friend, is nothing if not evanescent. Captain Marlow's story may grow in interest if we note that it stresses a view of human life closer to Mrs. Rochester's—the actions of our past form a lasting chain that leads us to our present—while also observing that the frame narrator's concluding remarks sound much like those in Mr. Carraway's narrative that he has already alluded to: '[O]ur weary eyes looking still, looking always, looking anxiously for something out of life, that while it is expected is already gone—has passed unseen, in a sigh, in a flash—together with the youth, with the strength, with the romance of illusions.'"

Marlow's chuckling drew the attention of all of us. "Jane, do you still think that what we do and say in our tales will be enough to counteract habits—and interests—of listeners? Ah, ah, that's a rhetorical question. But yes, there are also listeners who try to become, if not one of us, then one with us, listeners who seek to read out the vision we press into the story with the first-person pronoun. All of you I know want to be such listeners, so let me pick up, turn over, try on what you've said. Who knows, seeing the story through your eyes may change my vision. Pass the whiskey.

"One of the ironies of the story is that the title can apply as much to the forty-two-year-old narrator as to the twenty-year-old character: I was a youth at the narrative game and the story's a beginner's effort. Oh, I'd told a lot of stories in my time, but nothing on that scale before. At forty-two, though, I wasn't about to have a romantic experience. I got a thrill from holding the attention of my audience, from looking around the table and seeing their eyes gazing back at mine, seeing their emphatic nods when I was done. But that thrill is nothing next to the feeling associated with my first sight of Java. Now to some of you, this revelation may be disappointing. But to me it's not because this failure of the telling to equal the action is actually predicted by the story. If I felt about something I did at forty-two the way I felt—and still feel—about my first sight of the East, then my story would be as empty as last week's whiskey bottle.

"As I said, 'Youth' is a beginner's effort. For once, Jane and I, well, let me say, partially agree. The interests of the story are those of adventure, persistence, seeking a goal that proves impossible through no fault of your own. Very different from—and Stevens, to my mind as well as hers, inferior to—the interests of *Heart of Darkness* or *Lord Jim*. But at the risk of stating the obvious, there is a story running underneath the one about flood and fire, the account of my own growing confidence. My vision of the East would not have been as powerful or as enduring if I had not so recently discovered, by being forced to command my own boat, 'how good a man I was.'"

"I do—and did—see the connection between your sense of confidence and the impression that the East makes upon you," Jane interjected. "But my dear Charlie, your story still has problems. You never show us that you *doubt* your own confidence or abilities—or that you or we have any reason to. Your path from hardworking second mate to confident commander of his own boat is as straight as any flown by a gull from ship to shore. Further, is it because I am a woman and a Christian that I find your conception of goodness rather paltry—a combination of technical skill, masculine brawn, and youthful foolhardiness that has little to do with a true strength of character rooted in sound moral principles?"

"Ah, Jane, relentless as always. Yes, I fancy the story would be more satisfying if the trajectory of my growth were less smooth—but, I'm not going to change the facts, and I can't believe a woman of your rectitude would want me to. For once—indeed, for the very last time—in my life I did make steady, straight-line progress. So there you have it.

"But your point illuminates something else—the reaction of those who find me too focused on and too satisfied with my own success. There's a taboo against us character narrators telling straight-line success stories. The punishment for violating this taboo is having our readers insert the crookedness—usually within us. And so it's happened with me.

"Now for my paltry idea of goodness. By your Christian lights, I am sure I am paltry. And I'm similarly lacking by the lights of many others. But I never claimed to be a paragon, never anything more than a man trying to figure out the significance of different events, people, institutions. Being 'good' in 'Youth' just means being a decent sailor—no more. But also no less. The sailor's code of hard work, commitment to goals, maintaining a modicum of courage, and developing one's resourcefulness—there is something morally attractive in that.

"Now the measure of ambition that the code fosters and that is part of my self-portrait in 'Youth' is more morally ambiguous, something that, like pride, can bring out both the best and the worst in us. If you see that ambition, it's because I wasn't trying to hide it. Pass the bottle."

Stevens seized the opening created by Marlow's pause. "Captain Marlow, I for one don't find you all that self-satisfied. Indeed, I very much enjoyed those parts of the story where you adopted what I would call a bantering tone and poked fun at your former self. My favorite example, because it relies so much on what is not said, is your description of attempting to enter the cargo hold to put out the fire: 'No man could remain more than a minute below. Mahon, who went first, fainted there, and the man who went to fetch him out did likewise. We lugged them out on deck. Then I leaped down to show how easily it could be done. They had learned wisdom by that time, and contented themselves by fishing for me with a chain-hook tied to broom-handle, I believe. I did not offer to go and fetch my shovel, which was left down below.' It must be a considerable comfort to you to look back on your former self and be able to banter in this way about your behavior. You seem to have escaped the misfortune of regret—and in my experience it's a rare man who so escapes."

"Thank you kindly, Stevens. But be sure to be around when we discuss *Heart of Darkness*—you may end up deciding with a great number of other readers that there's much to regret revealed in that story.

"Now Carraway, what's on your mind?"

"Just this: if you were to tell the story again today, now that you're no longer a beginner, would you do anything differently—especially with your handling of the relationship between narrator and character?"

"I worry sometimes that the garrulous forty-two-year-old obscures the audience's vision of the younger man. You'll notice that I do proportionally less time-of-the-telling ruminating in *Heart of Darkness* and even *Lord Jim*. In 'Youth,' though, part of the point is that the events are still with me, so making myself as teller prominent seems justified.

"The summary at the opening though—about the voyage as a symbol of existence in which all tasks are impossible—I might drop that as too heavy-handed and as giving too much away. An adventure story ought to have more suspense.

"Your question also makes me think about differences between your story and mine. Unlike me, you practice fairly consistently the virtue of restraint about your present perception of things. But your deviations—especially at the beginning and the end—make it clear that you see things differently at the time of telling—and that your narrator's vision is ethically superior. In 'Youth,' the forty-two-year-old's vision is not—on the ethical axis—radically different from the twenty-year-old's. The intervening twenty-two years do allow me to see my former self in a broader context and to see the interconnections among my youth, my actions, and my feelings. I have distance on myself, but unlike you, have no regrets about what I did, no sense that I'd made some serious errors in judgment—and thus, I have no moral *éclaircissement* to report. At forty-two, I can make fun of my youthful earnestness but I also endorse that young man's vision. Interestingly, that move gets me in trouble with some readers, who regard that endorsement as a dangerous romanticization and even an effort to escape from my own aging and disillusionment. I think that what is going on here is not all that different from what is going on when readers' supply the crookedness in my path toward self-confidence.

"I object more strongly to this objection. The straight-line, no-internal-conflict story has problems but what, I ask, is wrong with the forty-two-year-old sharing the vision of the twenty-year-old?"

Seeing I had no answer, the governess spoke. "Captain Marlow, is my vision flawed or can you see now, if not then, the gap between your story and the frame? Does the frame narrator's concluding eloquence suppress, inadvertently or otherwise, a good half of what your story is claiming?"

"My compliments to your vision, ma'am; I was wondering if any one else would ever notice that. To be sure, there is a doubleness to my story's claims: youth is fleeting; youth can endure through vision, memory, narrative itself. The frame narrator, bless his soul, sees and hears only its evanescence. When quizzed about this gap in his telling, he was completely surprised; he genuinely hadn't seen it. From that point on, I've been thinking about the way the interests and habits of our readers affect their responses to our stories. But what do you make of his blindness?"

"I no longer think of myself as an exemplary reader, but I can venture a hypothesis: the blindness makes a point, for us, about you and your companions: you share the fellowship of the sea with them, but your decision to stay a seaman also separates you—or perhaps the intensity of your experiences on the sea, like the experience in Java, makes you stay a seaman. You, Captain Marlow, are, in any event, the romantic's romantic."

As Marlow nodded, I tried one more question. "Marlow, does this conversation teach us anything about why we're such suspicious characters, such suspicious narrators?"

"Well, Nick, age makes one increasingly wary of sweeping generalizations, so I'll confine myself to the controversy about my tales. 'Youth' gets in trouble for violating some conventional expectations about character narrator stories—the growth plot is too easy, the mature narrator too completely supports the youth. *Heart of Darkness* is of course much less straightforward; it had to be that way—despite my temporal distance from the action my narrator's vision was a lot cloudier—and, indeed, was still being formed as I told the story. Yes, I could see the ravages of European imperialism in Africa, but no, I could not see all the ways in which my attitudes were shaped by my own inevitable Eurocentrism.

Was I right to lie to the Intended? I still don't know how to answer that question; all I know is that at that moment I couldn't tell her the truth. When you get a suspicious character—a *toujours déjà* suspicious character—telling a story in which he's not fully aware of or fully in control of the ethical judgments, you'll have the kind of controversies we have about *Heart of Darkness.*

"Once again I've gone on too long. Next time I promise to shut up and listen to one of you. Pass the whiskey."

We nodded, each thinking our own thoughts about our own suspicious narrations, and each, I'm sure, sufficiently suspicious of Marlow's not to believe his last promise.

# Glossary

This glossary seeks to define, with clarity and concision, the set of terms and concepts fundamental to my conception of narrative as rhetoric in general and to my ideas about character narration in particular. In most cases, there are fuller discussions of these concepts in the preceding chapters, though in a few cases those discussions presume an understanding of the definitions offered here. My definitions of narratological terms such as *paralipsis* and *paralepsis* are inflected by my commitment to the rhetorical approach; for more formal narratological definitions, see Gerald Prince, *A Dictionary of Narratology*. For fuller discussions of many of the terms and their related concepts, see the forthcoming *Routledge Encyclopedia of Narrative Theory*, edited by David Herman, Manfred Jahn, and Marie-Laure Ryan.

**addressee** The audience to whom an utterance is directed. When the source of the utterance is the narrator, the addressee is the narratee; when the source is the implied author, the addressee is the implied reader or authorial audience; when the source is the flesh-and-blood author, the addressee is the flesh-and-blood audience.

**authorial audience** The hypothetical, ideal audience for whom the implied author constructs the text and who understands it perfectly. The authorial audience of fiction, unlike the narrative audience (defined below), operates with the tacit knowledge that the characters and events are synthetic constructs rather than real people and historical happenings.

**authorial intention** The meaning and purpose of an utterance as designed by its implied author. It is much easier to define the term than to identify all the different stances critics and theorists have taken toward the concept.

**autodiegetic narration** The telling of a story by its protagonist. See also *character narration; homodiegetic narration; heterodiegetic narration.*

**axes of communication**   A metaphor designed to indicate that implied authors and narrators typically make three distinct kinds of communication to their respective audiences, each of which corresponds to one of the narrator's three main functions: (1) the axis of facts, characters, and events, which corresponds to the reporting function; (2) the axis of perception or understanding, which corresponds to the reading (or interpreting) function; and (3) the axis of ethics and evaluation, which corresponds to the regarding (or evaluating) function.

**character**   An element of narrative that has three simultaneous components—the *mimetic* (character is like a person); the *thematic* (any character is representative of one or more groups and functions in one way or another to advance the narrative's thematic concerns); the *synthetic* (character plays a specific role in the construction of narrative as made object).

**character narration**   Narration in fiction or nonfiction by a participant in the story events.

**coduction**   The production of interpretation or evaluation through conversation with other readers.

**cultural narrative**   A story that circulates frequently and widely among the members of a culture; its author, rather than being a clearly identified individual, is a larger collective entity, at least some significant subgroup of society. Cultural narratives typically become formulas that underlie specific narratives whose authors we can identify, and these narratives can vary across a spectrum from totally conforming to the formula to totally inverting it.

**dialogism**   The presence of multiple voices within a narrative and the relationships among them. See also *double-voicing.*

**dimensions** and **functions**   The attributes of a character that create the potential for signification within the progression are dimensions. The realization of that potential creates functions. On the mimetic level, an attribute is a trait; when one trait combines with others to form a portrait of a possible person, that mimetic dimension is participating in a mimetic function. On the thematic level, an attribute is a trait considered as representative (e.g., a character's race) or as an idea (e.g., a character's belief in the supernatural); when the progression turns in some way on the presence of this trait, then it is being thematized, or, more formally, the thematic dimension becomes a thematic function. On the synthetic level, dimensions are always functions because dimensions are always already parts of the construction of the narrative. The synthetic functions can, however, be more or less foregrounded; in realistic narrative, they tend to remain in the background; in metafictional narrative, they tend to move to the foreground.

**disclosure functions** and **narrator functions**   The two *telling functions* available to the implied author, each identifying a different track of communication. Disclosure functions refer to the communication along the track from the narrator to the authorial audience, while narrator functions refer to the communication along the track from the narrator to the narratee. Character narration is an art of indirection because the implied author must use the narrator to communicate with the authorial audience and the narrator is unaware of that audience. This situation occasionally leads to conflicts between the disclosure and the narrator functions, and in such conflicts the disclosure functions will typically take precedence over the narrator functions.

**discourse**   The set of devices for telling a story, including vision or focalization (who perceives), voice (who speaks), duration (how long it takes something to be told), frequency (whether something is told in singulative or iterative manner), and speed (how much story time is covered by a stretch of discourse). In structuralist narratology, discourse is regarded as the "how" of narrative, distinct from the "what"—character, event, and setting.

**distance**   The relation between the norms of an implied author and those of a narrator. Distance will always be greater in unreliable narration than in reliable narration. In some autobiography, there is no distance and, consequently, some theorists say that in such narratives the implied author and the narrator are identical. I believe, however, that the distinction between the implied author and the narrator is worth maintaining even in such cases because it allows us to differentiate between the agent who designs the entire text, including the narrator, and the agent who reports, interprets, and evaluates the events of the narrative.

**double-voicing**   The presence of (at least) two voices in one utterance. In unreliable narration, for example, we hear both the narrator's voice and the implied author's voice undermining the narrator's.

**dual focalization**   A narrative situation in which the perceptions of two agents are communicated simultaneously; the most relevant situation for character narration involves a narrator perceiving his former self's perceptions.

**elliptical narration**   A narrator's report that leaves a gap that the narrator and the implied author expect their audiences to fill. Elliptical narration can be either reliable or unreliable.

**fabula**   The what of narrative before it is rendered in discourse; the sequence of events in chronological order.

**focalization**   The answer to the question "who is perceiving?" in narrative discourse. Genette noted that the term "point of view" conflated two distinct aspects of narrative discourse: voice (the answer to the question "who is speaking?") and vision or focalization. Since Genette's identification of the concept, narratologists have been debating how best to describe it and account for its effects.

**heterodiegetic**   Genette's term for what I call noncharacter narration—narration in which the narrator exists at a different level of existence from the characters.

**homodiegetic**  Genette's term for what I call character narration—narration in which the narrator exists at the same level of existence as the characters. When the character narrator is also the protagonist, homodiegetic narration can be further specified as autodiegetic. All nonfiction narration is homodiegetic.

**ideal narrative audience**  The hypothetical, ideal audience for whom the narrator is telling the story. See also *narratee; narrative audience.*

**implied author**  The streamlined version of the real author, an actual or purported subset of the real author's traits and abilities. The implied author is responsible for the choices that create the narrative text as "these words in this order" and that imbue the text with his or her values. One important activity of rhetorical reading is constructing a sense of the implied author.

**implied reader**  The audience for whom the implied author writes; synonymous with the authorial audience.

**instabilities** and **tensions**  Unstable situations upon which narrative progressions are built. Narrative moves by the generation, complication, and (sometimes) resolution of instabilities and tensions. An instability is an unstable situation within the story: it may be between or among characters; between a character and his or her world; or within a single character. A tension is an unstable situation within the discourse, consisting typically of a discrepancy in knowledge, judgments, values, or beliefs between narrator and authorial audience or between implied author and authorial audience.

**lyricality**  That which makes a given text a lyric. The rhetorical approach identifies two aspects of lyricality: a textual and a readerly dynamics. It further identifies two main kinds of textual dynamics: (1) somebody telling somebody else on some occasion for some purpose that something is—a situation, an emotion, a perception, an attitude, a belief; (2) somebody telling somebody else on some occasion about his or her meditations on something. The most important part of the readerly dynamics is that the authorial audience participates in the speaker's perspective rather than observing it from the outside and judging it.

**mask narration**  Character narration in which the character narrator is not only a reliable spokesperson for the implied author but also serves as an effective means for conveying the implied author's views along the axes of perception/understanding or of ethics/evaluation.

**mimetic/mimesis**  Mimetic refers, first, to that component of character directed to its imitation of a possible person. It refers, second, to that component of fictional narrative concerned with imitating the world beyond the fiction, what we typically call "reality." Mimesis refers to the process by which the mimetic effect is produced, the set of conventions, which change over time, by which imitations are judged to be more or less adequate.

**narratee**  The audience directly addressed by the narrator; the narratee may or may not coincide with the ideal narrative audience.

**narrative**  In rhetorical terms, the act of somebody telling somebody else on a particular occasion for some purpose that something happened.

**narrative audience**  The observer role within the world of the fiction, taken on by the flesh-and-blood reader in that part of his or her consciousness which treats the fictional action as real. The narrative audience position, like the narratee position, is subsumed within the authorial audience position.

**narrativity**  That which makes a text a narrative. The rhetorical approach identifies two aspects of narrativity, a textual and a readerly dynamics. The textual dynamics involves the representation of a sequence of related events during which the characters and/or their situations undergo some *change*. The readerly dynamics involves the authorial audience's role as observer and judge of the characters and events in that sequence.

**narratology**  The theoretical movement, rooted in structuralism, whose initial goal was to define the essence of narrative as a mode of discourse, to describe its fundamental structure, and to delineate the nature of its particular elements—author, narrator, narratee, character, event, setting, and so on. Over time these goals have been modified as narratology has interacted with other developments in critical theory including feminism, psychoanalysis, and rhetorical approaches.

**narrator**  The teller of the story.

**narrator functions**  See *disclosure functions* and *narrator functions.*

**observer narration**  Narration by a character narrator other than the protagonist.

**paralepsis**  A device in which a narrator's discourse reflects a greater knowledge than he or she could presumably have—in other words, a device in which the narrator tells more than he or she knows.

**paralipsis**  A device in which a narrator's discourse does not reflect his or her full relevant knowledge—in other words, a device in which the narrator tells less than he or she knows.

**portraiture**  That which makes a text a character sketch. The rhetorical approach identifies two aspects to portraiture, a textual and a readerly dynamics. The textual dynamics is most clearly seen in one kind of dramatic monologue, where the speaker's telling progresses according to the logic of the dramatic situation, while the audience's understanding progresses toward a deeper knowledge and understanding of the speaker. The readerly dynamics involves the audience in the role of external observer of the speaker, but that role involves comprehending and contemplating the character rather than judging him or her.

**progression**  The movement of a narrative from beginning to end, and the principles governing that movement. Progression exists along two simultaneous axes: the internal logic of the narrative text and the set of responses that logic generates in the authorial audience as it reads from beginning to end. Though this description focuses on the movement of narrative through time from beginning to end, a concern with progression is more than a concern with narrative as a linear process, precisely because it recognizes the dynamic, recursive relationships among the authorial audience's understanding of beginning, middle, and end.

**redundant telling**   A narrator's apparently unmotivated report of information to a narratee that the narratee already possesses. The motivation for redundant telling typically resides in the implied author's need to communicate information to the audience, and so it can also be described with the longer phrase *redundant telling, necessary disclosure*. In redundant telling, the disclosure functions take precedence over the narrator functions of the narration.

**reliable narration**   Reliable narration is that in which the narrator's reporting, reading (or interpreting), and regarding (or evaluating) are in accord with the perspective and norms of the implied author.

**restricted narration**   A technique marked by an implied author's limiting a narrator to only one function or axis of communication—reporting, reading, or regarding—while requiring the authorial audience to make inferences about communication along at least one of the other axes as well. Restricted narration may be either reliable or unreliable.

**serial narration**   The use of multiple narrators, each taking turns, to tell the tale.

**sjuzhet**   The fabula rendered in a specific narrative discourse; the synthesis of story and discourse.

**story**   The what of narrative: character, events, and setting are parts of story; the events in chronological order constitute the story abstracted from the discourse.

**suppressed narration**   The omission of significant information that the narrative itself otherwise indicates is relevant to the character, situation, or event being reported on, thereby creating either a gap in the text that cannot be filled or a discrepancy between what is reported in one place and not reported in another.

**synthetic**   That component of character directed to its role as artificial construct in the larger construction of the text; more generally, the constructedness of a text as an object.

**telling functions**   The communicative functions between the teller(s) and the receiver(s) of narrative. There are two kinds of telling functions, one referring to the communicative track between the narrator and the narratee called narrator functions, and the other referring to the track between the implied author and the authorial audience called disclosure functions. Sometimes the functions reinforce each other, but occasionally they conflict. See also *disclosure functions* and *narrator functions*.

**thematic**  That component of character directed to its representative or ideational function; more generally, that component of a narrative text concerned with making statements, taking ideological positions, teaching readers truths.

**unreliable narration**  Narration in which the narrator's reporting, reading (or interpreting), and/or regarding (or evaluating) are not in accord with the implied author's. There are six main types of unreliable narration: misreporting, misreading, and misregarding; underreporting, underreading, and underregarding. The two main groups can be differentiated by the activity they require on the part of the authorial audience: with the first group—misreporting, misreading, and misregarding—the audience must reject the narrator's words and reconstruct an alternative; with the second group—underreporting, underreading, and underregarding—the audience must supplement the narrator's view.

**voice**  (1) in structuralist narratology, the answer to the question "who is speaking?" in narrative discourse; (2) in a rhetorical approach, the term also can refer to the synthesis of a speaker's style, tone, and values.

# Works Cited

Adams, Timothy Dow. *Telling Lies in Modern American Autobiography.* Chapel Hill: University of North Carolina Press, 1990.

Altieri, Charles. "Lyrical Ethics and Literary Experience." In *Mapping the Ethical Turn: A Reader in Culture, Ethics, and Literary Theory,* ed. Todd F. Davis and Kenneth Womack, 30–58. Charlottesville: University Press of Virginia, 2001.

Anzaldúa, Gloria. *Borderlands/La Frontera: The New Mestiza.* San Francisco: Spinsters/Aunt Lute Press, 1987.

Appel, Alfred, Jr., ed. *The Annotated Lolita* by Vladimir Nabokov. New York: Vintage Books, 1991.

Bakhtin, Mikhail. "Discourse in the Novel." In *The Dialogic Imagination: Four Essays,* ed. Michael Holquist and trans. Caryl Emerson and Michael Holquist, 259–422. Austin: University of Texas Press, 1981.

Bal, Mieke. *Narratology: Introduction to the Theory of Narrative.* Trans. Christine van Boheemen. Toronto: University of Toronto Press, 1985.

Battersby, James L. "Fact, Fiction, Belief, and Emotion." In *Unorthodox Views: Reflections on Reality, Truth, and Meaning in Current Social, Cultural, and Critical Discourse,* 109–28. Westport, CT: Greenwood Press, 2002.

Bloom, Harold, ed. *Lolita* by Vladimir Nabokov. New York: Chelsea House, 1993.

Booth, Wayne C. *The Company We Keep: An Ethics of Fiction.* Berkeley: University of California Press, 1989.

——. *Critical Understanding.* Chicago: University of Chicago Press, 1979.

——. *The Rhetoric of Fiction.* 2nd ed. Chicago: University of Chicago Press, 1983.

——. "The Struggle to Tell the Story of the Struggle to Get the Story Told." *Narrative* 5 (1997): 50–59.

Brenner, Gerry. *Concealments in Hemingway's Works.* Columbus: Ohio State University Press, 1983.

Browning, Robert. "My Last Duchess." In *Robert Browning's Poetry: Authoritative Texts, Criticism,* ed. James Loucks. New York: Norton, 1980.

Byerman, Keith. *John Edgar Wideman: A Study of the Short Fiction*. New York: Twayne, 1998.

Carter, Forrest. *The Education of Little Tree*. Albuquerque: University of New Mexico Press, 1986.

Caruth, Cathy. *Unclaimed Experience: Trauma, Narrative, and History*. Baltimore: Johns Hopkins University Press, 1996.

Case, Alison. *Plotting Women: Gender and Narration in the Eighteenth- and Nineteenth-Century British Novel*. Charlottesville: University Press of Virginia, 1999.

Centerwall, Brandon. "Hiding in Plain Sight: Nabokov and Pedophilia." *Texas Studies in Language and Literature* 32 (1990): 468–84.

Chandler, Raymond. *The Big Sleep*. In *The Raymond Chandler Omnibus*. New York: Knopf, 1975.

Chatman, Seymour. *Coming to Terms: The Rhetoric of Narrative in Fiction and Film*. Ithaca: Cornell University Press, 1990.

——. *Story and Discourse: Narrative Structure in Fiction and Film*. Ithaca: Cornell University Press, 1978.

Cisneros, Sandra. "Barbie-Q." In *Woman Hollering Creek and Other Stories*, 14–16. New York: Random House, 1991.

Clark, Miriam Marty. "Hemingway's Early Illness Narratives and the Lyric Dimensions of 'Now I Lay Me.'" *Narrative* 13 (2004): 167–77.

Cohn, Dorrit. "Discordant Narration." *Style* 34 (2000): 307–16.

——. *The Distinction of Fiction*. Baltimore: Johns Hopkins University Press, 1999.

Conrad, Joseph. *Lord Jim*. Ed. Thomas Moser. New York: Norton, 1968.

——. "Youth." In *Youth, Heart of Darkness, The End of the Tether*, ed. John Lyon. London: Penguin, 1995.

Crossen, Cynthia. "Know Thy Father." *Wall Street Journal*, March 4, 1997, A16.

Culler, Jonathan. "Omniscience." *Narrative* 12 (2004): 22–34.

Davis, Todd F., and Kenneth Womack, eds. *Mapping the Ethical Turn: A Reader in Ethics, Culture, and Literary Theory*. Charlottesville: University Press of Virginia, 2001.

DeFalco, Joseph. *The Hero in Hemingway's Short Stories*. Pittsburgh: University of Pittsburgh Press, 1963.

Dickens, Charles. *Dombey and Son*. London: Chapman & Hall, 1907.

Diengott, Nilli. "The Implied Author Once Again." *Journal of Literary Semantics* 22, no. 1 (1993): 68–75.

Donne, John. "A Valediction: Forbidding Mourning." In *Songs and Sonnets of John Donne*, ed. Theodore Redpath. London: Routledge, 1967.

Dubrow, Heather. "Lyric Forms." In *Cambridge Companion to English Literature, 1500–1600*, ed. Arthur Kinney, 78–99. New York: Cambridge University Press, 2000.

——. *Shakespeare and Domestic Loss: Forms of Deprivation, Mourning, and Recuperation*. New York: Cambridge University Press, 1999.

Eakin, Paul John. *How Our Lives Become Stories.* Ithaca: Cornell University Press, 1999.

Edmiston, William F. "Focalization and the First-Person Narrator: A Revision of the Theory." *Poetics Today* 10 (1989): 729–44.

Faulkner, William. *As I Lay Dying.* New York: Knopf, 1990.

Fitzgerald, F. Scott. *The Great Gatsby.* New York: Charles Scribner's Sons, 1995.

Fitzsimmons, David. "I See, He Says, Perhaps, On Time: Vision, Voice, Hypothetical Narration, and Temporality in William Faulkner's Fiction." Ph.D. diss., Ohio State University, 2003.

Flora, Joseph. *Hemingway's Nick Adams.* Baton Rouge: Louisiana State University Press, 1982.

Fludernik, Monika. "Ficton vs. Non-Fiction: Narratological Differentiations." In *Erzahlen und Erzahltheorie im 20.Jahrhundert: Festschrift für Wilhelm Fuger,* 85–103. Heidelberg, Germany: Carl Winter, 2001.

Flynn, Elizabeth A., and Patrocinio Schweikart, eds. *Gender and Reading: Essays on Readers, Texts, and Contexts.* Baltimore: Johns Hopkins University Press, 1986.

Fournier, Nina. *Father, Mother, and Son: A Study of the Manuscripts of Ernest Hemingway's "Indian Camp," "Now I Lay Me," and "Fathers and Sons."* M.A. thesis, Trinity College, CT, 1991.

Friedman, Susan Stanford. "Lyric Subversion of Narrative in Women's Writing: Elizabeth Barrett Browning and Virginia Woolf." In *Reading Narrative: Form, Ethics, Ideology,* ed. James Phelan, 162–85. Columbus: Ohio State University Press, 1989.

Frost, Laura. "After Lot's Daughters: Kathryn Harrison and the Making of Memory." *a/b* 14,no. 1 (1999): 51–70.

Frye, Northrop. *Anatomy of Criticism.* Princeton: Princeton University Press, 1957.

Genette, Gérard. *Narrative Discourse: An Essay in Method.* Trans. Jane Lewin. Ithaca: Cornell University Press, 1981.

——. *Narrative Discourse Revisited.* Trans. Jane E. Lewin. Ithaca: Cornell University Press, 1988.

Gerlach, John. "The Margins of Narrative: The Very Short Story, the Prose Poem, and the Lyric." In *Short Story Theory at a Crossroads,* ed. Susan Lohafer and Jo Ellyn Clarey, 74–84. Baton Rouge: Louisiana State University Press, 1989.

Gilmore, Leigh. "Jurisdictions: *I, Rigoberta Menchú, The Kiss,* and Scandalous Self-Representation in the Age of Memoir and Trauma." *Signs* 28 (2003): 695–717.

——. *The Limits of Autobiography.* Ithaca: Cornell University Press, 2001.

Gornick, Vivian. Preface to *Living to Tell the Tale: A Guide to Writing Memoir* by Jane Taylor McDonnell. New York: Penguin, 1998.

Graff, Gerald, and James Phelan, eds. *Adventures of Huckleberry Finn: A Case Study in Critical Controversy.* 2nd ed. Boston: Bedford Books, 2004.

Green, Martin. "The Morality of *Lolita.*" *Kenyon Review* 28 (1966): 352–77.

Grice, H. P. *Studies in the Ways of Words*. Cambridge: Harvard University Press, 1991.

Harpham, Geoffrey Galt. *Getting It Right: Language, Literature, and Ethics*. Chicago: University of Chicago Press, 1995.

———. *Shadows of Ethics: Criticism and the Just Society*. Durham: Duke University Press, 1999.

Harrison, Kathryn. *Exposure*. New York: Random House, 1993.

———. *The Kiss*. New York: Random House, 1997.

———. *Thicker Than Water*. New York: Random House, 1991.

Hemingway, Ernest. *The Complete Short Stories of Ernest Hemingway: The Finca Vigia Edition*. New York: Charles Scribner's Sons, 1987.

———. *A Farewell to Arms*. New York: Charles Scribner's Sons, 1929..

———. "Now I Lay Me" manuscript. Ernest Hemingway collection. Item 618. John F. Kennedy Library, Boston.

Herman, David. "Hypothetical Focalization." *Narrative* 2 (1994): 230–53.

———. *Story Logic: Problems and Possibilities of Narrative*. Lincoln: University of Nebraska Press, 2002.

———, ed. *Narratologies: New Perspectives on Narrative Analysis*. Columbus: Ohio State University Press, 1999.

Herman, David, Manfred Jahn, and Marie-Laure Ryan. *Routledge Encyclopedia of Narrative Theory*. London: Routledge, forthcoming.

Hovey, Richard B. "Hemingway's 'Now I Lay Me': A Psychological Interpretation." *Literature and Psychology* 15 (1965): 70–78.

Ishiguro, Kazuo. *The Remains of the Day*. New York: Knopf, 1990.

Jahn, Manfred. "Windows of Focalization: Deconstructing and Reconstructing a Narratological Concept." *Style* 30 (1996): 241–67.

Jones, Nancy J. "Vladimir Nabokov's *Lolita*: A Survey of Scholarship and Criticism in English, 1977–95." *Bonner Beitrage* 54, no. 2 (1997): 129–47.

Josephs, Allen. "Hemingway's Out of Body Experience." *Hemingway Review* 2 (1983): 11–17.

Kafalenos, Emma. "Lingering along the Narrative Path: Extended Functions in Kafka and Henry James." *Narrative* 2 (1995): 117–38.

———. "Not (Yet) Knowing: Epistemological Effects of Deferred and Suppressed Information in Narrative." In *Narratologies: New Perspectives on Narrative Analysis*, ed. David Herman, 33–65. Columbus: Ohio State University Press, 1999.

Kauffman, Linda. *Special Delivery: Epistolary Modes in Modern Fiction*. Chicago: University of Chicago Press, 1992.

Lanser, Susan S. *Fictions of Authority: Women Writers and Narrative Voice*. Ithaca: Cornell University Press, 1992.

———. "The 'I' of the Beholder: (Non)Narrative Attachments and Other Equivocal Acts." *Blackwell Companion to Narrative Theory*, ed. James Phelan and Peter J. Rabinowitz. Forthcoming.

———. "(Im)plying the Author." *Narrative* 9 (2001): 153–60.

Lehmann-Haupt, Christopher. "Life with Father: Incestuous and Soul-Deadening." *New York Times*, February 27, 1997, C18.

Levinas, Emmanuel. *The Levinas Reader*, ed. Sean Hand. Oxford: Blackwell, 1989.

McCourt, Frank. *Angela's Ashes*. New York: Scribner, 1996.

——. *'Tis*. New York: Scribner, 1999.

McDermott, Alice. *Charming Billy*. New York: Farrar, Straus, and Giroux, 1998.

McDonnell, Jane Taylor. *Living to Tell the Tale: A Guide to Writing Memoir*. New York: Penguin, 1998.

Melville, Herman. *Moby Dick*. New York: Modern Library, 2000.

Miller, J. Hillis. *The Ethics of Reading: Kant, de Man, Trollope, Eliot, James, Benjamin*. New York: Columbia University Press, 1987.

Moddelmog, Debra. *Reading Desire: In Pursuit of Ernest Hemingway*. Ithaca: Cornell University Press, 1999.

Nabokov, Vladimir. *The Annotated Lolita*, ed. Alfred Appel Jr. New York: Vintage Books, 1991.

Nelles, William. "Historical and Implied Authors and Readers." *Comparative Literature* 45 (1993): 22–46.

Newton, Adam Zachary. *Narrative Ethics*. Cambridge: Harvard University Press, 1995.

Nünning, Ansgar. "Deconstructing and Reconceptualizing the Implied Author: The Resurrection of an Anthropomorphized Passepartout or the Obituary of a Critical Phantom?" *Anglistik. Organ des Verbandes Deutscher Anglisten* 8 (1997): 95–116.

——. "Unreliable, Compared to What?: Toward a Cognitive Theory of Unreliable Narration: Prolegomena and Hypotheses." In *Grenzuberschreitungen: Narratologie im Kontext*, ed. Walter Grunzweig and Andreas Solbach, 53–73. Tubingen: Gunther Narr Verlag, 1999.

Nussbaum, Martha. *Love's Knowledge: Essays on Philosophy and Literature*. New York: Oxford University Press, 1990.

Olson, Elder. "An Outline of Poetic Theory." In *On Value Judgments in the Arts and Other Essays*, ed. Olson, 268–89. Chicago: University of Chicago Press, 1976.

Olson, Greta. "Reconsidering Unreliability: Fallible and Untrustworthy Narrators." *Narrative* 11 (2003): 93–109.

O'Neill, Patrick. *Fictions of Discourse: Reading Narrative Theory*. Toronto: University of Toronto Press, 1994.

Orwell, George. *1984*, ed. Irving Howe. New York: Harcourt Brace Jovanovich, 1982.

Patnoe, Elizabeth. "Lolita Misrepresented, Lolita Reclaimed: Disclosing the Doubles." *College Literature* 22 (1995): 81–104.

Phelan, James. *Narrative as Rhetoric: Technique, Audiences, Ethics, Ideology*. Columbus: Ohio State University Press, 1996.

——. *Reading People, Reading Plots: Character, Progression, and the Interpretation of Narrative.* Chicago: University of Chicago Press, 1989.

——"Present Tense Narration, Mimesis, the Narrative Norm, and the Positioning of the Reader in *Waiting for the Barbarians.*" In *Understanding Narrative,* ed. Phelan and Peter J. Rabinowitz, 222–45. Columbus: Ohio State University Press, 1994.

——. "Sandra Cisneros's 'Woman Hollering Creek': Narrative as Rhetoric and as Social Practice." *Narrative* 6 (1998): 221–35.

——. "Why Narrators Can Be Focalizers and Why It Matters." In *New Perspectives on Narrative Perspective,* ed. Willie van Peer and Seymour Chatman, 51–64. Albany: SUNY Press, 2001.

——. *Worlds from Words: A Theory of Language in Fiction.* Chicago: University of Chicago Press, 1981.

Piercy, Marge. "Barbie Doll." In *Norton Introduction to Literature,* 7th ed., ed. Jerome Beatty and J. Paul Hunter, 821. New York: W. W. Norton, 1998.

*PMLA.* Special issue on ethical criticism. May 1999.

Pogrebin, Robin. "The Naked Literary Come-On." *New York Times,* August 17, 1997, 2.

Powers, Elizabeth. "Doing Daddy Down." *Commentary* (January 1997): 38–41.

Preston, Mary Elizabeth. "Homodiegetic Narration: Reliability, Selfconsciousness, Ideology, and Ethics." Ph.D. diss., Ohio State University, 1997.

——. "Implying Authors in *The Great Gatsby.*" *Narrative* 5 (1997): 143–64.

Prince, Gerald. *A Dictionary of Narratology.* Lincoln: University of Nebraska Press, 1987.

——. "A Point of View on Point of View or Refocusing Focalization." In *New Perspectives on Narrative Perspective,* ed. Willie van Peer and Seymour Chatman, 43–50. Albany: SUNY Press, 2001.

Rabinowitz, Peter J. *Before Reading: Narrative Conventions and the Politics of Interpretation.* 1987. Columbus: Ohio State University Press, 1998.

——. "Lolita: Solipsized or Sodomized?; or Against Abstraction in General." In *The Blackwell Companion to Rhetoric,* ed. Wendy Olmstead and Walter Jost, 325–39. Oxford: Blackwell Press, 2004.

——. "'A Lot Has Built Up': Omission and Rhetorical Realism in Dostoevsky's *The Gambler.*" *Narrative* 9 (2001): 203–9.

——. "Truth in Fiction: A Reexamination of Audiences." *Critical Inquiry* 4 (1977): 121–41.

Rader, Ralph. "The Dramatic Monologue and Related Lyric Forms." *Critical Inquiry* 3 (1976): 131–51.

Rafferty, Terrence. "The Lesson of the Master." *New Yorker,* January 15, 1990, 102–4.

Raphael, Linda S. *Narrative Skepticism: Moral Agency and Representations of Consciousness in Fiction.* Madison, NJ: Fairleigh Dickinson University Press, 2001.

Riggan, William F. *Picaros, Madmen, Naifs, and Clowns: The Unreliable First-Person Narrator.* Norman: University of Oklahoma Press, 1981.

Rimmon-Kenan, Shlomith. *Narrative Fiction: Contemporary Poetics.* New York: Methuen, 1983.

Romberg, Bertil. *Narrative Technique of the First-Person Novel,* trans. Michael Taylor and Harold H. Borland. Stockholm: Almqvist & Wiksell, 1962.

Ronen, Ruth. *Possible Worlds in Literary Theory.* Cambridge: Cambridge University Press, 1994.

Ryan, Marie-Laure. "The Narratorial Functions: Breaking Down a Theoretical Primitive." *Narrative* 9 (2001): 146–52.

St. John, Warren. "Kathryn Harrison's Dad Responds to Her Memoir." *New York Observer,* April 21, 1997, 1+.

Scafella, Frank. "'I and the Abyss,' Emerson, Hemingway, and the Modern Vision of Death." *Hemingway Review* 4 (1985): 2–6.

———. "Imagistic Landscape of a Psyche: Hemingway's Nick Adams." *Hemingway Review* 2 (1983): 2–10.

Scholes, Robert, and Nancy Comley. *Hemingway's Genders.* New Haven: Yale University Press, 1994.

Schwarz, Daniel. "Performative Saying and the Ethics of Reading: Adam Zachary Newton's *Narrative Ethics.*" *Narrative* 5 (1997): 188–206.

Schweikart, Patrocinio. "Reading as Communicative Action." *Reader* 43 (spring 2000): 70–75.

Sebold, Alice. *The Lovely Bones.* Boston: Little, Brown, 2002.

Shaffer, Brian. *Understanding Kazuo Ishiguro.* Columbia: University of South Carolina Press, 1998.

Shaw, Harry. "Loose Narrators: Display, Engagement, and the Search for a Place in History." *Narrative* 3 (1995): 95–116.

Smith, Sidonie, and Julia Watson. *Reading Autobiography: A Guide for Interpreting Life Narratives.* Minneapolis: University of Minnesota Press, 2001.

Sokal, Alan. "Transgressing the Boundaries: Toward a Transformative Hermeneutics of Quantum Gravity." *Social Text* 46/47 (spring/summer 1996): 217–52.

Steinke, James. "Hemingway's 'In Another Country' and 'Now I Lay Me.'" *Hemingway Review* 5 (1985): 32–39.

Tikener, Christina. "Time in *Lolita.*" *Modern Fiction Studies* 25 (1979): 463–69.

Toker, Leona. *Nabokov: The Mystery of Literary Structures.* Ithaca: Cornell University Press, 1989.

Toolan, Michael. *Narrative: A Critical Linguistic Introduction.* London: Routledge, 1988.

Trilling, Lionel. "The Last Lover—Vladimir Nabokov's *Lolita.*" *Encounter* 11 (October 1958): 9–19.

TuSmith, Bonnie, ed. *Conversations with John Edgar Wideman.* Jackson: University of Mississippi Press, 1998.

Twain, Mark. *Adventures of Huckleberry Finn,* ed. Gerald Graff and James Phelan. 2nd ed. Boston: Bedford Books, 2004.

Wall, Kathleen. "*The Remains of the Day* and Its Challenge to Theories of Un-reliable Narration." *Journal of Narrative Technique* 24, no. 1 (1994): 18–42.

Wideman, John Edgar. "Doc's Story." In *The Stories of John Edgar Wideman*, 147–53. New York: Pantheon Books, 1992.

Wolff, Tobias. "Literary Conceits." *New York Times*, April 6, 1997, 4, 19.

Wood, Michael. "*Lolita* Revisited." *New England Review: Middlebury Series* 17, no. 3 (1995): 15–43.

Yacobi, Tamar. "Narrative Structure and Fictional Mediation." *Poetics Today* 8 (1987): 335–72.

Yardley, Jonathan. "Daddy's Girl Cashes In: Kathryn Harrison Writes a Shame-ful Memoir of Incest." *Washington Post*, March 5, 1997, D2.

# Index